MW00637620

THE SILENT SERVICE IN WORLD WAR II

THE
SILENT SERVICE
IN WORLD WAR II

*The Story of the
U.S. Navy Submarine Force in the
Words of the Men Who Lived It*

EDITED BY **EDWARD MONROE-JONES** AND **MICHAEL GREEN**

CASEMATE
Philadelphia & Oxford

Published in the United States of America and Great Britain in 2012 by
CASEMATE PUBLISHERS
908 Darby Road, Havertown, PA 19083
and
10 Hythe Bridge Street, Oxford, OX1 2EW

ISBN 978-1-61200-125-8
Digital Edition: ISBN 978-1-61200-137-1

Cataloging-in-publication data is available from the Library of Congress and
the British Library.

10 9 8 7 6 5 4 3 2 1

Printed and bound in the United States of America.

For a complete list of Casemate titles please contact:

CASEMATE PUBLISHERS (US)
Telephone (610) 853-9131, Fax (610) 853-9146
E-mail: casemate@casematepublishing.com

CASEMATE PUBLISHERS (UK)
Telephone (01865) 241249, Fax (01865) 794449
E-mail: casemate-uk@casematepublishing.co.uk

CONTENTS

PART THREE: LATE WAR STORIES (1944–1945)

ACKNOWLEDGMENTS

The editors wish to thank the many World War Two veteran submariners who have contributed their experiences to the sources from which this anthology was compiled. Those sources include the following:

- Submarine Veterans of World War II, its Board of Directors and its 2008 President, Mr. Clarence Scott.

- The editors of *Polaris Magazine*, a publication of Submarine Veterans of World War II.

- The United States Submarine League, its quarterly journal, *The Submarine Review* and its editor, Captain James Hay, USN (ret.).

- The National Museum of the Pacific War, Center for Pacific War Studies and its research staff.

- Submarine Research Center and the many veteran submariners contributing their experiences directly to the construction of this anthology.

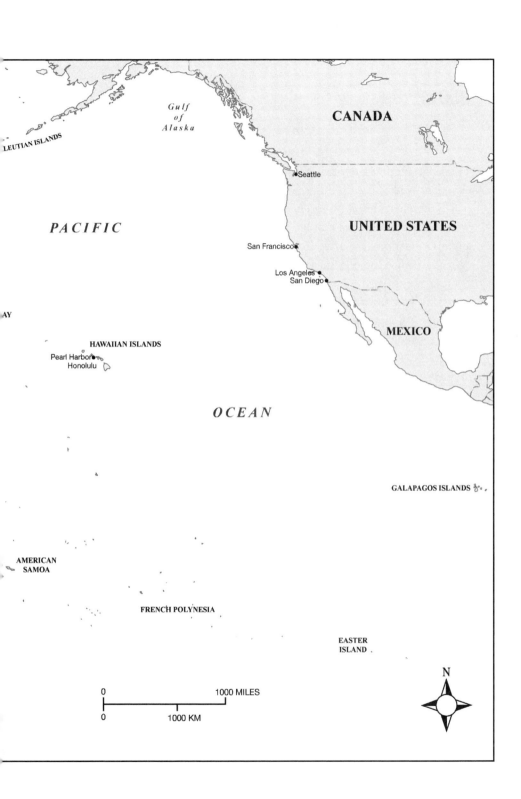

CANADA

Gulf
of
Alaska

LEUTIAN ISLANDS

•Seattle

PACIFIC

UNITED STATES

San Francisco•

Los Angeles •
San Diego•

AY

MEXICO

HAWAIIAN ISLANDS
Pearl Harbor•
Honolulu

OCEAN

GALAPAGOS ISLANDS

AMERICAN
SAMOA

FRENCH POLYNESIA

EASTER
ISLAND

N

0   1000 MILES

0   1000 KM

GLOSSARY

Those submariners contributing to this anthology of Second World War experiences have used phrases and words that were peculiar to the parlance of submarine technology and procedure. To help the reader gain an understanding of the language usage a few of the more common expressions and abbreviations are listed below;

The **1MC** is the general announcing system made up of speakers in all compartments with microphones in control, conning tower and bridge. It is used to give information to all hands in the boat at the same time.

The **7MC** announcing system is a series of microphones/loud speakers in the torpedo rooms, maneuvering room, control room, conning tower, and bridge. It is used when maneuvering the ship and when at battle stations. It is used to quickly convey information without disturbing off-watch crew members.

Answering Bells were used to signal speed changes. A fleet-type submarine's bells could signal stop, ahead one-third, ahead two-thirds, ahead standard, ahead full, and ahead flank. There were also backing bells: back one-third, back two-thirds, back full, and back emergency. Since the boat had twin screws a maneuvering bell might refer to the port screw, starboard screw or "all," meaning both screws. For example a tight turn could be made by "dragging" the inboard screw. The order might be "All stop. Starboard ahead standard, port back two-thirds." When the turn is completed the ordered bell might be "All ahead full."

Approach is synonymous with torpedo attack. It is the process of bringing the submarine into a position which will allow it to deliver torpedoes with maximum chance of hitting the target. Most World War II approaches were conducted on the surface at night. Some were conducted during the day when weather made detection less likely. Submerged approaches made using the periscope were handicapped by slow maneuvering speeds.

Christie, Admiral Ralph was commander of the submarines operating out of Fremantle before being relieved by Admiral Fife.

Conn, conn., or **conning** refers to the person designated by the captain to run the ship in his absence. When on the surface the ship's safety was in the hands of the conning officer, when submerged the conning officer was stationed in the conning tower. He gave orders for course, speed, and depth, and informed the captain when had concerns for the safety of the ship. Conn or conn. also refers to the conning tower as the place from which the boat was conned when it was submerged and where attacks were conducted.

Cubicle referred to the maneuvering room enclosure that housed the dangerous high-voltage switching equipment for the main propulsion plant.

Dinky was the auxiliary diesel engine. A fleet-type submarine had four propulsion engines and a small auxiliary engine for charging batteries and powering the housekeeping load. It sometimes was called upon to propel the submarine when all four main engines were out of commission.

DR or **Dead Reckoning** is the term that refers to the simple navigational process of using course and speed to determine a submarine's location.

Exec, exec., or **XO** refers to the executive officer who is the number two person in charge of the boat. His duties include all the paperwork of the submarine as well as being navigator and operations officer when another officer has not been so designated. He acts as assistant to the captain during battle stations and is in the conning tower next to him giving advice on an approach to a target.

The **Gangway** or **Brow** was the short platform which stretched from boat to boat or boat to pier when it was tied up alongside.

Gangway Watch or **Topside Watch** refers to the enlisted person assigned to protect the ship's safety when tied up in port. His station was on the quarter deck, except that submarine's really had no quarterdeck, so he simply stationed himself next to the brow or gangway where he could keep an eye on people coming aboard the submarine.

Green Board referred to the green hull opening lights on the Christmas Tree hydraulic panel which meant that all openings were shut and the boat was safe to submerge. It was usually combined with, "Pressure in the boat," when a small amount of compressed air was internally released. If the barometer needle remained constant the boat was airtight and therefore watertight.

Fife, Admiral John was commander of the submarines operating out of Brisbane and later out of Fremantle and Subic Bay.

Lockwood, Admiral Charles was Commander Submarines Pacific (ComSubPac) during the war. His headquarters was at Pearl Harbor.

Maneuvering Watch refers to the stations manned by the crew when the ship is being conned in close waters such as a harbor, alongside a pier, in a nest (a group of submarines tied up sided-by-side, typically next to a submarine tender), or in a river. Battle stations during the war referred to either making a torpedo run or using the deck weapons. The former was referred to as, "Battle stations—torpedo" and the later as "Battle stations—gun action."

MBTs or **Main Ballast Tanks** were the saddle tanks used to give the submarine positive buoyancy on the surface when dry or negative buoyancy submerged when flooded. They had flood ports on the bottom and vent valves on the top. Compressed air blew them dry when the vents were shut. To submerge it was only necessary to open the vents and water would displace the air, which escaped through the open vents. Some saddle tanks were fuel ballast tanks that carried diesel fuel until empty at which time they were converted to main ballast tanks.

OD or **OOD** was the abbreviation for Officer of the Deck. This was the name given to the officer who conns the ship when it is on the surface. His station is on the bridge where he communicates with the various stations throughout the ship via the 7MC, 1MC, or by a telephone talker who stands beside him on the bridge and relays messages to each compartment. A JOOD is a junior officer of the deck, typically a young, more junior officer who is still learning his trade.

PCO stands for prospective commanding officer. Officers selected for command of a submarine were required to attend the PCO school, which included making practice torpedo approaches.

Perth and Fremantle in Western Australia should be considered synonymous in the accounts in this book. Fremantle is the port at the mouth of the Swan River adjoining the city of Perth. The submarines were located in Fremantle, but the pubs were located in Perth.

Zero Float was the term for maintaining the battery at full charge by either using the Dinky or by skimming some propulsive power from the main engine.

INTRODUCTION

On December 7, 1941, the day that Japanese aircraft bombed Pearl Harbor, the United States Navy had 111 submarines, but they were a collection of First World War type boats, several one-of-a-kind boats, mine layers, and a few newer *Gato*-class fleet-type submarines. The older boats were 0, R, and S-class boats. America had seen the World War II approaching and had accelerated its submarine building program. By December, 1941 there were 73 fleet-type boats being built.

While the European war against Nazi Germany absorbed a good share of the Navy's ships, submarines were given the primary task of bringing the war to Japan in the Pacific. The old 0-boats were used for training purposes at the submarine training facility in New London, Connecticut and the R-boats were assigned to Key West, Florida where they provided services for anti-submarine warfare (ASW) destroyers. Some of these boats were also assigned to the Navy's Coco Solo submarine base on the Atlantic side of the Panama Canal.

S-type submarines and fleet-type submarines had been assigned to the Navy's Pacific bases including Pearl Harbor and Manila/Cavite in the Philippines. Following Pearl Harbor when it became obvious that the United States would not be able to prevent the Japanese from taking Manila/Cavite, Commander, Submarines Pacific (ComSubPac) who worked for Commander-in-Chief, Pacific Fleet (CincPacFleet) began the process of establishing submarine bases in Australia. The two primary bases were at Perth/Fremantle on the west coast and Brisbane on the east coast.

The narratives contained herein are primarily by men who served on S and fleet-type boats. As submarines tend to be somewhat complicated creatures a short explanation of the S and fleet-type submarines may assist readers in visualizing the action.

The S-series of American submarines were small. They displaced between eight hundred and nine hundred tons. By today's standards they amounted to little more than toys, but to the men who sailed them the S-boats were a source of remorseless problems and sluggish solutions. They were about 240 feet in length and had a 200 foot test depth. This was the maximum depth that designers estimated a submarine could descend before its hull collapsed. The truth was that many S-boats had riveted hulls that had become so eroded by age that they were confined to depths of under 100 feet. Although S-boats varied somewhat in length and equipment they generally had a single hull. This meant that ballast tanks were internal. Electric Boat Company had a patent on the U-shaped internal ballast tank and championed the superior performance of these tanks. Portsmouth Naval Shipyard installed saddle tanks that wrapped around the pressure hull, but they were partial and extended above the water line. Having tanks above the water line resulted in slower dives, definitely a problem in combat conditions.

Both fuel ballast tanks and main ballast tanks had flood valves called Kingston valves that were operated from levers on the starboard side of the control room. The range of the S-boats was so limited and the demands made on the boats were so great that many captains used all of the tanks as fuel ballast tanks. Of course, this reduced the freeboard and made cruising in heavy seas dangerous.

S-boats generally had five compartments: a torpedo room forward followed by a single battery compartment. Aft of the battery compartment was the control room, which was called the central operating compartment, an engine room, and a motor room. Above the control room was a tiny conning tower. Later S-boats had two battery compartments and were therefore longer. Each compartment was separated by a watertight bulkhead. In most S-boats, however, these bulkheads had not been tested to the two hundred foot test depth of the submarine.

Earlier S-boats had just one battery under the crew's and officers' berthing. Battery power could be supplied in series for maximum power and in parallel for maximum endurance. Large knife switches in the after part of the battery compartment were handled by electricians who responded to the diving officer's shouted orders.

On the early S-boats, the conning towers had little ports and men (it only held two people) in the conning tower could watch the fish. Periscopes extended down into the control room, next to the bow and stern plane wheels. On a few boats a short periscope stopped in the conning tower. In the portside after corner of the control room was the radio room that accommodated the large transmitting and receiving stacks. Communication was by Morse code and the radioman rate was critical to safety. Antennas were primitive, usually a half or quarter wave, end-fed, long line from the shears to the stern.

Passive and active sonar had been developed by other nations in World War I. S-boats could listen on a broadband frequency receivers that were housed in rubber shells called "rats" in honor of their shape. Another device was the Y-tube that was the fore-runner of more advanced sonar. Boat-to-boat underwater communication was by a Fessenden oscillator. This was a Morse code, keyed transducer that was good for eight miles in ideal conditions and about a half mile in typical underway conditions.

The U.S. Navy could not come up with a reliable submarine engine. Pre-World War I boats had gasoline engines that were undesirable not only because they were dangerous due to the flammability of the fuel, but because of its volatility when fumes from the fuel permeated the boat. The U.S. Navy first went to German made MAN (Mannheimer, Augsburger, Nuernburg) diesel engines and then finally to American made diesel engines. The engine room accommodated two engines, which had clutches and thrust bearings at the rear of the compartment. The clutch levers were thrown by enginemen while the battery-driven motors were operated by the electricians. The propulsion motors were on either side of centerline in the motor room.

Summing up the S-boats: they were cramped, leaky, primitive vessels that should have been taken out of service earlier, but were forced to fight in World War II as a stop-gap measure while the new fleet-type boats were being built.

In comparison, the fleet-type submarine was a modern, well designed series with all-welded, mild, low carbon steel hulls. They were 312 feet in length and displaced about 1,750 tons. Where the S-boats had crews of about forty men the fleet-type boats had crews of about eighty with some missions calling for up to a hundred men. The fleet-type boats normally had five or six officers.

The early fleet boats had test depths of 312 feet. These were referred to as "thin skinned" boats. The later *Tench*-class fleet-type boats had a 15/16 inch thick hull with a test depth of 412 feet. It should be noted that captains of the World War II often ran their boats down to 600 feet when evading Japanese depth charge attacks.

The fleet boats had saddle ballast tanks made from steel only a quarter inch thick. They were outside the pressure hull, open to the sea and therefore thin. These tanks surrounded the pressure hull and were divided between main ballast tanks and fuel ballast tanks. As fuel was used these tanks were could be flooded with seawater allowing them to function as main ballast tanks. The fleet boats had ranges exceeding twelve thousand miles, enough to carry them from Pearl Harbor to Japan where they could remain on station for about a month.

The pressure hull consisted of a long cylinder with six torpedo tubes forward and four aft. Thus, the two end compartments, the forward and after torpedo rooms, carried twenty-four torpedoes. The forward torpedo room had an escape trunk, and the after torpedo room had a reversible sleeve that allowed escape from the rear of the submarine. Behind the forward torpedo room was the forward battery compartment. This housed 126 cells that made up half of the fleet boat's battery. Above the forward battery cells were the officers' berths and their wardroom. Behind the forward battery compartment was the control room, which was topped by the conning tower. Below the control room was the pump room where many of the boat's electric motors driving various pumps resided.

The control room had two large wheels, one of which operated the stern planes and the other the bow planes. The planes were small wing-like plates that tilted to push the extremity of the boat up or down. The purpose of the bow planes was to keep depth, while the action of the stern planes was to keep the desired angle of the hull.

Just forward of the bow and stern plane wheels was the hydraulic manifold. This operated the valves for hull openings and ballast tank vents. It also controlled the flood valve for negative and safety tanks. Hull openings, ballast tank vent valve status and main/engine air induction valve status were shown on a panel of red and green lights called the "Christmas Tree." When the submarine dove the vent valves to the ballast tanks were opened, the tanks filled with water, the boat became heavy, and down went the submarine. On surfacing these vent valves were shut and compressed air from the air manifold on the other side of the compartment blew the water out the flood ports at the bottom of the ballast tanks.

The diving officer used trim tanks at both ends of the boat to help in keeping the boat level. Auxiliary tanks at the midpoint of the boat could be flooded or pumped to help the diving officer in achieving a submerged neutral buoyancy and relatively horizontal fore-aft trim. The manifold for moving water from tank to tank in the system was called the trim manifold.

The radio shack occupied the after end of the control room behind the housing for the periscopes, which ran from the boat's keel to the top of the periscope sheers above and behind the bridge.

The conning tower was a small cylinder that was mounted on the pressure hull. It had a lower and upper hatch; the lower to the control room and upper to the bridge. It contained the torpedo data computer, radar, sonar, helm, two periscopes and a small chart table.

Aft of the control room was the after battery compartment which housed the other half of the 252 cells and a refrigerator/freezer in the lower level with the galley, crew's berthing, and crew's head, with the crew's mess on the upper level. The crew's mess was the social center of the submarine in addition to providing eating tables so that a crew could eat a meal in three sittings of about thirty men each.

Two engine rooms, forward and after, housed four 1,600 horse-power diesel engines with generators on each engine. The speed of the engines and the output of the attached generators was controlled by electricians in a small compartment aft of the after engine room. It was called the maneuvering room and within its lower space were the main propulsion motors driving shafts that went to the screws. On the upper level the electricians manipulated large levers, generator rheostats, battery output, and engine speeds to turn the screws at speeds ordered by the conning officer in the conning tower. The job of the electricians was to switch from engine power to battery upon diving without interrupting the train of power to the screws.

Fresh air came into the fleet-type boat via the main induction. This consisted of a thirty-six inch valve and piping that had to be able to withstand full sea pressure at test depth. This piping dumped air into the submarine for the crew and into the engine rooms for the engines. The valve itself was behind the bridge in the superstructure.

HOLLYWOOD AND AMERICAN SUBMARINES

Several Hollywood motion pictures have fictionalized life aboard fleet-type submarines during World War II. They vary in accuracy depending upon the use of sets rather than real submarines. Cameramen trying to shoot inside an actual fleet-type submarine were hampered by the lack of open space within the boat; there is little room to place large movie cameras, necessary lights, and actors. Using sets is a more feasible option, but with the result that a submarine's interior appears relatively spacious, especially when compared to the real thing. (This is also true of belowdecks on surface ships, which even though spacious compared to submarine interiors, are also tight.) World War II boats were cramped and smelly and not hospitable to Hollywood production needs. Early submarine movies such as *Crash Dive* (1943) with Tyrone Power used sets and were the least accurate, while later ones such as *Submarine Command* (1951) with William Holden was entirely shot on the USS *Sterlet* (SS-392) and was therefore fairly accurate.

There are a few common misconceptions about life in a fleet-type submarine that have arisen from Hollywood motion pictures. Here are twelve more accurate descriptions:

- Submariners seldom wore hats in submarines. They got in the way and presented hazards around machinery.

- There were no pajamas on submarines. Men most often slept in their clothes, but a few of the more fastidious stripped down to underwear when in the bunk.

- Submariners didn't gather around the torpedo tubes to swap stories about girls back home. They swapped plenty of girl stories, but in the crew's mess.

• When under depth charge attack, submariners didn't stare at the overhead. They were too busy trying to hang on or keeping a piece of equipment from falling.

• Submariners didn't twist a convenient valve to stop a leak that sprang from a depth charge explosion. Leaks were stopped by damage control parties that had kits to cope with a variety of leak sources.

• Submariners ate the best food in the U.S. Navy, as long as it lasted. Long patrols meant lack of fresh everything, but ice-cream machines in submarines helped to boost morale. Officers ate exactly what the crew ate since meals for every person on board were prepared in the boat's single galley.

• Submariners smelled awful. A submarine's smell was a mixture of diesel oil, cork insulation, cigarette smoke, body odor, and cooking. Fresh water was limited. The purest water went for the batteries. The crew drank what was left. Showers were limited to a twenty-second dowsing once a week, if even that.

• Submariners were issued sandals which were worn in the tropical waters of the Southwest Pacific. A T-shirt, dungaree trousers and sandals made up the enlisted wardrobe. Officers wore khakis.

• Submariners were not modest. Space didn't allow for it.

• Submariners were profane. Swearing was a custom that had been honed to a fine art over their years of service by the chiefs, senior chief petty officers who could flavor the English language by inserting swear words to give it rhythm and spice. Young submariners stumbled through speaking with synthetic profanity as they tried to emulate the older salts.

• Submariners were polite and demanded good manners at mealtime. Since men were squeezed into such a small space, rudeness could not be tolerated. Prevalent in the submariner's language were, "please" when at the table, and, "excuse me" when moving through the boat.

• Every submariner was proud to be qualified in submarines and wore his dolphin emblem with patrol badge on every uniform while in port.

All in all, the submariner was an intelligent, thoughtful person dedicated to the safety of his boat. He went out of his way to ensure that every other man in his crew knew as much about his job as he did. Every submariner had to know the operation of every piece of equipment on the submarine.

PART ONE

*Prewar and Early
War Stories (1941–1942)*

SUBMARINE SCHOOL

BY CORNELIUS R. BARTHOLOMEW

Gunner's Mate Third Class Cornelius Bartholomew reported to Submarine School, New London, where he underwent physical and psychological tests to determine his aptitude for submarines. His first ride on an old boat left him doubtful that submarines were for him.

I rolled down my cuffs and squared my hat as the bus slowed. The August 1940 humidity made my blue uniform stick to my body. Wondering why I had to travel in dress blues, I handed my orders to the gate sentry at the New London, Connecticut, Submarine Base. He directed me by pointing at the school office. Inside the red brick building, I handed my orders to a yeoman in a cool white uniform. While he logged me aboard, I glanced at the name board. "Captain H. M. Jensen, USN, Commander Submarine Base. Lieutenant Commander G.C. Crawford, USN, Officer in Charge, Submarine School," it read.

"Bartholomew, report to the master at arms down the passageway. He'll fix you up with a bunk and locker. At 0800 tomorrow report to sick bay for your submarine physical," said the yeoman between yawns.

I dropped my seabag and hammock in front of my assigned locker. Looking out the window, I stared at the tall structure resembling a silo near the Thames River. There were other buildings, but no submarines in sight. The extent of my submarine knowledge was reading that Leonardo da Vinci had designed one. Weary from traveling, I stowed my gear, made my bed, ate supper and turned in. After breakfast, I reported to sick bay.

I wanted to ask why I should take another physical, but refrained. The lengthy medical history questionnaire taxed my memory. A doctor looked into my eyes, ears and nostrils. He kneaded my stomach like it was bread dough. A rubber hammer tested my reflexes. During the long examination, the doctor mumbled his findings. I was certain I had failed.

Commander C. W. Shilling, Medical Corps, U.S. Navy, Submarine Medical Psychologist, queried me for an hour. Some questions baffled me. Other questions made me extremely uncomfortable. Sweat dripped from my armpits. I wanted to flee. The commander laid down his pencil. "Bartholomew," he began, "Submarines do not carry doctors, when at sea, a highly skilled pharmacist's mate is the extent of medical services available. The extensive examinations you just completed probed for defects. The physical and emotional standards for submarine duty are far above the average for the Navy." Slumping in the chair, I realized that he was trying to be tactful. To my surprise he said, "Congratulations. You passed the first test."

Ecstatic, I wanted to celebrate, but I faced more tests. I stood next to the machine called a two-hand coordinator. Using both hands, I turned cranks as ordered. After a half-hour the instructor said, "Your eye hand coordination is excellent." Next, a pitch discriminator tested my hearing.

The next morning I stopped outside a classroom. The sign over the door got my attention. It read, "Their want of practice will make them unskillful and their want of skill, timid. Maritime skill, like skills of other kinds, is not to be cultivated by the way or at chance times. *Thucydides* 300 BC."

A tall, lean, young chief petty officer, in pressed work khaki, stopped next to me. A man in dungarees was with him. The chief introduced himself, "I'm Chief Larson. This is John Anderson, torpedoman first class. We'll be your instructors." The chief pointed at the sign. "Take the words seriously," he said.

I followed them inside. Colorful diagrams covered the walls. The side view showing the interior of a fleet-type submarine caught my attention. Other sailors entered the room. I took a seat in the front row. The chief, standing in front of a desk, glanced around the room. He introduced himself and his assistant. "This course is exact and demanding," he began. "Use your time outside of the classroom to study. We expect you to be bright-eyed and bushy-tailed every morning. If you drink, do it moderately. A hangover may allow you to miss something important that could save your life and the life of others. Did all of you bring swim suits and towels?"

Fifteen heads nodded. I immediately liked the chief. He wasn't one of the old, salty chiefs with bellies making them look like pregnant women.

His tone of voice was threat free. That was a pleasant change from barked orders.

The chief continued, "This morning, we'll march to the lower base and take the pressure test. Then we'll train in the submarine escape training tower. Submarines are safe. If an accident happens, the Navy has tested rescue measures. The submarine rescue chamber is pear shaped. A disabled submarine, like the *Squalus*, last summer, carries a releasable buoy. The yellow buoy rises to the surface. A brass plate on the buoy states, 'Submarine Sunk Here, Telephone Inside.' The buoy pinpoints the submarine's location and provides communication between the rescuers and the submarine crew."

My instruction continued. After the S-4 disaster in 1927, modem rescue procedures developed. The rescue bell could withstand pressures down to 600 feet. It could rescue eight people at a time. Every sub had specially designed hatches so the bell could attach itself to it. The equipment used in the submarine escape-training tank was similar to the bell. The torpedoman told us that we would learn how to use the Momsen lung. It would allow us to breathe while escaping if the bell wasn't available. He ended by saying, "Pay attention to the instructors. Being qualified in submarines, and some are also divers, they know their business. Let's get going.

Marching toward the lower base, I decided the silo-like tower was the submarine escape-training tank. Our group entered a building next to the tank where we put on our bathing suits. After changing, I ducked into a large cylinder. I took a seat on the bench. The white interior made the chamber look large. After the fourteen others squeezed in, the heavy door slammed shut. The instructor secured the door. "I'll bleed in air slowly, allowing you to adjust to the increasing air pressure," the instructor said. "If you have trouble popping your ears, work your jaws. Or pinch your nose, close your mouth and blow."

The hissing air created a mist. The gauge was calibrated in feet and its needle showed that we were under pressure equivalent to fifty feet beneath the surface. The instructor turned off the air. My ears cleared, and I understood what popping meant. The instructor opened a bleeder valve. The hand on the pressure gauge slowly returned to zero. After that test, my class climbed the spiral stairs to the top of the hundred foot water filled tank.

Several instructors in swimsuits were waiting. One held up a black rubber bag. "This is a Momsen Lung. There's a nose clip and mouthpiece. Chemicals in the lung allow you to breath under water. Come here," he said pointing at me.

He fastened the lung to my chest with straps around my body and fixed the clamp over my nose. I fit the mouth piece over my teeth and bit down. "Can you breathe?" asked the instructor. I nodded. Happy because I had no problems, I made escapes from eighteen and fifty feet. My final test was from the bottom of the tank, hundred feet below the surface. After entering a cylinder large enough to hold five men, called the escape lock outside the bottom of the tank, I wondered if this would be as easy as the other escapes. The instructor said, "This escape lock is just like the ones on submarines. It works the same. I'll open this valve and water will enter. The water will rise until the inside and outside pressures equalize. Then, I'll open the side hatch and we'll duck out into the tank and begin our ascent. Any questions?" he asked me. I shook my head no.

As the water rose, the inside pressure increased. If ever a person would have claustrophobia this was the time. I popped my ears and kept calm. Then I fitted the nose clamp and mouthpiece. The pressures equalized. The instructor opened the hatch. One hundred feet of water stood between me and the top of the tank.

I grasped the ascending line. Easing my grip allowed me to rise. I concentrated on what the instructor emphasized. Stopping at each ten foot marker allowed nitrogen to leave my body. Otherwise I would get the bends.

The first marker hit my hands. I clamped them shut and counted ten deliberately slow breaths. Every ten feet, I stopped. I lost track of the number of markers and time. My head popped out of the water. I wanted to shout with joy, but I didn't. The escape elated me and filled me with confidence. I wanted to repeat the escape, but time ran out.

The next day in the classroom the complex workings of a modern submarine unfolded. The fleet-type submarine is a 312 foot, welded, double hull vessel. It is sixteen feet wide in the middle. The pressure hull is inside the outer hull. Between the two hulls are the water and fuel tanks. There are eight compartments inside the pressure hull and one, the conning tower, attached above the control room. The torpedo rooms are at the bow and stern. The two battery compartments, two engine rooms and a maneuvering room are the other compartments.

The two torpedo rooms, in addition to their torpedo storage and tubes, are berthing space for some of the crew. Others sleep in the after battery compartment; it holds thirty-six men. The galley is also in the after battery compartment. The forward battery compartment has rooms for the officers, the chief's quarters and a ship's office. The battery well is under the living quarters in each battery compartment. Each contains 126 cells for storing electricity. Battery power propels the submarine when submerged. Each engine room contains two 1,600 horsepower diesel engines. The engines drive the sub on the surface. The maneuvering room contains the equipment needed to control the diesel engines and electric propulsion motors.

Throughout all compartments run electrical, hydraulic, water, and oil lines. There are watertight doors separating every compartment. Every compartment has external salvage connections. The pump room is under the control room. It contains pumps and air compressors.

Before I could qualify in submarines, I would have to submit a notebook that would contain my hand-drawn diagrams of every system aboard. The qualification examination would be oral and practical. The chief of the boat will test my knowledge first. I will have to operate all apparatus in the boat and answer questions about each piece of equipment. When the chief says I am ready, a board of qualified officers will give me the final test. "It's worth the work," said the instructor "People look up to qualified submarine sailors."

I wondered if I would earn the coveted dolphins, the distinguishing mark of a qualified submarine sailor. As I absorbed submarine knowledge, my confidence grew. Practical experience on the diving control trainer followed two months of classroom instruction. The device simulated actual diving conditions on board a submarine. I had a natural knack for controlling the depth and angle of diving using the bow and stern planes.

The day came when I and my classmates were to go to sea on a submarine. As I stepped onto the narrow topside deck of one, built in 1914, I wondered if had made a mistake volunteering. The R-Boat was 180 feet long and I guessed about ten feet wide. Images of the submarine *Squalus* sinking the year before filled my mind. My shins got scrapped climbing down the narrow hatch, further distressing me. I ducked my head often to miss overhead valves below deck. The cramped compartments didn't improve my disposition. It wasn't at all like the fleet-type boats we had studied in the classroom. I disliked the taste of the foul air. Engine noise filled my ears as the sub got under way. The creaking old submarine wobbled, traveling down the Thames to the operating area. *"OOGHA, OOGHA,"* caught me off guard. Kingston valves clanked open. Hissing air filled the control room.

"Green board, pressure in the boat," the chief shouted. The submarine tilted down. When it leveled off at periscope depth, I took control of the bow planes; making the submarine respond to depth changes. I forgot my fears. After that dive, I eagerly looked forward to the next one. The challenging course, the dangerous diving excitement and the camaraderie of the instructors and crew filled me with enthusiasm.

Upon graduation I received orders to a real submarine. I eagerly looked forward to the USS *Sargo* (SS 188), a fleet-type submarine.

Chapter 2

DECEMBER 1941

SEA DRAGON'S PROP WASH

BY A.J. KILLIN

A. J. Killin, a crew member aboard USS *Sea Dragon* (SS-194), was on the bridge when the Japanese attacked Cavite Naval Base, Philippines. The accurate bombing sank *Sea Lion* (SS-195) and badly damaged *Sea Dragon*, but Killin rode her south to Perth, Australia.

I was on a submarine, the U.S.S. *Sea Dragon* (SS-194), in World War II. As part of the Asiatic Fleet, we were stationed in Manila, Philippines. In December of 1941, we were at the Cavite Navy Yard for an overhaul. On the same day that Pearl Harbor was bombed, the Japanese wiped out all the air fields in the Philippines, thereby eliminating our air protection.

On December 10, 1941, at 12 noon, the Navy yard was heavily bombed. Three flights of 27 Mitsubishi bombers flew over our Navy yard, dropping 500-pound bombs. We did not have a gun that could touch them. They didn't even break formation. They completely destroyed the Navy yard and the ships in dry dock.

Our *Sea Dragon* submarine was tied up to the dock, and our sister ship, the U.S.S. *Sea Lion* (SS-195), was tied up outboard of us. The *Sea Lion* took a 500-pound bomb down the after-torpedo room hatch, sinking her. At that instant, one of our officers and I were on the bridge of *Sea Dragon*. That officer was killed by the impact of the bomb which destroyed *Sea Lion*.

While I was rushing down the ladder into the conning tower, another concussion knocked me fourteen feet below to the control room deck. Four knobs about two inches long were all that remained of the ladder railing into control. I fell onto one of the knobs sticking up, landing full force on the tip of my spine. I lay there senseless on the control room deck for quite awhile, and then heard the captain yell, "Abandon ship!"

By the time I picked myself up, managing to get top-side and was started down the dock, the captain was then telling everyone to get back on board.

After the bombers had flown away, a salvage ship, the U.S.S. *Widgeon*, tied up to our stern and with some effort pulled us clear of the destroyed *Sea Lion*. Our sub had also caught a lot of shrapnel from the *Sea Lion*, but luckily the pressure hull was not ruptured. We had many holes in the superstructure, and a lot of the deck was gone.

We managed to get over to Manila where we tied the submarine up to the tender, U.S.S. *Canopus*. For three days, work was performed on the *Sea Dragon*. We worked all night long, preparing the boat to once again become seaworthy. Work was done on the *Sea Dragon* under the cover of darkness at night, and during the day we would have to lie on the bottom of Manila Bay until it turned dark again. The reason for this was that the Japanese chose daylight to attack.

Finally ready for sea on December 13, 1941, we departed for Surabaya, Java, in the Netherlands East Indies. When we passed Corregidor and started south, we saw three Japanese destroyers patrolling the entrance to Manila Bay. Corregidor was an Army island fort at the entrance of Manila

Bay. As we proceeded to dive, the Japanese gave us our first taste of depth-charging. After about two hours, the three destroyers finally left. We surfaced, and after a few days we finally reached Surabaya, Java. We went into a Dutch dry dock and they fixed us up as best they could.

After our overhaul by the Dutch, we went out on our first offensive patrol run. We were assigned a patrol station off French Indochina. We were located outside Cam Ranh Bay, a big Japanese naval base. We made an approach on a heavy Japanese cruiser. Our captain ordered firing four torpedoes as the cruiser was going into their base. The torpedoes all missed. We were using Mark XIV torpedoes and having trouble with them, as was everybody else. The miss was costly. We were depth-charged pretty heavily.

After fifty-five days we ended our patrol. We could not go back to Surabaya because the Japanese had already captured it. Our orders were to go to Perth, Australia.

Tokyo Rose broadcasted that a Japanese destroyer had sunk a red pirate submarine off the coast of French Indochina. This crock of prop wash was supposedly us, the U.S.S. *Sea Dragon*! We made five patrol runs from Perth and as the torpedo problems were solved so our score got a lot better.

Chapter 3

DECEMBER 1941

A VANISHING DAY-DREAM

BY CORNELIUS R. BARTHOLOMEW

> Bartholomew had been promised that submarine duty would mean exotic, Oriental dancing girls, but he found only sweaty men in a smelly submarine.

A black tropical night catapulted me into manhood. Eighteen hours earlier I had been a carefree nineteen year old Gunner's Mate 3rd Class. I returned from Liberty in Manila, Commonwealth of the Philippines. The message, "hostilities exist," arrived west of the international dateline at 0300 Monday, December 8, 1941. Before that morning my concern about war had been as short-lived as a mouthful of beer on a hot afternoon. Although the USS *Sargo* (SS 188) and I had practiced war for months, neither was ready.

I felt a singular bond to *Sargo*. I was born in St. Paul, Minnesota. I liked to believe *Sargo*'s steel came from the Mesabi iron ore range in northern Minnesota. She was launched June 6, 1938 at Electric Boat Company Groton, Connecticut while I had chased girls in high school. During July of 1939 *Sargo* joined the Pacific Fleet to practice war. As I had bewailed the Army type life in the Civilian Conservation Corps camp I had no idea that she would become my life.

The CCC camp's officer was a lieutenant junior grade in the United States Naval Reserve. He had listened to my moaning and told another sea story. His sea stories always ended in romantic encounters with exotic dancing girls playing a ukulele. Those romantic stories propelled me to a Navy Recruiting Office. After boot training and submarine school I had reported aboard the USS *Salt Lake City* en route to the Mare Island Naval Shipyard where *Sargo* was completing an overhaul.

I dropped my sea bag at the brow of the submarine. The deck watch wore his .45 caliber pistol low like a western gunfighter. He stood in rubble on a black hulk with large red splotches. From all segments of the hulk, black spaghetti-like lines ran helter-skelter. Minnesota mosquitoes, CCC [Civilian Conservation Corps] and boot camp looked like the Garden of Eden compared to the wreckage I was boarding. I could hardly believe it was a submarine.

The deck watch shouted down the hatch, "Chief, fresh meat on deck." My stomach tightened as a khaki hat popped out of the forward torpedo room hatch. Following it was a smiling chief in dungarees. "Welcome aboard. I'm chief of the boat," he said pleasantly. I followed the chief down the hatch. Below decks looked like a giant ant farm. Tall, short, fat and thin men bustled about.

I quickly donned dungarees and helped piece *Sargo* together. After we got underway for sea trials, the leading seaman became my buddy. His sea stories were irresistible. On liberty in Vallejo he took me in every bar on Georgia Street where I found no exotic girls, just tawdry dark saloons.

My pal promised me that Hawaii was overflowing with exotic girls in grass skirts. Exotic girls filled my daydreams, but practice war had been the plan of the day. We performed every emergency drill and completed every submarine function for our skipper. He was pleased, but the schedule of practice had continued.

The closest I ever came to an exotic girl was a poster on the bulkhead at the SubBase Pearl beer hall. Dismayed, I hung onto my fading daydream as we got underway on a forty-day practice war patrol to the west. Passing battleship row that September day in 1941, I had nudged my buddy and said, "Do you think we're going to war?"

"Are you nuts? Look at them battleships with their awnings rigged. They have sixteen-inch guns and eighteen inches of armor. Who would be dumb enough to fight them?" he answered with certainty.

"Where are we going on patrol?" I asked.

"Between the Marshal Islands and Midway Island. Those islands are over-run with exotic girls," he guaranteed. The war patrol had ended at Midway Island. The only occupants were a Pan-American Airline employee, a tent city of U.S. Marines and a million gooney birds. Drinking beer with an aged Marine sergeant, I watched the Pan American Clipper disappear into the Western sky.

"China is the place for exotic girls," the sergeant said wiping tears from his eyes. I started daydreaming about oriental exotic girls. *Sargo* put to sea and we steamed west. One day I asked permission to come on the bridge. It was a quiet day of steaming and I asked the officer of the deck if he thought we were going to have a war with Japan. He shook his head and said, "They can't leave port since our President cut off their oil supply." It seemed logical.

Friday afternoon, December 5, 1941, we entered Manila Bay and moored to buoy number three. Saturday as we loaded exercise torpedoes, a Japanese passenger ship sped past and anchored near Fleet Landing. I wondered about that ship and again asked my buddy about the possibility of war. Undaunted by my pessimistic question he opened the, "Strip-ship for War" book.

"It says here that when war is imminent, we're to off-load all combustibles including awnings, paint and dress uniforms. The awning is rigged. A seaman is painting. We still have our dress uniforms," he said with conclusive conviction. He slammed the book indicating he won another argument, but I still thought of that Japanese ship.

On Sunday, December 7, 1941 my buddy declared that he had found our exotic girls. My war thoughts vanished. That night I drank Geneva Gin and Sarsaparilla at the Santa Anna Dance Pavilion. They were there alright. For ten cents a sailor could dance with one. It wasn't what I had dreamed of.

As the sun peeked over the horizon on Monday, December 8, I took a taxi back to the boat. I boarded *Sargo* and was confronted by the topside watch who told me that Pearl Harbor had been bombed by the Japanese. I plunged into preparing her for war. The awning came down. Combustibles were off loaded. Exercise torpedoes were exchanged for torpedoes with war heads. After fueling and topping off with supplies, we got underway, sped past Corregidor Island and anchored in Mariveles Bay to await darkness.

At midnight I relieved the lookout watch as *Sargo* made standard speed toward her assigned war patrol area. *Sargo*'s bubbling wake disappeared astern. Land passed from sight. With my last glimpse of land, my exotic daydream vanished; replaced by the urgency of war.

Chapter 4

JANUARY 1942

OPERATIONAL READINESS ON DECEMBER 7, 1941

BY FRANK E. PERRY

Frank Perry was aboard SS-141 that went to the Philippines where the boat sank a Japanese freighter, then, with equipment breaking-down on a daily basis, the old boat finally met her end, high and dry on a reef.

The keel of the SS-141, later to be the USS S-36, was laid in December of 1921. Launched a year later, she was placed in active commission early in 1923. I was also conceived and christened at about the same time, but, paradoxically, when our paths crossed on the 6th of April 1940, I was a green, untried young seaman and she a respected and venerable lady of standing in the Asiatic Fleet.

After having passed the required tests I received permission to wear the coveted embroidered dolphin insignia on my sleeve. I continued learning submarine lore in the ensuing months of local operations in the Philippines. This activity was punctuated by an annual ritual; the ten-day Readiness for War Patrol Inspection, and, as a finale, it was highlighted by a summer deployment to Hong Kong, Shanghai and Tsingtao, China. However, the heightened international tension prompted the decision to cancel our annual operations in Chinese waters in the spring of 1941. Later in the year, with war clouds unmistakably gathering, the scenario for the final chapter of the USS S-36 was set.

Lieutenant J. R. Mcknight, Jr. had assumed command, relieving Lieutenant R. R. McGregor. Our new skipper, having served on the more spacious and comfortable fleet-type boats, recalled that he was astounded by the cramped quarters and primitive living conditions on board the vintage boat, but that he had no real reservations as to her ability, or that of the crew, to cope with whatever operational assignment was handed her.

On December 2, 1941 the captain received a radio dispatch summoning him to the tender, USS *Holland*, for a briefing. Oddly, prior to leaving the boat, he ordered the executive officer, Lieutenant junior grade J.M. Seymour, to stop all scheduled ships work outlined for our routine refit period and, in its stead, issued orders to him to make all preparations for getting underway in full war-readiness condition. Returning from a brief leave, I arrived on board and was greeted by a frenzied level of excitement I had never seen before. Quickly changing into dungarees, I joined the bustling activity to assist in getting the boat ready for sea. I noted soberly, that a strip ship order was being expedited.

Our captain had not had any advance notice of the instructions he was about to receive at the briefing. He did, however, have a very strong hunch about it, and the hunch paid off. We were underway just before midnight, well before any other boat in our division was readied for sea. We left behind such non-essentials as our tiny brow, the hatch covers, topside awnings and our mooring lines.

Although the crew did not know our destination, it was literally impossible to maintain that type of secret on board such a small boat. Soon, all hands knew we were bound for Cape Bolinao, just north of Lingayen Gulf. The following day we sighted two Yangtze River patrol boats on reverse course, headed for Manila. These craft, we knew, had been ordered out of China in response to the rapidly worsening political / military climate in the Far East. Following a smooth passage, during the late afternoon of 4 December, in an idyllic picture-postcard setting, we glided serenely into Bolinao harbor. Anchoring in the calm, water, a modified steaming watch was set. Those of us not on watch were assembled at quarters and the captain very briefly related to us that a war message, originating from Commander in Chief, Asiatic Fleet, Admiral Thomas C. Hart, had come down advising that war with Japan was imminent and that we had been ordered to Bolinao as a preparedness measure and were to remain there until further orders.

The excitement of being on alert quickly wore off and, like military men everywhere, we began to grouse and complain. And although the crew made light of what was possibly ahead, there was an undercurrent of serious resolve behind the wise cracks and skylarking. I think most of us felt that war was coming and that it was better to adopt a philosophical tack since there was really very little that we could do about it.

In the very early morning of December the 8th, we received the fateful message, "Hostilities have commenced, govern your-self accordingly." We topped off the batteries with a quick charge, and about noon, slipped our anchor and receipted for specific instructions as to our assigned patrol area off Lingayen Gulf. Shortly before getting underway, a sloop that had been anchored nearby signaled to us. Its crew, understandably panicked by the shattering news, requested that they be allowed to accompany us. Since they were Americans it was indeed difficult for us to tell them they would simply have to make it somehow on their own. They trailed forlornly behind us as we stood out of the harbor, and later, after we had submerged and established our trim, she was glimpsed through the periscope, on a southerly course, presumably for Manila. I have never ceased to wonder as to her fate.

As the hot, sweaty days slowly passed it was increasingly apparent that the obsolescent and creaky old S-boat was truly showing disturbing symptoms of her advanced age. Without air-conditioning the tropical heat and humidity reached almost unbearable levels. And, as an adjunct, the tiny rivulets of condensation that slowly trickled down the bulkheads contributed to the many electrical grounds that plagued the electricians. Machinery that was nearly twenty years old first became balky and then failed completely. The electrical steering system, after being repaired twice, stubbornly resisted all further efforts to be restored. The main exhaust valves began leaking excessively and, ominously, a cracked cell was found in the after battery. And, annoyingly, we could receive radio traffic, but we were apparently unable to transmit. So, after a very frustrating period of attempting to keep S-36 operational, plus the added bad luck of sighting only a few friendly interisland small craft and an occasional enemy aircraft, we were recalled to Manila.

After anchoring off Mariveles Bay following a glitch in ship-to-shore recognition procedure, we entered Manila Bay and moored inside the breakwater alongside a sampan and beneath a camouflaged netting that was painted to resemble another sampan when viewed from the air. There the soft patch was removed and the crew hurriedly completed what other repairs that could be made while the cracked cell was replaced in the after battery. Shortly, after refueling and replenishing our dry stores and fresh provisions, we headed south to our next patrol station at Verde Island Passage.

On New Year's Day the captain decided to investigate the small harbor of Calapan, and luck was with us. Inside the harbor and moored to a seawall during unloading operations was a small Japanese transport. Skillfully maneuvering the boat inside the narrow confines of the harbor, the captain crept as close as he dared and fired one torpedo. *BAM!* The explosion was much louder than I think any of us anticipated and the dust sifted down from the overhead frame spaces along with a small rain of paint chips accompanying the flying debris were triumphant grins. One fish, one hit and one ship. Not bad. The captain, observing that the explosion was on the far side of the target, concluded correctly that the fish had run deep and had detonated on impact with the seawall, against which the ship had been moored. This was confirmed as the target listed heavily and sank, presenting her untouched flank toward us.

With spirits elevated we continued our patrol. On the 8th of January, with the toll of daily engineering and electrical casualties rapidly mounting, it became clear that the distance and time factors to our nearest friendly port, the Dutch East Indies, were critical. The problem lay with the high rate of battery water consumption. It had become prohibitive in light of the fact that our ancient Nelseco exhaust evaporators [sea water distillers] simply could not supply the batteries with the water they required. Reluctantly we headed south, and that night, the port air compressor failed. Despite working long, fatiguing hours in the oppressive heat, the weary engineers were unable to repair it. Two days after the port compressor went out the starboard compressor also began to exhibit a lack of interest in remaining operational. Then with no warning the port main motor succumbed to a myriad of commutator [rotary electrical switch] short circuits and the starboard main engine lubricating pump began to malfunction.

With but two main engines, mechanically clutched to two main motors, it was obvious that a casualty to any single unit in this array would be crippling. But, if say, the starboard motor and the port engine became inoperable that would be a terminal condition since two motors would be required to maintain speed and depth control while submerged. Similarly, at least one healthy engine in tandem with a functional main motor would be needed on the surface to recharge the expended batteries. Thus, it was clear that lacking full capability of both engines and both motors, the operational potential of our submarine was reduced to zero.

The crew was very tired. Men who were not engineers, some who didn't know an injector from a chipping hammer, had volunteered to help in the searing, strength-sapping heat of the engine and the motor room. Each day that came seemed to bring yet another mechanical or electrical failure. Each brought forth a yet more determined effort on the part of the exhausted crew.

In the early morning darkness of January 15th, with half of the port main motor's innards littering the deck of the after battery, the bridge received word that a delay was necessary in our scheduled morning dive since the starboard main motor had lost lube oil pressure. Nearly simultaneously, the starboard lookout reported an island on the starboard beam. The OD, puzzled because there should not have been land visible, trained his binoculars on the reported bearing and was horrified to see that the island was a Japanese destroyer which was closing fast. The captain arrived on the bridge, and swiftly appraised the situation. He then hurriedly blurted his favorite expression of, "Great Balls of Fire!" This immediately was followed by the order to, "Take her down."

The aggressive Jap tin can, in a determined effort to ram, loomed menacingly close aboard as our hatch thumped shut and we began to slide beneath the surface. His thrashing propellers, clearly audible through the hull, sounded like a passing freight train, and for a few seconds was accompanied by a strange thrumming noise that we later were to discover was the rubbing of his hull over our after clearing vanes. The Jap skipper, obviously a member of the Hirohito's [Emperor of Japan] first team, had immediately sensed that his ramming attempt had not succeeded. He accurately straddled us with a pattern of seven depth charges that exploded close aboard with a vicious, collective roar. Then, in numbing succession, we lost power to the bow and stern planes, the starboard lighting circuit and the main gyro. With all compartments aft of the control room momentarily in darkness, the starboard main motor, starving for lube oil, began to emit a rhythmic screech. The sum of our casualties meant we were with but one screw for propulsion and both planes were now in hand operation. As a result, we lost depth control and began rapidly to sink. As the depth gauge approached 260 feet, well past our test depth of 200 feet, the captain faced a rapid and unchecked descent. He ordered a bubble placed in number one main ballast tank. Then in a beautifully timed order, he flooded and vented the tank, neatly stopping our elevator-like rise to the surface at about ninety feet. It was truly a remarkable feat.

The destroyer methodically continued its search, pinging continuously, as our depth also continued to fluctuate wildly between seventy-five and two hundred feet. Some of our gyrations were deliberate, but most were only a matter of trying to keep up with our problems. The captain ordered the gun crew to assemble and stand by in the forward battery. At the same time the word was circulated to, "Stand by to abandon ship." Life jackets and Momsen lungs were issued and those without vital battle stations proceeded to their assigned areas. As the minutes trickled by it looked as though we had eluded the destroyer. By mid-morning, the captain, still maintaining the conn, had, with the planesmen, begun to solve the tricky feat of maintaining our depth and trim. Shortly, we lost contact with the destroyer, and thankfully, he with us.

We had experienced a very close call both from the attacking destroyer and also from our own very critical materiel deficiencies.

A key element in our survival was attributed to a gutsy seventeen year old fireman apprentice who remained in the almost unbearable heat of the motor room for a period of over two hours while he doggedly squirted oil from a hand gun onto the starboard shaft pedestal bearing. The bearing had been so overheated that the babbitt bearing surface was melting and oozing out onto the rotating shaft. His courageous action saved the boat. And, to this day, his timely action and persistent determination, remains one of those unrewarded feats that somehow, inexplicably, seems to get lost in the vast history of war.

We continued south on a heading for Soerabaja, Java as the exhausted electricians, performing like zombies, continued work on the port main motor. That night, unbelievably, the motor was again in commission. However, after assuming the load of the battery charge, in about six hours it began to smoke again. In addition, the starboard main motor lubrication supply again failed.

At dawn we submerged. Men, many in an advanced state of exhaustion and some dehydrated, dropped to the deck where they stood and slept like babies.

Just before noon a fire broke out in the main motor auxiliary circulating pump. It was quickly extinguished, but the boat was filled with acrid, irritating fumes that burned our eyes, causing us to cough and retch. After surfacing that night we reveled in the cool, fresh air being sucked down through the conning tower hatch by our one good engine as the men on watch continued their stubborn efforts to repair the ailing old S-boat. At 2300 we passed North Watcher Island abeam to starboard and obtained a good navigational fix. On the 17th of January we receipted for orders directing us to proceed to Soerabaja. During the day both the port and starboard shafts were alternately out of commission because of failure to the main motor lube oil pumps. The pumps were repaired, but several men, including myself, collapsed from the heat and exertion. The following day, the pumps doing their job, marked the first day since the 7th of January that no major part of the engineering plant was out of commission.

We continued down through Makassar Strait and, during the night of the 19th, we were able to get in a full battery charge. Shortly after 0300 the charge was secured and we were treated to both engines on the line for propulsion. Fate must have leered knowingly at our apparent good fortune because the additional speed gained from both engines contributed to the doom of the gallant old boat.

With the resilience of youth, I had recovered from the heat exhaustion I had previously suffered. After coming off watch at midnight, I had luxuriated in an alky [alcoholic] rubdown, a bucket face-wash and a shave. Feeling refreshed and chipper, I requested and received permission to go to the bridge. While enjoying the balmy night breeze, the OD rang up a standard bell. Soon, with some assistance from a quartering sea, we were making an estimated ten knots.

Just after the change of watch at 0400, 1 was in the forward battery compartment and I felt and heard a light scraping noise accompanied by a slight up angle along with a rapid deceleration of our forward movement. This immediately became a grinding, bouncing roar that culminated in a jarring crash that brought us to a full stop.

The captain went immediately to the bridge and shortly the order came down for one man to come topside with a lead line. I scrambled up on deck, noting as I did, that we already had a list to starboard. I could not read the lead line in the darkness but I had felt the lead strike bottom almost as soon as I released it and passed this information to the bridge. A full astern order was given which resulted in a terrific vibration as the screws chewed uselessly into the rock and coral that had entrapped us. A plain language message was transmitted, "Aground and sinking. Request immediate help." Chlorine was reported in the forward battery compartment and all hands were ordered topside where they huddled miserably in the lee of the conning tower, braced against the waves sweeping the deck.

The boat was now listed sharply to starboard. As the coming dawn lightened the sky the receding tide exposed the jagged coral and protruding rocks. A large coral head lay just under the port stem plane fairing, while a huge rock, the size of a Buick, had pierced number one MBT [main ballast tank] and the pressure hull, allowing water into the forward battery compartment. Ironically, those few extra knots that we had been so happy to attain was sufficient inertia for the boat to have planned up and over the outer ring of the nearly invisible reef while maintaining enough speed to clear it completely before smashing down into a mini lagoon studded with rocks.

The sea, estimated by the captain as Force Two, alternately lifted the boat clear of the rocks, then, as each wave passed the boat came smashing down again with a shuddering crash that shook her from stem to stem. Various suggestions were made and then discarded; lighten ship by firing torpedoes, jettison the fuel, and others. None of these measures could remove the huge rock that held us firmly, impaling us in a death grip. With each up and down movement of the boat, the mortal wound in her side was widened and deepened. After a wet and sleepless night a Dutch launch, dispatched from Makassar City, hove into view. A decision had been made to off-load all but a select crew of volunteers and await conditions that might be more favorable for salvage. All but fourteen men, I, being one of them, plus one officer and the captain were transferred without incident.

The boat continued to absorb the unmerciful pounding as the day wore on and the seas came up. We were by now all drenched and sunburned from the equatorial sun, and, it became increasingly clear to all of us that any salvage effort was doomed to failure. In mid-afternoon a Dutch freighter, the SS *Siberote,* nosed slowly into the reef, bow into the sea and lowered a lifeboat. After rigging the boat for flooding we disembarked, in orderly fashion, leaving the stricken old S-boat for the last time. We had given our best to save her, having fought the good fight. Now it was time to go.

Later, I was assigned to the USS *Sargo* (SS-188) and en route through Makassar Strait to our assigned patrol station, I was on watch in the control room. Word came down that I was wanted in the conning tower. As I heaved myself up the ladder, the captain winked at me and asked, "Wanta' see your old home?"

From a range of about 2,500 yards, with periscope in high power, I could only distinguish a thin black finger angling skyward, touched occasionally with a feather of foam. A rush of nostalgia washed over me as I thought of the old 36 boat and her scrappy crew. Now, there she was, defiant as ever and still braving the sea in her tomb of coral and rock. She had been a courageous and gallant lady.

Chapter 5

JANUARY 1942

REST AND RECREATION

BY FRANK KIMBALL

> Frank Kimball's submarine was chased south from the Philippines by advancing Japanese naval forces. He wound up at Surabaya, Java, where a Dutch facility offered great recreation . . . including a Dutch wife.

The morning of December 7, 1941 broke the news of Pearl Harbor to us when we were tied up to a Submarine Tender in Manila Bay. The news led to a flurry of activity as we topped off our fuel and provisions and headed for sea so that we, too, would not be caught like sitting ducks. I was beginning my first war patrol on a Fleet Submarine.

During the next six weeks or more, we received our baptism of fire, having every size shell carried by the Japanese Navy fired at us, from machine gun bullets up to eight-inch shells. There were so many depth charges dropped on us that I had lost count. We had avoided floating and submerged mines and torpedoes. In fact, we even avoided getting rammed by patrol boats bent on sinking us any way they could.

I had spent so many hours on regular watches and at battle stations that I was bone-weary, cross-eyed, punch-drunk, and close to becoming a zombie. Our air conditioning machinery broke down, making the heat and humidity almost unbearable, and on top of that, all of our perishable food was exhausted. Fresh salads, eggs, and even meat were distant memories, and everything put on the table came out of cans. Milk was powdered Klim, meat was canned Spam to go with canned spuds. When the cook opened a can of powdered eggs the stink went from one end of the boat to the other, and we were gagging before we even started for the crew's mess. Dreams of a platter loaded with fresh, scrambled hens' eggs and a tall glass of milk were top priority in my list of pleasurable dreams.

It was good news then, when on January 19, 1942 we were ordered into Balikpapen, Borneo, where a Dutch Army Depot would refuel us and give us what provisions they could spare. No sooner had we tied up to the fueling dock than we had to throw the lines over the side and skedaddle as the first wave of Japanese bombers came over and literally obliterated the base. Ninety miles at sea the fires could still be seen as the oil storage tanks burned.

On the 30th, we docked at a Dutch Navy Yard in Surabaya, Java. Once we had submitted our list of urgent repairs to the Navy yard representative, the crew was granted shore leave, except for the duty watch. We were advised to get some rest while we could, as our schedule was so uncertain.

As I climbed the ladder and stuck my head up into the first sunshine I had seen in two months, I received the first of several unpleasant surprises. I thought I had been stabbed in the eyes with knives, and I had to go back below and wait dusk. Then, I tried again, along with my buddy, Jack, intending to proceed to a restaurant only a block and a half away and fulfill that dream of fresh, scrambled eggs, and milk. We had walked only a half a block when the second experience hit us—we could not walk that far. Our feet and legs were no longer capable, and they rebelled. We immediately hailed a pedicab and rode the rest of the way in style. We had one-track minds and would have crawled if necessary.

Night had already fallen, the blackout curtains were all shut, and our destination was lit only by several small candles, and we could barely see the table at which we sat. The waiter came over barefoot, but dressed in glistening white, from a huge turban to a Nehru jacket to pantaloons that buttoned at the ankles. Local custom was to drop cigarette butts, chicken bones and such on the floor and we watched, fascinated as our waiter trampled over live butts without even flinching. However, we had a new problem—he spoke no English and we spoke no Dutch or Javanese. Our orders were met with blank looks, and our hand signs and Pidgin English were no more understandable.

Finally, in desperation, we signaled the waiter to follow us, and headed for the kitchen. That was evidently forbidden territory, and cost us a bribe. By the time we reached that area we had collected quite an entourage of cooks, waiters, various kitchen employees, and even the manager. Of course, all of this cost more bribes.

I finally found a basket of eggs, but they were small, like pigeon eggs. However, that no longer mattered. It would only take more. Then I looked for milk; not knowing there were no cows raised in that climate, so when

I did find a container of milk, little did I know it was from a water

We now had most of the necessary ingredients. Continuing to hand out more money to everybody who objected, I found two huge glasses, filled them with milk, nestled them in a pan of crushed ice, and was ready to scramble eggs. But first, we had to wrestle the monstrous cockroaches that seemed reluctant to turn our bowl loose, and Jack finally had to hold on to one side and fight them off with his other hand while I broke eggs into it and added milk. Once we had the mixture in a pan on the hot stove, the bugs conceded defeat and left, but not far.

Accompanied by a large following of natives who gathered to see some crazy Americans eat the mess we had prepared, we began our meal. We had everything set in place on a snowy white tablecloth, with Jack and I impatient to dig into food that was fit for the gods. We were both sitting in near darkness as I reached for the salt and pepper, lifted the containers and gave each several shakes, ignoring the protests of those watching.

In that country there were no lids on the shakers. A person poured a little in the palm, and then, taking a pinch, sprinkled a bit onto the food. I had emptied both containers on my eggs, but because of the dim light could not see my error.

Of course, those beautiful scrambled eggs ended up on the floor, as I hurriedly reached for my glass of cold milk. Once again, I did not know that our waiter had been trying to be helpful and figured if we wanted an iced drink the ice belonged inside the glass. The meal was a disaster. After all our months of anticipation, to have it end like that was a disappointment beyond description, and we were both still weak from hunger. So, sadly we left that place of despair, went outside, caught another pedicab, went to the establishment next door, sat down and ordered a bottle of sarsaparilla.

We had now been in port four hours. The following morning, word was passed that the Dutch commandant had extended the use of their submarine rest camp to our crew. It was high in the mountains, would be cool and relaxing, and it would be free. Half the crew could go at once, and upon their return, the other half could go. I was in the first group, so hurriedly gathered some toilet articles and headed topside to board the waiting bus, which took us into town and left us at the railroad station. We were soon loaded onto a small train resembling the famous, Toonerville

Trolley. We headed up a steep, winding climb into the mountains. It was a beautiful trip, what with all the lush, tropical vegetation, and as it started to cool off, I thoroughly enjoyed the ride.

When we arrived at the camp, we were informed that a nearby, luxurious, tourist resort had also extended an invitation to us to use their facilities, and that too was free. So, once again I boarded a bus, and we rode over to the lodge where we found swimming, sauna, gymnasium, tennis courts, and other luxuries available. I elected to go horseback riding, along with half a dozen others, so we were soon on our horses, and, guided by a native employee, riding through a maze of rice paddies, on a caribou path that more or less followed an irrigation ditch.

The roar of hundreds of planes caused us to look over our shoulders, and we saw wave after wave of Japanese bombers and fighter planes coming up behind us, and no doubt heading for the air field several miles ahead. Our glistening white uniforms stood out like sore thumbs, and a fighter pilot decided he would pick up a bonus. With machine guns blazing, the plane angled over and came after us. We could see the water riffling as the bullets struck, and the line of spray headed right for us. There was only one thing to do, and I wasted no time in diving off the horse and into the irrigation ditch. I scrambled for the bottom, trying to find a handhold to enable me to burrow deeper into the mud and slime, and held my breath for as long as possible, then surfaced cautiously. The bullets had evidently bounced off the surface, or at least been deflected enough that no one was hurt, and the planes were by then busily engaged in wiping out the air base. They had also obliterated the tourist resort as they went over, but fortunately had not bombed the rest camp.

Again, we had no choice, as we hiked back to the rest camp. We arrived there, still wet, filthy dirty and bedraggled, with our formerly white uniforms looking as though we had mud-wrestled in a vat of very strong coffee. My room boy, shaking his head, brought me one of his native sarongs and took my clothing to the laundry to be washed and ironed. I felt kind of silly, parading around barefoot in a piece of brightly colored cloth tied at the waist. But I had company, and no one paid us much attention.

Following our evening meal, I returned to my room, where a wooden platform covered with a thin reed mat awaited me. That would be my bed, but to make it even worse, I could not find any bedding. It was already dark and raining outside, really cooling off, and I had nothing on except my little sarong. While I stood there the air raid sirens started wailing and a Dutch Marine pounded on the door and pointed towards the air raid shelter.

Running outdoors and in the direction indicated I fell into a six-foot deep slit trench, which was where I spent the next several hours. It was really raining by then, a real monsoon. I had to hold my head down, close my eyes and breathe through my mouth to keep from drowning. Of course, the trench had a couple of feet of water in it, and I thought I would freeze before the all clear sounded. Then, when I returned to the barracks I found that the camp's generator had been secured for the night, so the showers were icy cold. I had to bribe my room boy for a second one of his sarongs.

Once again I searched for bedding, but without success. I was becoming desperate as well as cold, so I called the room boy again. He, in turn, had to procure an interpreter, who informed me that no one used bedding up in the mountains. It was too hot. However, if I wished, I could go to the supply depot and draw a Dutch wife for the length of my stay, but that was all that was available. I did not have the heart to defy local custom and didn't want to risk hurting the feelings of my hosts. If that were the custom, then I would happily cooperate. In fact, I felt it was my patriotic duty to investigate this offer and then report to my shipmates back on board, so they would not be ignorant of local customs. A Dutch woman sounded just fine to me.

Down to the supply depot I went. Stepping boldly up to the window, I stated, that I would like to be issued a Dutch wife for the night.

When the supply clerk returned, he handed me what looked like a big pillow. It was about a foot in diameter, and about thirty inches long, covered with bright cotton cloth, tied at both ends. Of course, I didn't understand. I had been expecting to see a beautiful girl walk out of the storeroom and say, "Welcome."

Fortunately, the clerk spoke English and was able to explain this custom. He said that when Dutch forces first took over the island, during the days of their colonial empire expansion, dependents were billeted in bachelor quarters, guarded by sentries. As Java was almost on the equator, the troops started suffering from heat rash and other tropical problems. Then, someone stuffed a pillow full of down and used it to throw an arm and leg over. That allowed air to circulate, and sleeping was cooler and more comfortable. As this became popular and refined, the present bolster evolved, and they were called, "Dutch wives." Eventually, young children used a smaller version that increased in size as the child grew.

However, I was looking for warmth, and this object was of no use to me. While I was debating with myself how to handle the problem without causing hard feelings by returning it, the sirens opened up again. I quickly thrust the bolster back through the window and made a dash for the now familiar and rain-filled trench where I had to remain until dawn.

Following the all clear, I returned to the barracks, and, as the generator was now running, I had a hot shower and donned my clean, dry uniform. Then the room boy came in with a steaming pot of tea, and while I was on my second cup, we were called to breakfast.

Upon arrival in the dining room, I was introduced to another local custom. This was the main meal of the day, and the tables groaned from the weight of dozens of cold cuts, meats, fish and poultry, along with many unrecognizable foods. There were no bacon and eggs or other American dishes, just wafer-thin slices of sandwich material. I started making myself a Dagwood. I was beginning to feel nearly human again, and that was a good thing, because the loudspeaker was turned on and someone with a Dutch accent ordered, "All American sailors back to the ship."

When we hurried over the brow a little later, we found the crew furiously passing cases and crates of canned goods down the hatches. Most of them had labels that read, "*Hutspot Me Clapstuk*." That turned out to be beef stew with gravy. It would probably taste better than Spam, which by then was all gone.

As the last supplies went down the hatch, the air raid sirens started up and the planes were visible on the horizon. We simply shut the hatches, opened the vents and settled on the bottom, right where we were. However, we found the water too shallow to get all the way under, and our shears and periscope stuck up like a beacon. After the raid the captain said, "Men, this rest and recreation is going to be the death of us. What do you say, let's go back to sea."

Chapter 6
FEBRUARY 1942
THE FIRST AND ONLY PATROL OF S-27 (SS-132)
BY GEORGE J. HEROLD

> George J. Herold rode the trusty old S-27. Caught in a fog the boat grounded on an island near Kiska. His hair-raising account has become a submarine legend.

It was nice weather in San Diego in October 1941. I had almost six months in the Navy and had gone through Submarine School right after boot camp at Newport, R.I. Paul Whiteman and his orchestra were playing at the Orpheum Theater in downtown, San Diego. A couple of S-boats were tied up at the destroyer base, but things were lazy for us in the months just before Pearl Harbor. This was Southern California and I was a Seaman Second, and felt like a big shot.

Around the first of November, I was put on a liberty ship bound for Pearl Harbor. The posters were right: "Join the Navy and see the world." I went to signal school at SubBase, Pearl and was there during the bombing on December 7, 1941. The experience was devastating and I was a different person when I took the trip back to San Diego on another liberty ship sometime in February 1942.

The S-27 had just returned from yard overhaul at Mare Island [California], and I went aboard around the first of March. Along with the S-28 we worked with the sound school for a while. I was glad to be back in California. Honolulu was in a state of continual emergency where the war was pervasive on everybody's lives.

Something was in the wind on board S-27. The married men aboard ship were getting nervous. Then it happened. We sailed out of San Diego on our first war patrol. On the way to Dutch Harbor, we had some trouble with our main motor and put in to Port Angeles, Washington. We were tied up near the USS *West Virginia* and those of us who had never seen a really big ship before went aboard. This was a bit of a shock. I had been at Pearl Harbor on December 7th, but had not really seen any damage up close. The steel decks on the West Virginia were like rolling hills and there was a lot of damage to the superstructure. It would be a long time before they would be ready for sea. We left Port Angeles, via Puget Sound, after the work on the main motor was completed. We stopped at Dutch Harbor to top off and found that the Japs had bombed it and the war in the Aleutians was on. The Japs had landed on Attu and Kiska Islands. The next month saw us patrolling the Kuluk Bay area south of Tanaga Island. That time of the year in the Bering Sea meant nineteen hour daylight and five hour nights, which in turn meant long dives on this old S-boat. I had my eighteenth birthday on this patrol and was standing quartermaster watches. We saw nothing but fog, rain and overcast skies except occasionally, when visibility allowed us to catch glimpses of some of the barren islands of the Aleutian chain. Sun lines and star sights were put on the shelf.

After surfacing on the night of 16 June 1942, we received a message directing us to leave our patrol area off Kuluk Bay and proceed to assigned area at Kiska Island via Amchitka Pass. Prior to leaving Dutch Harbor the captain had received verbal orders from the division commander to inspect Constantine Harbor on Amchitka Island for the presence of enemy activity.

The course was set to clear to northward of the islands by five miles, and the distance to travel indicated our arrival off Constantine about 0100 (Plus 12) on 18 June. We were able to obtain fixes until we rounded Gareloi Island and headed across Amchitka Pass on course 245T. At 2345 Capt. Jukes went to the bridge to see if Amchitka Island had been sighted and to be present if a landfall was made.

At 2400 when nothing could be seen ahead we changed course to 270T in order to make certain of landfall in case the current (of which we had no information) had set us to the south and east during the passage. After steaming for one hour at two-thirds speed (eight knots) on this course without sighting anything, the decision was made to circle with 10-degree rudder until light conditions were better. The captain was concerned about being unable to see, and because the coast pilot chart showed the entire island was low in elevation, we might not have been able to see it in time to prevent a grounding. This was done even knowing that the 0100 DR [dead reckoning] position still gave us seven and a half miles of open water.

At 0204 we steadied on course 090T and dived at 0207. From that time until 0556 we steered various courses until we picked up the island and obtained a fix. We patrolled until 1200 when we started rounding the southern end before time to surface and charge batteries. It was deemed advisable to stay submerged during daylight because the enemy was known to be within 70 miles and we had no reports of their air activity.

The decision was made to round the island to the southward was based upon the following factors:

1. Previous reports indicated the presence of the enemy on Semisopochnoi Island. Therefore, knowing they were at Kiska Island, it seemed likely that there might be air patrols between the two. A northern route might disclose our presence and we wanted to reach our area from the north of Kiska Harbor undetected if possible.

2. To enter this area from the north would have hemmed us in by Rat Island, Little Sitka Island and subsequently the unknown currents of Oglala Pass where some enemy surface shipping might be expected; whereas a southern approach left us free water rounding Amchitka to the south.

The latter option seemed the most logical route. After rounding the East Cape on Amchitka Island at 1330, numerous tangential fixes were obtained and a set to the north of about two knots was determined. Currents such as this were known to exist and had been previously encountered in other Aleutian passes. At 1735 we increased speed to about six knots and adjusted course in order to round St. Makarius Pt. In order to be at least five miles from the island prior to 2000, it would be necessary to surface and lie to for a battery charge for a period of at least four hours. This position should have removed us from the influence of the currents in the pass, or so we thought. No information on currents to be encountered in this area was available.

At 1920 the boat surfaced, visibility was two to three miles, and the island was not in sight because of a fog bank. In order to close the line to steer for our area we came to course 315T at a speed of eight knots and stopped at 2005 in order to start the battery charge. Our DR position at this time placed the boat five miles west of St. Makarius Pt. or any known enemy position. Also, this position provided the least chance of detection either by radar or visual search because of our blending with the shore background.

At 2010 the charge was started. Conditions at this time: Visibility two-three miles, sea calm, sky overcast and the island not in sight. The bridge watch was instructed to be especially on the alert for land. At 2200 the night order book was written and made available to the OD. In it were instructions to set course 305T speed six knots when one engine was released from the charge, to keep a careful watch for land, breakers or other indication of land as we may be set toward shore. Upon sighting any vessel dive immediately. Call the captain when charge is completed.

At 0027 the OD went ahead six knots on the starboard engine and came left from 050T to 305T as per instructions. He informed the captain of the course change and status of the charge. About 0043 the OD reported he was coming left to 225T with full left rudder as he thought he had sighted land on the starboard bow.

A dark object, believed to be land, suddenly loomed up about one point on the starboard bow and was sighted simultaneously by Boatswain Krueger who was the OD. Quartermaster Dick Lister, who was the starboard lookout and Seaman Stan Jorgensen spotted the land at the same time. Krueger immediately ordered, "Left full rudder, come to course 225. Report to the captain that I think I have sighted land on the starboard bow and am changing course to 225." As all this was happening, I was in my bunk in the forward battery compartment.

Immediately thereafter the OD saw small breakers about twenty-five yards forward of the bow and rang up, "Back Emergency" on both engines and sounded the collision alarm. The boat grounded as the captain was on his way to the bridge.

The captain arrived on the bridge at this time, followed by the executive officer, Mr. Smith. The captain relieved the OD. The port motor was backing and the starboard started backing within a few seconds. The boat was reported rigged for collision. We were bumping violently on the rocks and rolling about ten to fifteen degrees. The motors continued to back emergency, but to no avail. We were all awake and up by now and I heard Nelly ask, "Are we on railroad tracks or something?" Orders were given to blow the fuel from number three main ballast tank (which had been rigged as a fuel ballast tank), the after fuel group and all variable tanks.

We kept trying to back clear as the boat became lighter. But as we became lighter the stern began to swing to starboard and bang against the rocks. Then the starboard screw struck one and was disabled. We had to move the boat in order to clear the stern. During this period we found that the boat could be moved only about twenty feet forward or aft before it became fast on the rocks. We even sounded the area for a possible passage through which the boat might be warped, but none was found.

At 0115 we sent our first message, "To any or all USN [United States Navy] ships aground southeast side, Amchitka Island."

The rocks on the starboard side were high, almost as high as the bridge. When we backed down, the stern would go into a reef and ride up a little, and then shear to starboard. It was starting to get a little light now, and we could see another group of rocks just off the starboard quarter and on several occasions the stern got close against these rocks and we kicked ahead to clear them. We didn't do any good with this maneuver so we stopped for a while and took some more soundings all around the boat. They were all very shallow except ahead where there was one spot twenty to thirty feet deep. But there was apparently another reef beyond. The stern was pounding on the rocks. The bilge plating in the motor room was buckling in. Those on watch noticed it getting worse when she pounded on the rocks. After this had been noticed we secured the motor room, shut the water tight door and put pressure in the compartment.

Lt. Butler meanwhile was busy encoding messages to be sent. At 0145 we sent our second message. Pounding was increasing and we thought the tanks might give at any moment. The rubber life raft was brought topside and made ready. One officer and one man, both capable swimmers, were first sent to the beach, which looked like a calendar picture of a rocky Maine coast. They reported back that conditions were favorable once the raft cleared the first rocks close to the boat. A "ferry" system was then used with lines to the boat and the beach.

At 0440 another message was sent, "Wedged solidly, St. Makarius Point Amchitka X Port screw working on motor but motor room expected to flood at any time X Unable to back over rocks X Believe can be pulled clear by tug X All tanks dry X Pounding is bad X Am prepared to abandon X Heavy fog."

Provisions, dry and warm clothing, guns medical supplies and men were safely transferred to the beach. By about 1100 all but the captain and five men were landed. By this time breakers had increased so that further trips for provisions were not safe. The captain and those who remained aboard destroyed the coding machine, radio/transmitter, torpedo angle solver, torpedo approach data and secret publications.

At 1530 three of the remaining men were taken ashore. I think my buddy, Pugsley, was still aboard with the captain and someone else. At this time the heavy pounding had definitely loosened the side plating for it could be heard rattling at each jar of the boat. The torpedo room was slow flooding although air pressure had been built up in this compartment. An angle of six degrees down by the bow was noticed. The screws were now clear of the water.

At 1550, since nothing could be done further to help the boat, and the torpedo room was half flooded, the radioman, the executive officer and the captain came ashore. We were all in sort of an unsheltered cove and we had all these provisions (canned food and dry stores), some warm clothing, guns and the medical supplies piled up on this rock-strewn beach. We were all wet too, and it was cold. Fires were started and the wet clothing removed. No injuries were reported and, aside from being exhausted, we were in pretty good shape. We all had a couple ounces of grog [liquor] in hot coffee. We kept the fires going all night, but because of the very cold wind and rain, no one got any sleep. Another thing—wherever the Navy goes, watches must be stood. So, naturally the non-rated men got the call.

There was a cliff overlooking this cove. Here we stood watches, one hour to a shift, with a forty-five strapped on our hip. We were much closer to the enemy than we were to friends. Anyway, I had to relieve Scott Horton about 0100. When I got to the top of the hill it was dark. You could hear the breakers down below and also the boat grinding, scraping and banging on the rocks. I called out, "Horton"—but not too loud. I had visions of Jap soldiers sleeping in tents all around me. Scott was only a few feet away, but he must have seen the same movies I had and thought it was a Jap trick. I relieved him and went back down by the fires and stayed right there, keeping my eye on those fires until I got relieved.

The next day we had an experience. We had to hike to Constantine Harbor with all the supplies. Once we were away from the beach this island was just rolling tundra. It all looked the same so we stretched out in long lines so we could keep in a straight line. We knew there was a church and a few small buildings at Constantine. The captain had seen them through the periscope a few days ago before all this happened. When we got there we found six houses, one church and an underground storage bunker. Three of the homes were destroyed by aerial bombs and there were a few bomb craters around.

The former villages had a big bell rigged up to call people to meals. We had a man on it during daylight hours in case of a ship or plane sighting. And sure enough on June 26th that big bell rang and we ducked or took cover. But it was a PBY [Patrol Bomber, Consolidated Aircraft] and we were all up and waving as he started to circle. He sent a message by aldis [signal] lamp, saying he would send out our position and attempt a landing in the harbor. He did land and taxied as close to us as he could. They had to throw a lot of stuff over the side so the PBY could be made light enough for fifteen passengers. We waved good bye and they took off after a lot of kidding like, "How come you get to go first?"

The next day three more planes came back and took the rest of us to Chemofski Bay and to a converted four-piper called (I think) *Humbolt*. After a bath and examination, the first and last war patrol of the USS S-27 (SS132) was over.

Chapter 7
MARCH 1942
S-37'S VOYAGE HOME
BY ROBERT B. LANDER

Bob Lander endured a terrible depth charge attack in S-37. An American plane then bombed S-37 by mistake, but the "friendly" attack from the air was worse than that which the Japanese had handed out.

We were in Manila when the Japs attacked Pearl Harbor. Most of us had our personal effects, clothing, and uniforms either in apartments ashore, or in lockers aboard the submarine tender, *Canopus*. We never returned to claim our belongings. Instead, we began a war patrol, which took us down through the Philippine Islands and eventually ended in Australia. On the way we stopped in a small village on the island a Mindoro, where we were so hungry that we traded our mooring lines and deck anchor for chickens and coconuts. Our monthly commissary report to the Bureau of Supplies and Accounts would have made accounting history had there been a post office where we could mail it.

Our one remaining anchor was a mushroom type, which we used frequently for soundings. S-37 had no fathometer, and we were not certain of our navigation. The only chart for that part of the world was in a world atlas, a volume included in our meager ship's library. We didn't miss our uniforms, since the uniform for surface cruising was shorts, and for submerged running we wore only under-clothing. We kept a towel and bucket at arms-length. We would wipe off the sweat with the towel and wring it out in the bucket. S-37 was not what one might call a luxury submarine. For example, there were two heads' [toilets] one for the officers and one for the crew. These were the, "build up the pressure and blow overboard" type, requiring a master's degree to operate.

One dark night on our way south we were passing through Makassar Strait. Our executive officer, Bill Hazzard, was the duty officer. With eyes like a cat, he spotted four Japanese destroyers and got us in position on the beam about 1,500 yards away. We went to battle stations. The skipper, Jimmy Dempsey, came to the bridge. We got the torpedoes ready and, using a Braille pelorus [compass] system invented by the exec for night attacks, we fired one torpedo at each of the destroyers. Luckily, one of them hit the third destroyer. We watched it blow up, then as the rest of them turned to look for us, we submerged and went deep, which for us meant 200 feet, our test depth. The depth charges, which followed, were close enough to rattle the bulkheads, but there was no damage. The two heads, however, assumed a role of greater importance than before the attack.

We made it to Surabaja without further adventure. The Dutch treated us with great cordiality, but we were anxious to get on with repair work. One of the priority items of repair was our engine room hatch. During the Battle of the Java Sea, S-37 was attacked and mauled by a group of Japanese destroyers. We were able to evade the depth charges, but one blew out the engine room hatch gasket. The water poured in at an alarming rate, but we could do nothing about it until our tormentors departed and allowed us to surface. With the hatch repaired we were in fair shape to get underway.

We departed Surabaja with an escort through the minefields, remembering well our experience with mine fields the last time we departed Manila. On that night the giant rock of Corregidor loomed awfully close, when a signal light from the garrison informed us that we were in the middle of their minefield. All of their navigational lights had been turned off, putting us in an unknown and worrisome position. Fortunately, their mines were remote controlled, so we came through blindly and with great trepidation.

Our navigation turned out to be not much better after leaving Surabaja. Our charts were similar in quality to the World Atlas, which had led us out of the Philippines. We entered the Lombok Strait en route to Australia, and around midnight I was awakened by the sound of motors instead of the usual diesel engines which we used for cruising. Our diesels could not be reversed. Consequently any maneuvering had to be done with the motors. I could not imagine why we were backing down in the middle of Lombok Strait.

I soon found out that we had hit bottom and run aground. To make matters worse, there were shell tracers passing over us and the terrifying sound of gunfire could be heard from up on the bridge. This turned out later to be the Battle of Lombok Strait between many Japanese and American destroyers. We were unwittingly in the middle of it while stuck in the mud, but we were able to get clear after some maneuvering.

The destroyers ceased fire, and all was calm as we shifted to diesels and went on our way. The next day, however, it was very obvious that we had a bad leak in our fuel tanks. We were leaving a heavy oil slick in our wake. There was no doubt that we had a ruptured fuel tank and that our only recourse was to return to Surabaja.

Our tank was quickly repaired, and we departed on the day before the Japs overran and occupied Surabaja. Our voyage to Fremantle was without incident. The Aussies gave us a very warm welcome. We were taken into homes, wined and dined as though we were celebrities. Better yet, S-37 received a good overhaul. Our major engineering problems were overcome, and we departed for our long journey around the south of Australia, ending up in Brisbane. S-37 was moored to New Farm Wharf hence we earned the name "New Farm Wharf Rats."

We made several patrols from Brisbane to the Guadalcanal and New Guinea areas. We were near Rabaul one day when we sighted a seaplane tender. The captain was Tom Baskett. Our attack was successful. We watched the ship sink and went deep to avoid the escort. Our procedure for "Rig for Depth Charge" usually required all unnecessary lights to be turned off, including the Christmas Tree [hull opening indicator panel] which indicated by red or green [lights] the status of hull openings in the boat. At the same time we opened the main vents and the Kingston flood valves to allow a free flow of water under force from depth charges.

Our experience with the Japanese made us aware that the slightest noise could be picked up by their sonar, so we always tried to avoid speeding the motors or starting any pumps unless it was absolutely necessary. On this day we were running at our most silent speed, and the boat started to slowly sink. It was obviously too heavy and needed to be lightened by pumping out water, or else we needed more speed so that the bow and stern planes could hold the depth.

The Japanese were raining depth charges on us. We decided to open a high-pressure valve to the middle ballast tank to give it a shot of air and force a quantity of water out. The order was given, "Put a bubble in Two." Under normal conditions this would have lightened the boat without disturbing fore and aft trim. We would have been able to control the depth at slow speed. Nothing happened. We continued to slowly sink. We were passing our test depth. We gave the tank another shot of air and still nothing happened. Fortunately, the depth charges stopped. We put on a little speed and came up to 200 feet. Nothing was heard from the Japs, but after slowing to silent speed again we started to slowly sink. Another shot of air, this time a big one and we found no improvement, but since nothing could be heard from the Japs, we secured from our silent running. The lights came on, and it was then found that we had forgotten to close the main ballast tank vents before blowing high pressure into the tank. The air rising to the surface and expanding from a depth of 200 feet must have resembled a geyser to the Japs. This must have been evidence enough for them that the Yankee submarine had surely sunk.

We returned to Brisbane [Australia] to hear good news. We had been ordered home. We were being replaced by fleet-type submarines. We were to proceed to New Caledonia to refuel then head to Pearl and eventually to San Diego for overhaul and modification.

Our homeward voyage was made more interesting when we were ordered to make a sweep through the Gilbert Islands to report any enemy activity which could be observed along the beaches. The voyage was also a tribute to the engineer who computed the cruising range of this submarine. That range turned out to be exactly the distance from New Caledonia to Pearl Harbor minus ten miles, because we ran out of fuel at that point and had to proceed into Pearl Harbor on motors and batteries. Our destroyer escort flew an international signal flag hoist, which indicated, "Vessel, which I am escorting, is not under command due to lack of fuel."

Our reception in Pearl was rather cool, caused by the passengers we brought back from Australia including, parrots, cockatoos and a wallaby.

After taking on fuel and being fumigated, we left Pearl in high spirits, homeward bound.

In order to increase our speed, we pumped our variable ballast tanks dry. No one dreamed that we might be required to dive between Hawaii and San Diego. The weather turned bad. High seas and overcast skies extended all the way to the California coast. Except for the rolling and pitching, everything was tranquil until the day before we were supposed to pick up our escort and enter port. We sighted a beautiful cargo ship outward bound, flying the American flag. In spite of the waves breaking over the bridge we brought our signal searchlight up from down below and mounted it. We transmitted the prescribed recognition signal and hoisted our colors. After an interminable delay we spotted an answering flash from the cargo ship. This was followed by the splash of a shell landing close by. "Clear the bridge" orders were followed by the diving alarm. We knew that with dry variable ballast tanks it was going to take some time to get under water. As the bow crashed into the swells struggling to get under, the captain watched the splashes through the periscope getting closer and closer. After what seemed like an hour we passed through periscope depth and went down to safety. We surfaced after a short while and found nothing in sight. We had not received any damage.

Next morning we exchanged signals with our escort and proceeded into San Diego. Our escort informed us that we had been presumed lost, since our friendly cargo ship of the day before had reported sinking a submarine at the point where we were supposed to be. Despite rumors of our demise we were greeted by a boarding party heavily laden with publications outlining liberty hours, uniforms, conduct ashore and other welcoming information about San Diego.

Chapter 8

MARCH, 1942

BOB ROSE AND *SARGO'S* AUSTRALIAN WELCOME

BY DOUG RHYMES

> Doug Rhymes was in the control room when a Japanese destroyer attacked. He was on the stern planes when the boat passed test depth and a circuit breaker blew a ball of fire through the compartment. Rhymes survived to tell the story of *Sargo's* (SS-188) pounding.

I was torpedo and hull officer aboard the USS *Sargo* (SS-188). On 4 March 1942 we were cruising off the coast of West Australia. We were on the surface at eighty percent power and ninety percent speed on four engines, carrying a battery float on the Dinky. Our ballast tanks were dry except one fuel ballast tank. We had thirty-one evacuee passengers aboard, heading home and were about one day out of Fremantle, West Australia. The Bridge lookouts were Gunner's Mate Frank Kay, Torpedoman Jim Haywood, and Torpedoman Frank Perry, The quartermaster was Signalman Henry Bennett. I was Officer-of-the-Deck and conning officer. In the control room Electrician's Mate Mac McHenry was on the hydraulic manifold, Motor Machinist's Mate George Corbin was on the air manifold, and Lieutenant Johnny Lajaunie was diving officer.

Suddenly, Frank Kay spotted and reported a plane dropping out of the cloud cover, and coached me onto the bearing. We all recognized the plane as a Lockheed Hudson bomber, camouflaged in a mottle of brown, green and manure tones. It turned and headed straight for us. I ordered Bennett to flash the recognition signal, "Lemon Moon." Henry flashed it several times with no response. This American bomber, which we later learned was flown by an Australian crew, kept boring in with a zero angle on the bow. I cleared the bridge and sounded the diving alarm. As we passed forty feet the first pair of bombs exploded close aboard our port quarter. The force lifted our stern up to where the plane crew observed our propellers fanning the air.

Sargo went down out of control at a steep down angle with the stern planes jammed on hard dive. Frank Kay jumped in and helped Frank Perry unjam the stern planes. Jim Haywood put the bow planes on hard rise, and Lajaunie ordered bow buoyancy and safety blown, with little immediate effect.

At this point, our executive officer, Lieutenant J. D. Fulp, clawed his way up to the air manifold and braced Corbin as George blew all ballast tanks in addition to safety and bow buoyancy. Meanwhile, the engine room throttlemen were each hanging from the overhead with one hand while closing an inboard exhaust valve with the other hand. The acrobats were Motor Machinist's Mates Willie Green, Warren Morse, A.M. Davenport and C. W. Farmer.

Blowing all ballast pulled *Sargo* out of her plunge at around 300 feet and she started rising towards the surface like a cork. We vented the tanks as fast as we could, but McHenry reported that main ballast tank number seven was hung-up. Torpedoman Dave Johnson, in the after room, opened number seven vent by hand. As a consequence of upward momentum *Sargo* broached and rode the surface as we expected the worst. We started down again and this time at about fifty feet keel depth the second pair of bombs exploded; this time very close aboard our starboard beam. The detonations were tremendous jolts that even created optical distortions in some of the men. It may well have been that the pressure hull actually was dished in about a foot and sprang back in place as darkness descended and shattered glass rained onto the deck.

One evacuee passenger even swore to torpedoman H. D. Bise that he saw a five-inch shell go straight through the torpedo room. At this remark Bise almost swallowed his dip of snuff. The huge jolts of the second bombing knocked out all power by popping the overload relay breakers in the main control cubicle. The blasts shattered most lights and gauges. They shattered the optics in both periscopes. They damaged the conning tower lower hatch, the conning tower upper hatch, and the after battery hatch. We were taking water through each of these hull openings. We were in total darkness.

Each compartment had several emergency lights that were independent of the main lighting system. They came directly off the main batteries and were in steam tight fittings with separate switches. Unfortunately most of their bulbs were knocked out by the bombs. At the diving station, where Lajaunie, Haywood, Perry, and the helmsman were struggling to shift bow planes, stern planes and steering from power to hand operation, we could see by the glow of a flashlight that the indicator needles had been jolted off both 165 foot large depth gauges and the eight inch diameter 450 foot depth gauge. This left us a four and a half-inch diameter sea pressure gauge for calculating our depth at the ratio of forty-four pounds sea pressure per hundred feet depth.

Darkness and futility seemed forever, yet no more than ninety seconds could have elapsed before Electrician's Mate Bob Rose restored power to *Sargo* through an exceptionally courageous act. To truly appreciate the significance of Bob's daring actions, we must backtrack to pre-war days in Pearl Harbor.

Among the several times that the Bureau of Engineering used *Sargo* as an experimental guinea pig, they ordered the installation on *Sargo* of some experimental main power overload circuit breaker relays. They were ironically classed as depth charge resistant. These relays were installed by Electrician's Mate, A. C Pettingill and Bob Rose in super-confining areas of the main control cubicle where maximum clearances between bus bars carrying high voltage were about one-half inch. During installation a spring leaf of one relay fractured and shorted across bus bars with a huge flash. Pettingill sustained serious burns on his face, hands, and arms. He was taken to the after battery compartment where the doc tried to stop the pain. Bob Rose completed the installation of the relays.

The main breakers were kicking out as fast as they could throw them in. Bob told Ace to standby for a two-on-one sequence in which Ace would throw each breaker in, and keep pressure on the control lever, while Bob wedged the breaker closed with a wooden block. Bob Rose opened a safety door and entered the control cubicle in total darkness. By feel, he located each fickle overload relay breaker; by feel he wedged each one closed with a wooden block; all as Ace Koenig kept pressure on the control lever. Rose ran the risk of getting electrocuted. The Good Lord answered our many prayers and protected Bob Rose. *Sargo* had main power restored together with a little light.

Throughout the boat, there was a surge of confidence as we replaced light bulbs and got equipment back on the line. We experienced no panic or hysteria during this ordeal. We were a highly trained team of shipmates, with each man doing his assigned job to the best of his ability. It did make a great difference to be able to see what we were doing, and to have power to do it.

At the diving station we regained control of the boat at about seventy-five pounds equating to about 170 feet. Motor Machinist's Mate Jay Sears checked this gauge against readings of sea pressure gauges in the pump room and both torpedo rooms.

We remembered that somewhere on the way down water had stopped cascading out of the conning tower hatch. The leaky hatches had been warped from percussion shock of the bombs, but sea pressure had flattened out the warps. So *Sargo* cruised at about hundred feet until nightfall. We blew everything when we surfaced. As we headed for Fremantle, West Australia, Skipper Jacobs had Bill Wolfe radioed a report of the surprise attacks and the resultant damages. We were notified that the Aussie plane crew would be waiting on the dock to apologize. Our lead quartermaster, "Jump" Murphy, a feisty 130 pounder, made said, "When I see the pilot of that damn plane, I'm gonna knock him flat on his can."

After we tied up at New Farm Wharf and got the brow over, the Aussie plane crew came aboard. As we went through a session of handshakes, apologies, forgiveness, smiles, and expressions of friendship J. D. Fulp observed that the pilot stood about six foot four and tipped the scales at around two twenty. J. D. turned to the Gangway Watch and said, "Go get Murphy."

Murphy walked up rather quietly, shook hands with the pilot, and said, "How do you do, Sir?"

Chapter 9
MAY 1942
ESCAPE BY SUBMARINE

BY LUCY I. WILSON, UNITED STATES ARMY NURSE

> Lucy Wilson was a nurse on Corregidor when the Japanese invaded Manila. She escaped to ride *Spearfish* (SS-190) out of harm's way and tells her story of becoming an honorary submariner.

May 1, 1942 brought certainty that Japanese forces were capturing the Philippines. On the 3rd, eleven Army nurses, one Navy nurse, a Navy wife, six Army colonels, along with six Navy officers were loaded into a boat and left Corregidor about 6pm, heading out into Manila Bay, wondering why we had been selected for evacuating aboard a submarine. Soon, the Bay was bright with moonlight, shell fire and bombs. Suddenly, a big dark object rose out of the water in front of us.

They hurried us aboard the submarine, USS *Spearfish* (SS-190). The hatch was such a small opening that I didn't think I could do it, even though my weight by that time was only seventy pounds, after the starving and diarrhea over the past five months on Bataan and Corregidor. Others made it, so I did too! Safely below in the crew's mess, we couldn't believe our eyes. They had a single layer chocolate cake ready to serve us. It was so delicious! Of all the people I have ever known, those submariners were absolute tops and as each day went by, I knew they couldn't be beat.

Almost immediately after our boarding, we submerged and traveled for twenty-two hours without coming up. A crewman told me that while all our gang was coming on board, he was wondering where they would find a place for all of us to sleep. When he saw me, he thought, well, she can sleep with her father, as he presumed I was the daughter of one of the men coming aboard, because I was so skinny. We hadn't had the comfort of makeup for months and my hair was up in braids.

Our group increased the submarine's compliment by almost fifty percent. There was no extra space, other than for the crew, and very little for them in the first place. That first twenty-two hours seemed like it would never end. They warned us not to talk or move about, but they didn't have to do that, we couldn't. Because of so many people on board, the oxygen supply was insufficient and we struggled just to breathe. Many passed out from the lack of oxygen and I am sure the starvation contributed to that. They pumped more oxygen into the system and spread lime about to help cleanse the air. During this time, with no one moving around, there was no need to worry where we would sleep, but as soon as this was over, in the area where the bunks were, sheets were draped around four bunks. The "hot bunk" system was used; where the bunks and same linens are used constantly, changing shifts every eight hours. I was on the third shift and because I thought I would be the thirteen sleeper I slept on the deck. It was so hot, because it was directly over the batteries.

When I finally awoke, they told me Corregidor had surrendered May 6, 1942. Everyone was so quiet. It was so depressing.

The submariners were so good to us. They gave us some of their clothing, such as cut-off dungarees and T-shirts, as we had already lost everything we owned. My only possession was a small suitcase containing the white nurses' uniform that we wore, before they changed us to khaki, while serving on Bataan.

There were three heads in the sub and we were assigned to use one. The instructions to flush it was about half a page long and so complicated that they quickly decided to have one of the submariners do it for us after a couple of disasters. It was so embarrassing! The Philippine mess boy stationed nearby volunteered to come to our assistance.

Spearfish was supposed to surface for four hours every twenty-four hours to recharge batteries. I think it was the first time we surfaced, and before our four hours were up, we came in contact with the Japanese again and had to crash-dive. They sounded the alarm that sounded like a Model T Ford car horn, and we went almost straight down. This happened several times during our 3,000 mile trip. They had a small square hand-cranked Victrola [record player] and a few records. Whenever we crash-dived, everyone would grab the Victrola and records to keep them from breaking, as we plunged almost straight down. That was our only entertainment, other than talking and singing and we didn't want to lose them.

We didn't dare get rid of all the garbage as we were going under some of the Japanese Navy, so it was stacked around in bags. One was in the radio room and I would lie on it with my legs up the side of the bulkhead and sleep, for the lack of a better place —for the first several days I was so tired.

The only time that we got to look out was when we passed Bali. There was a very popular song about it at the time. Lcdr. J.C. Dempsey, captain of the Spearfish let us look through the periscope for a few seconds. All we saw was a dark blob on the horizon, but I saw it! We never saw daylight, for we only surfaced at night.

The submarine was long and narrow and when we surfaced to recharge batteries, it seemed like it would roll completely over. Nearly everyone got seasick at one time or another, including the crew. I was fortunate that it didn't bother me. Nancy Gillihan was sick the whole way. About the time she would stop vomiting, we would surface again!

Of course, the food was so much better and more of it than we had been having, and it was twice a day, we thoroughly enjoyed it. I must admit the first time we had navy beans for breakfast it was a shock for me, as I had never heard of it before, but they were so good, and now I knew why they were called navy beans! At times some of us would try to help out the cook. There was little else we could do to break the monotony, or do to help in any way. I like to think we helped morale in spite of the over-crowded conditions. The highlight of the whole trip was the traditional sea ceremonial of the Ancient Order of the Deep, when you cross the equator. There were too many "pollywogs" aboard to ignore it. The crew was very ingenious in fixing funny and remarkable costumes for the Royal Court: King Neptune, Davy Jones, the Royal Baby, among others that have slipped my mind. The fun and mystery during the preparations, plus the forewarnings we got of the awful things to come made the hot, monotonous trip more intriguing.

Finally, we arrived at zero latitude and I don't know how deep under the water in Macassar Straight we were, when each of us were issued a summons to court. We were blindfolded and barefoot and standing in a shallow pan of water while the charges against us were read. Mine were as follows:

1. Working on the sympathies of the crew and thereby talking

them out of their clothes, seats, food, and even in some cases, their hearts!

2. Being a cowgirl from Texas.

3. Always pouting.

4. Being hot tempered.

5. Telling tall tales about Texas.

6. Beating new-born infants around while a nurse in training.

7. Having been fortunate enough to get away from Texas, desiring to go back.

8. Asking if there was a beauty parlor on board.

9. Making insulting remarks concerning the persons of the Royal Shellbacks.

Therefore, appear and obey or suffer the penalty. This displeased the King and he sent an electric shock through the water and you can imagine the jumping and hollering that took place, which tickled the, "Court." Several other things were done which have escaped my memory. Once your initiation was over, you could watch the others. Then we became "Shellbacks". The whole affair provided discussion for days and helped break the tension as well. It made us one big happy family, who had just, and were still, going through some of the most horrible experiences the human body and mind can go through and come out alive, still fairly well balanced mentally and physically. Usually, in every group, there is at least one that is grouchy or "touchy" in some fashion, but I have absolutely no memory of any such person aboard the Spearfish.

Near the end of the journey, when it was determined that we would have plenty of water, they gave each shift a half-bucket of water, so we could bathe and wash our underwear. It was so refreshing and made the extremely rough waters of the Indian Ocean a little more bearable.

I do not know how to adequately express my gratitude to the submariners for all they did for us and making such an impossible trip so tolerable and enjoyable for us most of the time. Had it not been for the seventeen days of good food and relaxation, camaraderie and kind consideration, I do not know if I could have survived the busy times ahead in the States. I never noticed any bad odors aboard, probably because of hav-ing had such bad dust and odors in Manila Tunnel. Of course we knew of the danger we were going through daily, but at least it did not have the horrors of working twenty-four to forty-eight hours continuously, trying to sew bodies back together and wondering just how long they would live amid the constant bombing and shelling. A submariner not only has to perform his job perfectly, but must be able to get along with other people in extremely close quarters without very much else to do but work and sleep in unpleasant surroundings. They are the World's best to me!

Chapter 10

JUNE 1942

THE DOUBTFUL TALE OF THE S-36

BY ALFRED SIMS

> Al Sims rode the creaky old S-36 on her last patrol. The crew fought to save her, but her equipment failed and she foundered, never to sail again.

I was already qualified in submarines when I reported aboard S-36 in the fall of 1941. Having come from a fleet-type submarine I was appalled by what I found. It's never a good idea to start off a new boat experience with negative thoughts, but I couldn't ignore the decrepit condition of this old-timer, the S-36.

It had been built in San Francisco, California and launched on June 3, 1919. In 1925 she was assigned to the Asiatic Fleet and operated out of Cavite. For the next sixteen years she was in the Philippines while con-ducting a variety of chores in the South China Sea and adjacent waters. When I reported aboard she was due to return to the United States for a long overdue overhaul, but on December 7, 1941 the Navy was turned upside down. Everything that could float, or, in my case, submerge, was pressed into service. On December 8, the overhaul was canceled and S-36 was assigned to patrol the waters off Cape Bolinao.

As we were retiring from our operating area I conducted an appraisal of all equipment under my domain. At the end of her first patrol we were detected by a Japanese destroyer off Verde Island. We submerged and during the chase the depth charging damaged every piece of equipment on my doubtful inventory list and much of the equipment outside of my inventory list. We had severe air leaks in the ballast tank blow system, the radio transmitter tubes had blown, the electrical steering failed, the engine exhaust valve leaked, the port engine air compressor failed, the starboard engine air compressor lubrication failed, then the starboard engine seized. In addition, there were numerous seawater leaks requiring continuous bilge pumping.

Every crew member sweated in the foul atmosphere as we worked like dogs trying to repair enough equipment to get the submarine functioning. As we fought a futile fight of failing equipment those on watch lost control of the submarine. From depth charging we lost planes control, but the diving officer was able to keep the boat between one hundred and two hundred feet. Then, on the next round of depth charges the master gyro compass failed, but we managed to get it working again. Then the port main motor bearing began smoking and had to be hand oiled on a constant basis. The trim pump stalled. Depth was maintained by partially blowing the ballast tanks, then flooding them in short spurts to an approximate neutral buoyancy.

Meanwhile, above us, the Japanese destroyer gave up and left the area. We never knew if he ran out of depth charges or just got tired of banging away on the poor old S-36. The enginemen and electricians struggled with propulsion equipment as temperatures rose higher and higher. One man passed out and the doc attended to him. The port main motor bearing problem was partially repaired but the starboard main motor field remained grounded.

We surfaced during the night and the entire crew worked without letup to get the boat back into operation. It was my job to get the hydraulics in order and my back ached as I worked with inadequate tools. The only good news was that fresh air seemed to revive us and we crammed a little food down as we worked. At day-break the boat submerged. Just as I thought we had enough machinery working for us to relax a bit, the main motor auxiliary circulating water pump caught fire.

On June 17, 1942 we received orders to proceed to Surabaya, but both shafts seized from lack of lubrication. I and two others crammed ourselves into the motor room bilges and hand-lubricated the shafts. We were only able to make one third speed, but the boat was able to return to port where repairs were made on a catch-as-catch-can basis. These were the dark days of World War Two and the S-36 was pushed back out to sea. We doggedly put to sea and continued to operate with barely-running machinery while the crew labored to keep the boat going by hook or crook. We operated until January 20, 1943, when so much of the boat's machinery began breaking down that we couldn't keep up with it.

Then, to top off our agonizing existence, the old S-36 went aground on Taka Bakang Reef. We battled to get the boat off the rocks, but chlorine gas from a hull puncture in the forward battery compartment prevented a prolonged effort. A radio message was sent and a Dutch launch, the *Attla* took all crew members off the boat.

When rocking back and forth while sitting in the bottom of the launch I thought how lucky I was to have gotten off the S-36 before she took all hands down with her. At the same time I felt a certain sadness to see the end of the boat we had struggled so hard to save. I suppose it was just too much for the old girl. She was too tired to keep going.

Chapter 11
JUNE 1942
RIVETS IN THE 0-2

BY STANLEY LAMBKIN

> Stan Lambkin was a submarine school student. He went out in the old 0-2, a worn-out school boat, on his initiation ride in a submarine when the boat fell apart under him on her ultimate dive.

It should be pointed out that 0-9 had been operating in waters off New London (The Isle of Shoals) in June of 1941 when her hull had collapsed sending all hands to their death. Only two years before that the *Squalus'* main induction had failed to shut during a routine dive with resultant heavy loss of life. These events were well known to the students at New London Submarine School in June of 1942.

I had entered submarine school as a first class fireman (the equivalent of a third class petty officer). I found the school on the Thames River near New London, Connecticut to be not difficult. My prior experience with diesel engines and all the machinery that went with them made the engineering part of the curriculum pretty simple. The base was divided between the instruction buildings on the upper base and the shops and piers on the lower base. These were finger piers that stuck out into the Thames River which gave the officers ulcers because landing a submarine in its swift current was difficult.

Toward the end of the curriculum we were informed that we would be going to sea in one the school's boats. It was to be the 0-2, an ancient relic of the First World War. There was an audible groan from us students since we had talked about of the recent 0-9 disaster and the *Squalus'* main induction failure. These events were well known to the students at New London Submarine School in June of 1942, so we looked up a few details of the submarine we were to ride. The 0-2 was launched in May, 1918. Her pressure hull was riveted and her soft patches were bolted to the pressure hull. She was only 520 tons (surface) and 172 feet long.

I saw 0-2 chugging up and down the Thames River, but had never given the little submarine much thought. Now I took note of those daily trips into Long Island Sound which gave enlisted men a taste of what real submarining was all about. I had been in submarine school for eight weeks when my section was marched down to the piers for my first ride in a submarine. As we marched we whispered about the 0-9 disaster, but I tried to keep my mind on my own problems, and off the frightening tales swirling around me.

We students crossed the narrow brow onto the submarine's deck. Each student slithered down hatches with ladders on the sides of long tubes that dropped down into the bowels of the submarine. The smell was foul. They hadn't told us about the smell in submarine school. It came as a shock. We assembled below decks in small groups. As the boat got underway, I listened to an old-timer describe the torpedo tubes. He had made his speech so many times I thought he was going to fall asleep while talking. At the end his mouth closed and his eyes drifted into space. We stood, waiting for more, but when nothing more came from the torpedoman we started talking among ourselves. A chief appeared and moved us into the next compartment. Moving from learning-station to learning-station I and my fellow students wound up in the control room for the first dive of the day. Whether or not the submarine had been properly compensated for the trim dive was unknown to any of us. Indeed, we hardly knew that such a thing took place before the submarine could dive. At that point in my submarine career I only knew that the engines were back aft and the torpedo tubes were up forward.

It was an exciting business as the klaxon [horn] sounded the diving alarm and men jumped down into the control room from the bridge. A chief pulled some levers and the men who had come down from the bridge manned two large wheels. Between them was a depth gauge which showed the submarine's keel depth. The needle began to move. The captain looked at the needle and explained to the watching students what was going on as the diving officer gave orders to planes-men and others. I noticed that the diving officer kept giving orders to pump from here to there. The captain told the diving officer to make his depth forty-eight feet. The needle on the depth gauge hit forty-eight feet, but kept going.

I was comfortable, because the boat only had a five degree down angle, but I was wedged between other students and had to crane my neck to see what was happening at the diving stand. As the boat slid passed forty-eight feet the captain ordered eighty feet. The needle was moving faster now and the captain, seeing that it would not stop at eighty feet ordered a new depth of hundred feet. I discerned a new expression on the captain's face. Furrows crept across the captain's forehead. I would have recognized it as apprehension, except that all seemed to be going so well.

Again the depth gauge needle went passed hundred feet and kept moving. The captain now shouted for a new depth of 150 feet, but followed that quickly with a hot discussion with the diving officer. I couldn't hear what was said, but I thought I heard the captain use some expletives that were reserved for torpedomen. When the depth gauge needle swung on down passed the 150 foot mark, the veins on the captain's neck appeared blue against his reddening skin.

By now the diving officer was shouting while the captain, still trying to maintain his submarine aplomb, ordered a new depth of 200 feet. It seemed to me that the angle on the boat was decreasing, but the depth needle showed no sign of slowing. It now was apparent that all was not what it should be. The planesmen were sweating and the chief was looking intently at the captain waiting for an order that didn't come.

When the first bolt on the boat's soft patch blew and a shot of water hit machinery back aft the resulting panic came forward in the form of men shouting something about flooding. At this point I was fairly certain things were definitely not what they should be. I thought of the whispered references to the 0-9. A surge of undefined fear gripped upward from my shoes. My vision became blurred, but I saw the depth needle at 220 feet.

The captain's order to blow everything was almost drowned out by two more soft patch bolts having parted with more water pounding into the boat. Next to my ear, compressed air blasted into the ballast tanks. The needle stopped, then began to retrace its path, this time turning counter-clockwise. It accelerated as the up angle on the boat increased.

The boat broached the surface and the captain, diving officer, and planesmen quickly climbed the ladder. It seemed to me that their ascent was more like an escape than a routine evolution. I and the other students remained where we were in control. The chief and others in ship's company left below talked in whispers. It was obvious that they didn't want us students to hear what they said. Somebody from back aft reported that the flooding had stopped and the chief held up a hand in recognition of the report. Then he issued more orders with the apparent result that drain pumps went to work on the water in the bilges.

That had been the first dive of the day and what turned out to be also the last dive of the day. I talked to my colleagues about what we had just witnessed while the boat headed up the Thames River to the submarine base. Although I wasn't particularly perturbed about the dive, and the resultant flooding, one of the students had seen enough for him to know that the boats were far too dangerous for any sane person to seriously contemplate. He reasoned that no amount of sub pay could compensate for what he had just seen. References to the 0-9 loss seemed to confirm the man's theory.

The next week the event was capped off by the issuance of deep dive certificates to those students who had decided to stay with submarines in spite of the 0-2's unusual trim dive. I kept that piece of paper in my seabag as I went to a new construction fleet-type submarine. I was glad I didn't have to serve on an 0 boat.

Chapter 12

AUGUST 1942

AGROUND ON A REEF

BY FRANK BOWMAN

> Frank Bowman was aboard S-39 when she grounded in the Southwest Pacific. HMAS *Katoomba* rescued the crew, but the boat is still there.

I had been aboard S-39 long enough to know every rivet on the trusty old boat. True, she wasn't one of the new fleet-type boats coming off the ways at Groton and Portsmouth, but I was comfortable with the routine even if she wasn't the best boat in the fleet. The S-39 had been launched in 1919. As the political picture between the United States and Japan continued to deteriorate during the fall of 1941 our life consisted of training new replacements coming from the states and of providing ASW [antisubmarine warfare] services for the surface ships of our far western fleet. I worked mostly with the executive officer who was also the navigator. He was a good guy and I was lucky to be on S-39. Our old hull limited the boat's submergence to 200 feet, but in the end S-39 racked up five war patrols.

When the Japanese bombed Pearl Harbor S-39 was home ported in Cavite, but we were on patrol off of southern Luzon when the news came to us. We were ordered back to Cavite and our skipper, Lieutenant James Coe took us in. When we got there we found the base in an uproar. We took on provisions and two more torpedoes, then immediately went back out to sea together with *Seawolf, Sculpin, Skipjack* and *Tarpon*. All five of the boats patrolled off the southern tip of Luzon, but the seas were rough and it was miserable. We didn't spot a single ship.

On December 11th, 1941 we took a brutal depth charging from a Japanese destroyer in the San Bernardino Strait. We escaped by evasive action and in January, 1942 I was ordered to take S-39 south to Java to help stem the tide of Japanese expansion on the peninsula.

In the Java Sea we took up position with other boats. We were the western most boat. We were assigned to get a British big-wig off the island of Chebia. I volunteered and the captain brought us in close to shore. I and two others went into shore in a rubber boat. The Japs were everywhere. Little gun boats ran up and down the island. S-39 retired to sea and dove. We were on our own and were supposed to meet the submarine at midnight after rescuing the British officers. We searched through the jungle and came up with nothing. It was a tricky business and we weren't well suited to go prowling around the jungle. The insects were vicious, the heat unbearable and I expected a Jap to jump out from behind every bush. Even though we were empty-handed I was glad to get our boat back out to sea. I paddled like the dickens and sure enough, the old S boat surfaced right on time. I was never so glad to see my old buddies as I was then.

At one point we spotted a tanker. I think it was off Karimata Strait or the entrance to Makassar Strait. The boat out-ran the tanker and got ahead of her course. Then we dove and waited for the tanker to approach. It was a perfect set-up and for some reason the ship did not have an escort. We shot four Mk 10 torpedoes and three struck the big ship. It was enough to do the job. The captain and the executive officer watched the tanker go down bow first.

S-39 turned south and made port in Fremantle, then to Australia's eastern seaboard, Brisbane. On May tenth she put to sea on her fourth patrol lurking around the Louisiade Archipelago to the north of the Coral Sea. On this patrol we were plagued by engine troubles and when the executive officer had an attack of pneumonia she turned back to Australia. We put the sick exec ashore at Townsville. We had a new skipper by this time, Lieutenant Francis E. Brown.

We again put to sea and took station in and around the Louisiade Islands. The Archipelago was one of the remotest parts of Papua, New Guinea. It was situated in the extreme southeast part of Papua, almost midway between the mainland of New Guinea and the Solomon Islands.

Rossel Island was one of the many insignificant islands in the chain. It lay about 370 miles west of the Solomon Islands.

During the second week of August, 1942 the sea was very rough with enormous waves and high winds. There were no navigational aids and the navigator and I were relying on the accuracy of our DR [dead reckoning], but the weather had pushed the boat much closer to Rossel Island than what we had estimated.

On the night of August 13, 1942 as the U. S. Marines were battling the Japanese on Guadalcanal the S-39 tried to stay well clear of the coast-line of Rossel Island. It struck a reef and immediately took a list of thirty-five degrees. The heavy seas rolled into shore and the boat was pounded as each successive wave stormed into it. The captain backed on emergency diesel power. He then tried it on battery power. The effort had no effect and the batteries were drawn down in the backing maneuver. As each wave rose from the rear of the submarine the boat rose then fell heavily onto the reef. Fuel and ballast tanks were blown dry. Again the boat was backed, but to no avail. For most of this action I was in the conning tower and hanging on as the boat slammed against the reef. Since the boat was now high in the water, each wave had an even more devastating effect. Its stern swung to take the waves from the beam. This increased the punishment.

On the morning of the 14th the screws were backed and a twist was put on the boat in a last-ditch effort to free the submarine from the grip of the reef. The boat backed some distance but as soon as the power was reduced she slid back onto the reef, while still at a port thirty degree list.

The captain sent a message requesting assistance. Australia answered that HMAS *Katoomba* would be in the area on the following morning. As we awaited the arrival of the mine sweeper, the breakers increased in height and intensity. They were now hitting the boat from broadside and pushing it further over. I tried to spend as much time as possible on the bridge and I sure felt sorry for the others who had to endure the hammering while hanging on. The guys in the engine room had it the worst. The engines roared and the heat was terrific. Several battery cells were shorted and a battery charge became impossible. With what little remained in the bat-teries the captain again tried backing, but the screws had lifted partially out of the water and the effort had no effect.

The boat now had been driven farther onto the reef and was bouncing to a sixty degree angle on each brutal wave. The captain gave permission for an officer to try swimming to a high point on the reef where he would secure a messenger. He would then pull a line to the reef which would allow others to leave the boat and thus get to shore. It took two men to do the job, but at last a line was made fast and men began heaving themselves to safety. I was one of the first to go overboard. I pulled myself along the line and kept my eye on the pounding surf. When a big breaker came at me, I held my breath and gripped the line with clenched fist. Finally, I made it. So did all the others. We were a tired but determined bunch.

When HMAS *Katoomba* came in sight we were on shore and in good spirits. We waved and cheered. A small boat from the *Katoomba* made several trips to shore and picked up a few men off the submarine and the rest of us from the beach. The S-39 remained fast to the rocks of Rossel Island. As we pulled away from the reef I didn't have the courage to watch our boat in its death-throws. Somehow, I felt like we were abandoning the old thing. It had been my home. We had shared many a tough experience. It was like losing a good friend.

The crew members were taken to Townsville on the north east coast of Australia where we spent a pleasant week or two at the town's pubs. We were assigned to other boats in the course of time, but the S-39 never left the reef.

PART TWO

Mid-War Stories (1943)

Chapter 13

JANUARY 1943

POMPON EVADES TORPEDOES

BY CHARLES FOSKETT

> Charlie Fosket was an electrician aboard *Pompon* (SS-267) when a Japanese torpedo came straight at the boat. He lost the power load, the boat slowed, and the torpedo missed by a hair.

Australia, January 10, 1943: bound for a patrol area around the Truk Islands. Wednesday, January 16 at 2308 hours, two torpedoes fired at the *Pompon* (SS-267) from a Japanese submarine were sighted. Evaded torpedoes which passed ahead 400 yards, that's what the patrol report recorded for history.

Now I'll tell you the true story! A battery charge had ended and the bridge instructed maneuvering to answer bells on the battery and carry a zero float on number three main engine. I was the senior controllerman and Milton Dworkowski was the junior controllerman. We started work on orders received over the 7MC to shift the load from number three main engine to the auxiliary engine, answering a two third bell on the battery.

When the auxiliary engine was running and up to speed, we, the controllermen, proceeded to shift the load. Milton had never done the actual change-over before and requested that I perform the task. Having full confidence in his abilities, I agreed, instructing him to be sure the auxiliary engine generator voltage was the same or above the battery voltage. I also told him to inform me when he was ready to close the auxiliary engine breaker so that I could stop the propulsion to assure everything would proceed without any voltage fluctuation. He informed me he had a matching voltage and I ordered him to close the breaker.

As Milt started to close the breaker, the auxiliary engine inexplicably slowed down, dropping the generator voltage; and, thus dropping below the battery voltage. There was a loud explosion, smoke, and flames as the breaker closed. Milton was momentarily blinded, yelling, "I can't see." The hair on my neck stood up as I rushed to assist him. Meanwhile, we were without propulsion as I helped Milt to the control panel area.

The 7MC came alive wanting to know why we lost propulsion and steerage. As I was about to answer, I distinctly heard a look-out report, "Torpedo wakes crossing our bow." Without replying to the bridge and without orders, I immediately went to "Full" on the battery. Milton rang up "Start aft engines."

Meanwhile, we did not hear anything on the 7MC. Apparently, the bridge was now busy evading the torpedoes that had crossed our bow. As the engines were readied, we shifted propulsion to them and informed the bridge we had full power on four engines. But we still had a two third speed bell. After a few seconds, bridge gave us a full ahead bell. Hours later, we were ordered to standard speed on two main engines.

Later, after being relieved of the watch, we expected to be called to the wardroom. Surprisingly, nothing was ever said of the incident by any officer. Incidentally, after the breaker explosion, the auxiliary engine was again running smoothly until we ordered it secured. Sometimes I think that if that auxiliary engine hadn't malfunctioned which caused us to lose propulsion those torpedoes might well have found their mark.

Chapter 14
FEBRUARY 1943
GUN BOSS PAY
BY EDWARD CRAWFOOT

Edward Crawfoot was an electrician on *Pompon* (SS-267). He wanted the extra $5.00 per month pay for being a gun boss, so he volunteered for the deck duty. But, he hadn't counted on the enemy shooting back.

I joined the Navy in January of 1939 and was sent to boot camp at Newport, Rhode Island. Those sleek destroyers sitting out in Narragansett Bay looked like Greyhounds and that's how the instructors referred to them. Upon graduation we were asked if there were volunteers to go to the USS

Falcon. I assumed that it was one of the destroyers waiting for me. We boarded a bus which trundled us up to Portsmouth, New Hampshire where I saw a peculiar looking ship. It was smaller than a destroyer, was fat with big appendages hanging from its bulky superstructure and was altogether rather ugly. I turned to the chief petty officer in charge of us and was about to protest when he told us that we were to get aboard since the *Falcon* was going to sea to lift the *Squalus* off the bottom.

I scrambled aboard with the other seaman apprentices. We whispered about the sinking of *Squalus*; sharing what we knew from newspaper stories. After throwing our seabags onto hammocks we reported topside to handle lines. The *Falcon* was already heading out to sea. I did as I was told and during the next week I watched as divers went over the side time after time. What they did down there I didn't know, but it was fascinating to a young farm boy. Finally, the nose of *Squalus* appeared at the surface and we all cheered.

After the *Squalus* was safely in port, the same chief who had taken us on the bus to Portsmouth, talked to us one at a time. He told me I was being reassigned to the R-11. He explained that it was a submarine and that I was lucky to be assigned to her. I objected because I knew I hadn't volunteered for submarine duty and I remembered those wonderful destroyers riding at anchor. My words fell on deaf ears as the chief explained that when I had volunteered for the *Falcon* I had volunteered for submarine duty. It was an ASR [submarine rescue ship] and as such was a part of the submarine service. It all seemed perfectly logical and the next day I went aboard the submarine. It seemed really small and totally foreign. The topside watch told me to lay below and I pushed my seabag down a hatch. Inside the thing I was struck by the foul smell. The *Falcon* had a faint smell, but nothing like this. As I looked around at my new home a couple of guys took my seabag, shook my hand, and showed me into berthing. It was cramped, dark and filled with cranks, levers, dials, gauges, wheels and endless pipes. But I couldn't deny the friendliness of the crew who made me feel like a fellow submariner from the very beginning.

Having not been to submarine school I spent my every waking moment studying the systems of the R-11. I learned to love the old thing. It was a fascinating assemblage of every imaginable piece of equipment. Diesel engines, batteries, hydraulics, torpedoes, all beckoned for me to understand them. Soon I was qualified in submarines, but I was still only a seaman, second class. I was sitting on top of the world. My base pay was thirty-six dollars a month. Add in an extra fifteen dollar sub pay, five dollar dungaree pay and I had lots of money for beer. Being greedy I wanted more. A gun captain got an extra five dollars a month. It didn't make much sense to me, but I was determined to become a gun boss and get the extra dollars. Soon the chief of the boat made me the gun captain for our three-inch deck gun. Our drill consisted of running onto deck, unlocking the barrel support, dropping it to the deck, loading the gun, training it onto a target raft pulled by a tug, then pumping shells at it. We got pretty good, and the executive officer was pleased. Best of all, I was gun captain and was making sixty-one dollars a month.

We were sent down to Key West in 1941 to provide ASW services. R11 wasn't a front line submarine. It was built during World War I and had a test depth of only 200 feet. It had eye ports in the little conning tower and main propulsion controllers were throughout the boat. The series-parallel switches were in the after battery compartment and the rheostats for main motor voltage were in control. There was no crews mess, only a little table that hung by pipes. Crew members ate while standing. It wasn't much of a submarine so we were in the back-waters of the Gulf as a new war approached.

It was four days after Pearl Harbor and as usual we were running submerged at eighty feet when the destroyer escort signaled us to surface and to get back to port. She had two sonar contacts and the other one had to be a U-boat. We surfaced and started to race for Key West, but the captain thought it would be too dangerous to remain on the surface. He pushed the diving alarm and down we went. We were passing ninety feet when we heard the sound of a torpedo. It made a whine right through the hull and must have passed over us by only a few feet. We all looked at each other and at the time it seemed like a movie, except we were in it.

Six months later I went to Manitowok, Wisconsin where I was one of the crew who put USS *Pompon* in commission. We worked day and night on the submarine. By then I was a third class electrician and knew my way around submarines, but Captain Hawke made me re-qualify on *Pompon*. I didn't mind because after working so hard to get the submarine ready for its journey to sea I already knew all the systems. We took her through the lakes, through Chicago, than got off as others took her down the Mississippi River by barge. We had a pleasant train ride, than picked her up in New Orleans.

From there we went through the [Panama] Canal to Pearl and from there to Fremantle, Australia where the beer was nearly free and so were the girls. On our first patrol we went to gun action. I was still making my forty-seven dollars a month including gun captain pay. As we surfaced I saw a small junk-like boat with sail. From the bridge the captain told us to blow it out of the water. We trained our gun on him and put one shell into the sea. He sprayed our deck and bridge with machine gun fire. The captain yelled for us to get below. We dove through a hatch as the boat slid under. No one was hurt, but I sure wasn't enthused about being shot at.

The captain was indignant that this flimsy sampan should try to harm his submarine. In a pique of anger he took *Pompon* out of range of the machine gun and again surfaced. This time we took careful aim and hit the target with our first round. It sank and we submerged. The captain shook my hand on being such a crack shot. I didn't tell him I was really only interested in the extra five dollars a month gun-boss pay.

Chapter 15
April 1943
LOSS OF THE USS *GRENADIER,* (SS-210)
BY ROBERT W. PALMER

> Bob Palmer was in the maneuvering room when a plane attacked *Grenadier* (SS-210) while it was on the surface. The bomb badly damaged the aft end of the boat and Palmer found himself and his shipmates swimming in the ocean.

Pre-dawn on 21 April, 1943, USS *Grenadier* (SS 210) was making an end-around on two Japanese ships which had been sighted to the westward during the previous night. Her Fairbanks-Morse engines were each delivering full power, driving the boat on course 155 degrees toward Malacca

Strait and a predetermined position from which it was anticipated a successful torpedo attack could be made on the two ships.

At about 0835, still some ten minutes before diving, a single engine plane was sighted, at low altitude, approaching the port quarter. The captain yelled, "Dive, Dive, this is not a drill." He hit the bridge diving alarm twice. As the lookouts streamed below he pulled the upper conning tower hatch lanyard and told the helmsman to ring up an ahead-emergency bell.

The already tense atmosphere below at once became electrified. As 120 feet registered on the depth gauge a sense of safety was destroyed by the terrible sound of a bomb splashing into the water. I heard it through the hull as did my shipmates. We froze. Then came a click as the bomb armed itself. It was as though two express trains collided on top of us. The detonation occurred close by and to starboard above the after torpedo room bulkhead. The boat rolled violently to port. In the maneuvering room we were knocked about, but those in the after torpedo room became airborne, ending up between torpedo tubes and on the deck.

All power for propulsion, auxiliary equipment and lighting was lost. We switched to emergency lighting, which came directly off the battery. The sight of devastation staggered us in maneuvering. It was inconceivable that *Grenadier* could have withstood so much damage, and still could be more or less intact, especially from abaft the after engine room bulkhead. The after torpedo room was in complete disarray; tubes were askew, pipe lines, valves and gauges ruptured or rendered inoperative; equipment and bodies were in a jumbled mess on the deck.

We in maneuvering assessed the situation as best we could. The room was damaged beyond belief. Both propeller shafts were seized in a viselike grip by the twisted hull, which had been folded to port. To further complicate the situation, seawater was pouring in from the hard patch above the cubicle, the after torpedo room loading hatch, and numerous other hull openings. As we passed 200 feet smoke appeared in the cubicle. I passed the word, "Fire in maneuvering!" We grabbed fire extinguishers and battled the small blaze. While doing so we realized that the main motors were in immediate danger of flooding.

The fathometer indicated that we were in about 270 feet of water whereupon the skipper decided to settle on the bottom in lieu of surfacing.

The crew began their struggle for survival. A bucket brigade was formed. We had to keep the water level from reaching the main propulsion motors. The line of men stretched through the engine rooms, after battery, control and forward battery into the forward torpedo room. Hand over hand the buckets were passed forward. This continued until a jury rig could be established to power the main electrical circuits. We worked hour after hour to clear short-circuits and establish propulsion.

During the day, many a man passed out from fatigue, heat and foul air, even though oxygen had been released into the atmosphere and CO_2 absorbent had been spread throughout the interior. Finally at about 2130, preparations were made to surface. All tanks that would hold water had been filled in order to anchor *Grenadier* and keep her from moving in the fast current of Malacca. Banks of compressed air were bled into these and the main ballast tanks. Finally, and with reluctance, Grenadier moved upward, finally breaking the surface. Officers and men, totally exhausted and very short of oxygen, tasted sweet fresh air.

Throughout the night we struggled in hopes of reestablishing propulsion, but to no avail. The entire drive was out; shafts were bent, seals were distorted and screws were damaged. In addition, radio communication had been destroyed, and the 3 inch deck gun was inoperative.

Some of the men sewed mattress covers together and rigged the resulting sail to number two periscope, in hopes that enough wind could move the ship close to the Malaysia shore where it could possibly be submerged and made seaworthy. Dead calm belayed this effort.

There was no option but to take preliminary steps to destroy *Grenadier* should such action become necessary.

Shortly after 0800, another Japanese plane began an approach from ahead. Though we were a sitting duck, we were not incapable of some retaliation. The plane was a dive-bomber, referred to as a VAL and as it got close it began a strafing run down our starboard side. We opened up with two 20mm guns, two .30 caliber machine guns, a few rifles, some .45 caliber pistols, and some Tommy guns. The steward threw potatoes. Tracers revealed that the 20mm fire was effective. The plane wavered, pulled up and circled our stern making an approach up the port side. Again our automatic weapons blazed away. The plane was again hit several times. The pilot must have become discouraged for he released his bomb as he passed abreast to port. It detonated about 200 yards off the starboard bow.

By this time, surface ships were observed at some distance, approaching from both north and south. The coding machine was brought to the deck and smashed with hammers. A Tommy gun was emptied into the torpedo data computer, torpedoes were run hot in the tubes, radio gear smashed, all code books burned, documents thrown over the side in weighted bags. Time was running out! We would soon be surrounded, and being no match for Japanese destroyers, the skipper had to abandon ship. He then had ordered, "All hands on deck except the Chief of the Boat, wear life belts, inflate the rubber life boat and all hands over the side and away from the hull."

Then to the chief below he ordered, "Open everything and come topside." The Chief of the Boat, then the skipper, joined all other personnel in the water. *Grenadier* slid gracefully under the water for the last time. All hands were picked up by a Japanese armed merchant ship and taken to a commandeered Catholic school in Penang, Malaysia. Torture and inhumane treatment began immediately. Beating, burning, breaking fingers with bamboo or pencils between them were perpetrated on the men by Japanese soldiers who sneered and joked.

The men were divided half and half between the school rooms on the ground floor, stone decks; the officers in single rooms on the second floor, wooden decks. The rough treatment started the first afternoon, particularly with the men. They were forced to sit or stand in silence in an attention attitude. Any divergence resulted in a gun butt, kick, slug in the face or a bayonet prick. In the questioning room, Jap thugs used persuasive measures such as clubs, about the size of indoor ball bats, pencils between the fingers and pushing of the blade of a pen knife under the finger nails, trying to get us to talk about our submarine and the location of other submarines.

Maybe I would pass out and maybe not. Following this I would receive another club beating until I passed out. On coming to, they would try to get me to talk and when it was not forthcoming, I received more beatings. Finally I would be carried to my room and dumped on the floor waiting for a while until they decided to try again. Every time I would hear that warrant officer, assisted by his walking stick, come into the building, I would think it was for me again or maybe some other poor devil. We all had the same feeling for everyone received beating after beating, as like treatment was given to all hands. One became so stiff and sore it was almost impossible to move, let alone change position from standing or sitting or reclining, even if able to get away with it.

This was the beginning of twenty-eight and a half months of similar treatment for most all of the crew and officers alike. Work camps eased the brutality somewhat; however, the Japanese caused the death of four crewmembers. It was a miracle any of us survived.

Chapter 16

JULY 1943

MIDWAY, OUR REFUGE OF 1943

BY JACK QUADE

Seaman Jack Quade was stranded on Midway Island. He became a lifeguard and went into business catching langouste (spiny lobsters) until the officers' club confiscated his catch.

I was a seaman aboard *Skipjack* (SS-184) in mid-1943. The boat's diesels were throttled back to an idle and the boat, still making way, rolled slowly, in a dark but glassy sea. The deck watch and the lookouts aloft were scanning the horizon for any sign of that tiny coral reef known as Midway Island. Our radar was out and the overcast had compromised our getting a good star fix. We had heard our would-be escort plane, but he hadn't been able to sight us. We couldn't break radio silence to guide him. During the last fifty-three days we had operated mostly on the surface so we were low on fuel, and totally dependent on reaching the island. We had similar problems on previous patrols. Midway was small and stood barely forty feet above the water. It was hard to find.

One of the upper lookouts was the first to see the superstructure of a submarine tender, bearing almost dead ahead. The order went down to increase to standard speed. As we approached, the island came into view, surrounding the tender and giving the appearance that the ship had run aground. As we came closer a second, but smaller, island began to take shape just east of the tender. Between the islands was a narrow ship channel filled with white coral heads that passed under our keel. After maneuvering through the outer reef we executed a sharp turn to port allowing us access to a sizable inner lagoon.

To the north, five piers extended into the lagoon, providing berths for maybe ten boats. To the east, the tender occupied one of the piers, while a smaller drydock was moored further to the east. We turned toward one of the piers crowded with a band, officers and well-wishers, as the first throwing line hit the pier, the band struck up a musical welcome. Slowly the boat slid gracefully into a berth. We had made it. We had left this place almost two months before and we were back, safe within the refuge, the inner lagoon of this tiny island.

At this point the wounded were usually the first to go ashore, but we had only a single injured man, the captain. He had been on the bridge during a fire-fight and had been hit in the hand by a machine gun bullet. With his bandaged hand, he carefully descended the ladder to the main deck and moved forward to greet the admiral and his staff who were only then coming across the gangway.

In due course the captain would become the property of the medics. The rest of us began an unwinding process such as receiving mail, fresh fruit and ice cream. With packets of mail in hand, we retreated to the shade of pier sheds to read our letters, some stayed on board, leaning against the conning tower fairwater and sinking into a trance, feasting on every word from loved ones and home.

In short order, the relief crew began replacing us and we were shuttled off to a rest camp. The officers were transferred to the old Gooney Bird Hotel, a stone remnant of the 1930 China Clipper days, when passengers from those great flying boats would spend the night during their trans-Pacific flights. The enlisted men would be bunked in barren Quonset huts, with no amenities, but with very welcome showers.

We spent the next two weeks sleeping, eating, occasionally drinking green beer, playing cards, lying on the beach soaking up the sun and writing letters home. The usual course of events would be to return to the boat after a couple of weeks and take over from the relief crew, who had repaired and brought the old war horse back to operational status. And after a few weeks of trials we would stuff the boat with supplies, a full load of fuel, and new torpedoes. A rested crew, including me and some new faces replacing those transferred out, completed our readiness for sea. The refit completed, we headed out again, leaving the refuge, going back to the unknown, on patrol somewhere off Japan.

But not this time, the executive officer had been moved up to captain and we had a full complement of crew, but we did not have new patrol orders. The rumors were rampant, but there was nothing specific. There had been lots of talk in the recent past about the boat's age. The Skipjack was a thin-skinner, red lined at a depth of 260 feet, with only four tubes forward and four aft. She carried less fish and sported an old four inch deck gun from the First World War. Built in the 1930s she was mechanically and operationally outdated. She had been on ten patrols and was not drawing assignments equivalent to the more modern, better equipped, deeper diving boats. Now, without marching orders our futures became uncertain and the boat languished in her berth.

As the days progressed, some of the crew was assigned to active duty on the base. Normally, I would have been posted to the relief crew, working either in communications or navigation. But both groups were over-staffed so they posted me to the beach. Guard duty! A picture has survived to this day of me standing on the Midway Beach with three other life-guards, in a pith helmet, adjacent to a life-buoy marked Midway Beach, looking every bit the part of a Southern California beach boy.

In a matter of a few short weeks I had gone from standing watches aloft, next to the ice covered periscope shears of a submarine on patrol in the Sea of Okhotsk to being a beach bum on sunny Midway Island. It seemed unreal. North of Japan, sea temperatures had been below freezing and the interior of the boat had sweat with condensation. We had engaged the enemy, dodged depth charges, aerial bombs and mines and had been attacked on the surface. Now I was a life guard, heroically saving people from getting sunburned. Unless you were drunk, it wasn't possible to drown in the inner lagoon. It was a turquoise bathtub surrounded by a white coral beach.

Twice a day I passed the line of boats at anchor, where small signs identified the boat in each berth, names like, *Tang, Albacore, Silversides, Trigger, Bowfin, Sea Horse, and Sea Cat;* a never ending parade of boats coming and going. I didn't think about it then, but I was watching history in the making. Some of the legendary and the least known of the submarines of the war passed here and ultimately something like three thousand men would set forth from this refuge, never to return. At that time we knew little more than that they were, "overdue from patrol and presumed lost." Nothing about, why and where it happened. Some of my classmates from sub school were on those boats. Some were school mates from junior high school.

From 1942 to 1945, Midway was the last outpost where submarines could top off fuel tanks on their way to the war against Japan. Or, on their way home it was the first refuge for a submarine struggling back from the war.

With almost no responsibilities and a small motorized whale boat at our disposal, some of the other life guards and I began exploring the outer margins of the partially submerged reef. It was circular in shape and about five miles across with a central lagoon nearly fifty feet deep. What was most interesting was the sea life.

Clearly this place was both a home and a refuge for other creatures that had been here for eons before we came. Both inside and outside the reef were countless fish. Outside the reef, Bosun Birds followed schools of anchovies and sardines being feasted on by passing predatory schools of game fish, like albacore and tuna.

While diving along the inside edge of the outer reef we found a habitat of pools and ledges overflowing with Longusta, a critter that except for his green color and the absence of pincers was a lobster. Catching them by hand was a bit tricky, but not for kids born on the California Surf. In short order we had a steady supply of these rare delicacies.

Somehow the word got out and the base commander demanded that some of our goodies be delivered to his mess. Our sense of importance went way up, but it wasn't from saving lives. It was from supplying the commander's table.

There were other residents on these Islands, besides us. Sea birds of every description, waves of them on annual migrations stopped by Midway for a rest. They found it so nice many stayed to raise their young. The Albatross were completely protected and without fear of us, so they laid eggs everywhere, that soon became a cacophony of squawking mothers and chicks. The gooney-birds were the most amazing. At sea these birds were a picture of elegance, gliding effortlessly over the waves, hardly moving their wings. But on land they were clumsy, noisy and territorial, guarding every egg with aggressive lunges at anyone who entered their space.

Their landings and takeoffs were a constant source of entertainment. They glided in over the wet asphalt streets at high speed, landing gear down; instinctively thinking it was sea water and a soft place to land. But it wasn't. This resulted in some of the most amazing crash landings ever seen, never fatal, but most embarrassing.

For me this interlude would come to an abrupt end with the return of my wounded skipper with only one good hand, but a new boat, the *Plaice* (SS-390) and a need for a young sailor with great night vision, one who had served him well and would do so again. We returned to the waters off Northern Hokaido, to the winds off Siberia and to the destruction of the enemy. The cycle would be complete with our return to the refuge, but the cycle would not end for us, not until that eventful day in August of 1945.

Chapter 17

AUGUST 1943
LOOSE TORPEDO AT PEARL HARBOR

BY JAMES H. ALLEN

> Jim Allen watched from a submarine tender at the Pearl Harbor Submarine Base as an armed torpedo left the tube of a submarine tied up alongside and streaked across the harbor toward a ship on the other side.

It's tough to remember exact dates from fifty years ago, but I believe it was mid-1943, and I was in Submarine Division 102, on board the sub-tender, USS *Sperry*. We were tied at the long dock of the Sub-Base in Pearl Harbor. With no duties at the time, I wandered to the bridge where there was a great view of the base and Navy Yard. There were a few boats tied up at the finger piers off to port. One was firing water slugs from the stern tubes. For the uninitiated, this involves going through all steps to fire a torpedo except there's no torpedo involved, at least there's not supposed to be a torpedo in the tube. The tube is filled with water, and the procedure allows a full check of the firing circuits. Every time I would hear the *"whoomp"* of the water slugs, I would glance in that direction and note the disturbance of the water boiling up at the stern. When the third or fourth slug was fired, I was flabbergasted to see a torpedo wake streaking out across the harbor in the direction of the Navy Yard. The bridge of the *Sperry* must have been hundred feet above the water line, so I had a panoramic view. The wake was headed straight at the stern of a freighter docked broadside to the speeding torpedo. I believe I was the only eye-witness; however, I was sure the crewmembers who had fired the "slug" knew something was different. I remember thinking that maybe there was ammunition on board that freighter, but I could not move. I could not take my eyes off the wake.

The procedure for firing water slugs called for maximum depth setting, so when the torpedo was about 200 feet short of the freighter it must have hit bottom. There was a gigantic explosion. A geyser of mud and water shot into the air, the stern of the freighter seemed to lift twenty feet and slam back down. A shock wave traveled through the water and through the air, and jarred the *Sperry* when it hit. Water and mud came raining down out of the sky, and a big circular wave was rushing away from the point of detonation.

A period of calm followed, but it was probably only a few seconds. I heard running footsteps, and became aware that signal lights were flashing all over the place while the *Sperry* bugler was blowing General Quarters. Moments later General Quarters was sounded for the whole base and navy yard. The bridge of the *Sperry* quickly filled with more brass than I had ever seen in one place, and General Quarters was *"gonging"* away. Men in battle helmets and life preservers were rushing up and down ladders and along the deck. Ammunition was broken out for the 20mm and 40mm AA [antiaircraft guns], and the five-inch gun turrets came alive. Over the loud speaker "single up all lines, prepare to get underway.

I heard the captain order the signalman to ask the Water Tower at the Navy Yard (the center of communication), "Are we under attack?"

Gathering courage I stepped forward with a snappy salute and said,

"Sir, I can explain." That's as far as I got when one of the officers growled, "Do you have a battle station? Then get to it." Stammering, I said "But, but, Sir." That's all I got out. I was ordered to my battle station or the master at arms would have me on report. My battle station was in the magazine of the after five-inch gun, loading shells into a vertical hoist.

Eventually, the guys who fired the torpedo came forward and admitted their goof. In another few minutes we were secured from General Quarters and things just went back to normal. I never did come forward as probably the only eyewitness to the Great 1943 Pearl Harbor Attack.

Chapter 18
OCTOBER 1943
SECOND PATROL OF THE USS *BLUEFISH* (SS-222)
BY EDWIN J. SHEPHERD, JR.

Ed Shepherd Jr. witnessed his captain's chase of a fast convoy. A Japanese POW was in *Bluefish* (SS-222) until Ed found the poor man dead in his bunk.

On October 1, 1943, while aboard the submarine tender, *Pelias* in Fremantle, Australia, I was assigned to the USS *Bluefish*. The captain was Commander G. E. Porter and Lieutenant Commander Chester W. Nimitz, Jr., the son of the Commander in Chief of the Pacific Fleet, was the executive officer. I soon became aware of the crew's great admiration and loyalty to this pair.

We sailed for the *Bluefish*'s second patrol on October 15, 1943 from Fremantle. My assignment was lookout while on the surface and bow planes when submerged. The trip north along the coast was uneventful. At the northwest corner of Australia lay Exmouth Gulf where the navy had a signal station and a tanker of Dutch registry. This was a very barren and lonely place and duty at the signal tower and the tanker had to be among the most boring in the war. The surrounding desert had a sparse cove of scrub brush. One of our lookouts observed a large herd of kangaroos stampeding across the rolling hillside, kicking up a cloud of dust. The tanker topped off our fuel tanks and we were ready.

We departed Exmouth Gulf and set our course for Lombok Strait, the narrow passage between Lombok Island and Bali. The approach to the strait was made on the surface on a dark night, no moon. We entered the strait at flank speed to get through the dangerous passage as quickly as possible. I was the starboard, aft lookout and recall that the vibration was so great that resting my elbows on the railing made it impossible to use the binoculars. Our radar detected a sub chaser coming out from Lombok and the forward lookout said that he could see something, probably a wake. Our own wake was aglow with phosphorous which sparkled brightly as our screws sent it boiling astern. The sub chaser couldn't keep up with our speed and we proceeded into the Flores Sea.

Several days later we received a radio message that one of the coast watchers had sighted a convoy heading in our direction. This information included an accurate location, course and speed of the convoy. The convoy, containing six ships, was sighted, November 6, 1943 at 2052 hours.

After losing contact in low visibility the convoy was relocated the next day and we fell in astern. At 1730 hours, we commenced an end-around to gain position ahead. During the daylight hours of November 7 we proceeded ahead of the convoy while going ahead flank on the surface. During my lookout watch in the afternoon, I could occasionally see the tops of the mast of the leading ship.

The following is copied from Commander Porter's Patrol Report, now on file with the National Archives at College Park, Maryland November 8, 1943,

0100: In position ahead. Took convoy course and speed awaiting moonset at 0231.

0130: Everything was perfect until we sighted a small vessel broad on the port bow (Ship contact No. 7), probably a destroyer. Put our stern to same and increased speed to flank. The situation looked bad when he commenced signaling at us. When he disappeared from sight we worked over to the other bow of the convoy.

0231: Moonset. Manned the radar. Immediate contact. Large pips at 16,000 yards. Commenced tracking. Unable to determine the disposition of the ships as they varied all over the ocean. Speed checked perfect at 12.8 knots. Base course 007deg T

0336: Radar range 16,000 yards. Distance to track 8,000 yards. Built up to full power and started in. During this time I was scheduled to be a lookout. Capt. Porter had decided to be on the bridge, manning the TBT, with Chief Signalman, Richmond, the only lookout. I was seated on a sack of potatoes in the control room with the red night vision glasses on, ready to man the lookout station if needed.

Continuing with the patrol report:

0353: Stopped and opened the torpedo tube doors. Built up to full power again. At the range of 5,000 yards I saw a submarine commanding officer's day dream; six ships lined up in a column open order forming practically a continuous target with no escorts visible.

0357: At range of 2,800 yards, commenced firing bow tubes (Attack No 1). Fired two torpedoes at the first ship, one at the second, one at the third and two at the fourth. Ordered right full ruder and brought the stern tubes to bear.

0402: With a range of 1,350 yards, fired two torpedoes at the fifth ship and two at the sixth. Bluefish was maneuvered so that all torpedoes were fired with zero gyro angles. The fifth torpedo was a premature, very close aboard. The column of water wet down our bridge. The other nine were seen, heard and felt when they hit. The first ship fired at was a tanker. It blew up and sank. Two pips on the radar disappeared. Pulled out to range of 6,000 yards and commenced to reload torpedoes.

Within a little over five minutes the captain had fired ten torpedoes.

The forward room's six torpedoes were just reaching their targets as the four from the after room were being fired.

Continuing with the patrol report:

0427: One of the four remaining pips disappeared without opening range.

0441: Reload completed. There were still three pips on the radar and two ships were visible. Their ranges had been constant at 9,000 yards, 11,000 yards and 13,000 yards for about 20 minutes, bearing between 040 deg T and 070 deg T. Built up to full power and started in on one of the two remaining ships in sight. On the way in, with range decreasing, two of the pips became smaller and smaller and disappeared, at which time our chosen target disappeared. Closed on the only remaining ship.

It should be remembered that during all of this engagement the *Bluefish* remained on the surface with the crew at battle stations. The four lookouts on standby in the control room were ordered to get into their bunks and be rested for a later watch. I really did not want to give up my front row seat, but orders were orders. Of course sleep was out of the question.

Continuing with the patrol report:

0500: At a range of 2,000 yards fired a spread of four torpedoes (attack No. 2), all to hit amidships, at a tanker which was dead in the water. One torpedo ran erratic in deflection, one hit and two missed. This hit did not seem to affect the target. During this period the radar gave us a number of exciting moments by picking up numerous pips at 2,000 to 4,000 yards which we thought might be patrol boats, but it turned out to be lifeboats. Four torpedoes were fired to insure destruction of tanker before help arrived; keeping in mind the escort vessel seen this morning.

0509: At a range of 1,000 yards, fired two torpedoes (Attack No.

3) at tanker, both to hit. One hit and one miss. Target lower in the water. By this time dawn had broken, visibility was good and no other ships were in site.

0548: At a range of 1,000 yards fired two torpedoes (Attack No. 4) at tanker from the stern tubes, both to hit. Two hits. The one set at 20 feet rocked him hard and the one at ten feet started the most beautiful fire I have ever seen. Smoke rose and formed a cloud about 4,000 feet in the air. Took moving and still pictures.

At this time the captain permitted members of the crew to come to the conning tower and observe the burning tanker through one of the periscopes. By the time my turn came, a destroyer had been sighted, but the captain insisted that I have my turn. He used the second periscope to check out the enemy ship. His description of, "the most beautiful fire" was accurate, but the thought of the sailors caught in it was sobering. The space between the two periscopes is only a couple feet and I found myself bumping bottoms with the captain. This made me uneasy because I knew that his job was far more important to me and the rest of the crew than what I was doing, so I left, thanking him for the once-in-a-lifetime view.

The destroyer never sighted us and we submerged for the first time since leaving Exmouth Gulf. He began dropping depth charges randomly at a long range and although we could clearly hear them they were not close. The crew was ready for the sack and we took advantage of it. The torpedomen's job of reloading fourteen torpedoes in such a short time had been exhausting.

In mid-afternoon on November 8 we surfaced and set course to south toward dangerous ground. This course took us through the scene of the attack. Here we sited large oil slicks and empty lifeboats, which we looted. A very new looking box compass was recovered and later given to Admiral Christie. I had a life jacket, also like new. It was a kapok type, very bulky and I had no place to store it. The label printed on the canvas had the ship's name, *Kyokuei Maru*, and the maker's name, Joe Rose, Tokyo, Japan. I cut off the label, but regrettably lost it before I was discharged from the Navy.

The Official Chronology of the U.S. Navy in World War II by Robert

J. Cressman makes the following entry: "8 Monday November 1943 Submarine *Bluefish* (SS 222) sinks Japanese army tanker *Kyokuei Maru* in South China Sea off northwestern coast of Luzon. Although *Bluefish* claims five more ships, none are damaged; escort vessel *Tsushima* counter-attacks unsuccessfully."

There were several uneventful days, cruising on the surface in the dangerous ground area then we returned to the Sulu Sea. There we sighted a small vessel, ten to fifteen tons, with a Jap flag painted on the side of the pilot house. It was manned by about ten men. On the deck there were many large sea turtles, alive and on their backs. At first the captain thought the men might be fishermen, but their skin was not of the very dark complexion of the Mulocan natives. When ordered to stop, there was no reaction. We fired a few shots across their bow, but they continued on. Finally, we came close aboard, actually unintentionally ramming the port side of the vessel. The cracking of the wooden timbers could be heard from my position in the lookout shears. We spent a long time getting the crew to abandon ship. There were two outrigger canoes tied to the stern. We finally convinced the men in the water that they were expected to use them. Three or four of the Japanese were brought aboard the bow of the *Bluefish* to be questioned but they were uncooperative and were thrown back into the sea.

We shot a second four-inch shell into the boat and another man jumped overboard. The man who last jumped overboard was frantically begging to be brought aboard. We accommodated him. During all of this time, well over an hour in broad daylight, we on lookout were reminded repeatedly that we were only 340 miles from Manila and could expect Japanese aircraft at any time. None appeared.

Upon relief from watch I went to my bunk area. There were two bunks for lookouts. When I arrived I found the pharmacist mate with the prisoner standing in front of my bunk, holding on to the bunk above. The poor Japanese had eighty-five percent second and third degree burns. Since there was no bunk available I helped the pharmacist. About this time we learned from a radio message from Darwin that he was a Japanese Army communications man who had stayed on board calling for air support. The pharmacist gave him two shots of morphine and we put him into the bottom bunk and I crawled into the bunk above him and fell sound asleep.

When I was awakened for my next lookout watch at 0100 the pharmacist was called to check the prisoner who he found to be dead. He was the enemy, but it was difficult not to feel sorry for him. We buried the man at sea.

Chapter 19

OCTOBER 1943

S-48, MY FIRST BOAT

BY CHURCHILL "JIM" CAMPBELL

Reserve officer Jim Campbell was an expert on diesel engines. On S-48 and *Parche* (SS-384), under legendary submarine skipper Commander Lawson P. Ramage, he put his knowledge to good use.

To understand what a reserve officer went through during the war, you have to know a little of his background-mostly because commanding officers of all ships were looking for men that could fill in the blanks in their organizations in minimum time and could do a satisfactory job.

I had made a pretty good impression on my superior officers in San Diego primarily because of my education and training at Standard Oil Company. When I was accepted at Northwestern University's NROTC [Naval Reserve Officer Training Course] program, my commanding officer recommended me and suggested I should volunteer for submarine duty because of my electrical background.

After December 7, 1941, I volunteered for a commission as an ensign, engineering volunteer specialist and on February 1, 1942 was assigned to the Office of Industrial Management for the 11th Naval District in San Diego. At that time I was married and took a substantial cut in pay with an ensign's $125/month salary to work on the Broadway Pier in San Diego. That was not what I had hoped to do in the Navy so I volunteered for every school that was offered.

At Northwestern I had taken Navigation & Nautical Astronomy and a course entitled, The Mathematics of Naval Gunnery. I volunteered for a diesel engineering course (four months) at Purdue University. Diesel engineering included a course in lubrication and much experimental work with vibrations in two-cycle diesel engines. This was far and away the best time I ever had in the U.S. Navy. I lived in the student union on campus with maid service and everything furnished.

On completion of diesel school, I was assigned as an engineering officer on an LCI [Landing Craft Infantry] under construction in Orange, Texas. En-route from West Lafayette, Indiana to Orange, Texas, the train passed through Washington D.C. Remembering the recommendations of my NROTC commanding officer, I stopped off at the submarine desk in the Pentagon where I dropped off a resume and told the officer in charge, "I could make the service a good submarine officer." He laughed and said that I'd better get on down to Orange, Texas.

I put the LCI-83 into commission and sailed with her down the Sabine River to Sabine, Texas where four of the 8GM 6-71 diesel engines failed. The problem turned out to be sabotage from the shipyard. We had spotted the problem early enough that damage to the engines was minor, but it did take about ten days to make sure we had corrected all of the problems. It was at this point that orders to Submarine School in New London caught up with me.

Upon arrival at sub school, we were given the longest and most complete psychological examination that you can imagine. It went on at all hours night and day. After this, most of us were passed on to a most thorough physical exam. I was doing fine until one of the doctors said that I had excessive wax in my ears and assigned a corpsman to clean them. During the cleaning, the corpsman scratched one eardrum and they determined that I could not make the Momsen Lung escape from the hundred foot water tower.

Since I had apparently done satisfactorily through all of the examinations and preliminary testing I was assigned to the S-48 (SS-159) until such time as my ear healed and there was a vacancy in another submarine officer's class. I am sure that if I had not dropped off my resume showing an electrical engineering and diesel engine background on my trip through Washington D.C. I would have been sent back to surface craft right then and there.

I was very disappointed to be assigned to a submarine of World War I vintage. The S-48 had actually been commissioned in 1921; however, it was probably the best thing that could have happened to me.

The S-48 was used primarily as a training boat for prospective commanding officers on their way to new submarines. When I reported aboard, the executive officer asked my name and I said, "Churchill Campbell, sir." He simply said, "It's too long. What else can we call you?"

Since my middle name was James, I said, "Call me Jim." From that time on, until the end of the war I was called Jim Campbell.

I really got a thrill out of diving a submarine and so I worked very hard at doing it. In a very short time I became the battle stations diving officer and took the dive when the prospective commanding officers would make practice approaches on ships and convoys coming into Boston and New York harbors. The very senior submarine officers would critique the approach tactics of each PCO. I was able to stand at the diving station and absorb a number of very good lessons in how to handle a submarine and make a submerged attack. Then when we did get into New London, I spent most of my time in the attack trainer.

Finally on July 1st, I received orders to submarine school. By this time I had become the engineering officer of the S-48. The executive officer of the S-48 had been in that position for some time. Since she was a training boat the captains stayed for a very short time, while they awaited new construction boats. When I received my orders to submarine school, Commander McCrory wrote a letter to the SubBase commander stating, that in his opinion, because of my education and previous experience, I really did not need to go to submarine school. Instead, I took the final examinations at sub school and did quite well.

Prior to graduation from sub school, each officer was able to make three choices as to where he would like to go. It was understood that those with the highest class standing would get their choices first. My first choice was for a modern submarine in the Pacific; however, when I received my orders it was to a submarine named the *Parche* (SS-384) then under construction at Portsmouth Navy Yard.

When I arrived on the *Parche*, I found that my former executive officer from the S-48 was now the executive officer of the *Parche*, and that he had specifically requested that I be ordered to the boat. Kind of a nice way to start a new job, but from that time on he sure never showed me any favors! Very shortly I met the commanding officer, Commander Lawson P. Ramage. Captain Ramage had already made two war patrols aboard the *Trout* and had received a Navy Cross. He looked like God to me; a green Ltjg. in the Naval Reserve.

Captain Ramage was adamant that all officers who had not qualified on fleet submarines would start right there as if this were their first submarine and make all of the required system drawings and complete a qualification notebook. And, that he would personally take them through the boat while they described each piece of equipment and its operation.

The *Parche* was commissioned in October 1943. At that point I was assigned as the communication officer and assistant engineering officer. Since I just happened to have very good night vision, my battle station while on the surface was on the Target Bearing Transmitter (TBT). Once the TDC operator pushed the button that said he was on the target it was my job to keep those binoculars centered on the target no matter what!

We operated with the British in the North Atlantic for about three weeks and then headed down to Key West where we operated with the antisubmarine forces that were testing a new weapon known as the Hedge Hog. During one dive, while the surface ship was pinging on us, fixing the Hedge Hog, the *Parche* was running with her vents closed. As luck would have it, one of the dummy bombs from the Hedge Hog lodged in the after vent operating mechanism. At this point, we blew main ballast and surfaced in preparation for the next test run.

The fact that the small dummy bomb was lodged in one of the after tank vent valve mechanisms was not known. Consequently, the boat made her next dive with the after vent valve did not open and we started for the bottom head first. I was sitting in the yeoman's compartment next to the control room decoding a message. The officer who had the dive was relatively new and he panicked. Not wishing to die and having had considerable diving experience on the S-48, I relieved the diving officer, got a bubble into bow buoyancy, shut the vents, blew main ballast and ordered all back full. We got out of that one OK, but from then on the main ballast vents remained open until we were ready to surface. I was assigned as battle stations diving officer for the next four war patrols.

Diving the old S-48 was a thrill, but diving this new submarine was a thrill like I had never known and still have never experienced anything like it.

We were credited with sinking three ships with torpedo attacks from the surface during our first patrol.

The second run was really the outstanding patrol for the *Parche*. We had our patrol repairs done by the tender at Midway and headed for the South China Sea. Once again we were part of a three boat Wolf Pack. Captain Parks (a four striper) was on board as the wolf pack commander. The other boats were the *Steelhead* (SS-280) and the *Hammerhead* (SS-364).

During thirty days on station we tried to make an attack on an aircraft carrier, but we could never get into position for a torpedo shot. The *Hammerhead* experienced some damage and headed for Pearl Harbor.

Since *Parche* and *Steelhead* both had a full load of twenty-one torpedoes, Captain Parks requested and was granted permission for the wolf pack to remain on station. On the thirty-second day, Steelhead made contact on a large convoy and then passed its course and speed on to us. The night was very dark, but the *Steelhead* got into position for a submerged attack ahead of the convoy while we raced at full speed to catch up and get into the action.

When *Steelhead* made her attack, sinking a freighter and damaging a very large troop transport, all of the convoy escorts went to the point of attack and gave the submarine much depth charging. The convoy reversed course putting us almost in its middle without an escort destroyer in sight.

I was manning the target bearing transmitter [TBT] and Captain Ramage had the bridge. The first two torpedoes were fired at a small freighter, but because of the very short setup time, the data was not good and the target was able to avoid that one. However, we passed directly under his stern, opened the range to 400 yards and fired a single stern tube. The freighter disintegrated.

The captain selected a tanker as our next target. I settled the TBT on her center, the radar fed in the range and we fired three torpedoes. We made hits, the tanker started to bum, but she did not sink at that time. The captain then selected another tanker as the third target, and started to get into position while the crew loaded torpedoes in the forward room. This tanker took two direct hits and sank in short order. Ships in the convoy were firing all of their guns. I don't know what they were shooting at, but we were hit only by small arms fire and the captain had sent all of the lookouts and the quartermaster below. For some reason, some ship had fired star shells and those along with the burning tanker made it all bright as day.

The tanker that had been our second target was still burning, but refused to sink. So we made another attack and this time one more torpedo sent that tanker to the bottom in a hurry.

On several occasions we had passed close enough under the stern of a ship in the convoy that we on the bridge could hear commands being given on the Jap ship.

The captain next selected as a target a large freighter coming on to a perfect position for us to fire a torpedo so he ordered, "All stop." The freighter took a direct hit and sank very quickly.

At this time, I noticed an escort heading for us with the obvious intent of ramming and so informed the captain who then ordered right full rudder. At this point, I advised the captain that we were at, all stop. The captain instantly ordered, "All ahead flank."

The sudden thrust of both screws against a hard-over rudder drove us into a very sharp turn just as the escort slid by. The patrol report said that the escort had missed us by fifty yards, but in my estimation it was much closer to fifty inches.

We then pulled clear of the milling convoy to reload torpedoes. And as we started back toward the convoy there was a very large transport headed directly at us. The captain made one quick observation and then fired three torpedoes down the throat. One torpedo hit the transport and she stopped dead in the water. We swung out and fired one torpedo from a stern tube for a direct hit. The transport was observed sinking as we pulled clear of the convoy.

I had personally observed the sinking of five ships in a period of forty-six minutes. During this time the Parche had fired nineteen torpedoes.

After much research after the war, in the final analysis, the *Parche* was credited with sinking four and a half ships in that particular action. The transport that we sank was determined to be the same one that the *Steelhead* had previously damaged in her submerged attack.

With only two torpedoes on board and having been in the area for thirty-four days, we headed for Midway and then on to Pearl Harbor. For this action, Captain Rampage received the Congressional Medal of Honor and old Campbell received the Silver Star Medal that was pinned on by Admiral Lockwood who also gave me my gold dolphins. I was finally qualified in submarines.

For the third run, we were assigned primarily to lifeguard duty. The patrol was very long the only sinking was one small gun target. When the maneuvering watch was set on our return to Midway, the executive officer told me to take the deck and since nobody came topside to relieve me. I conned the boat through the narrow entrance channel and moored her alongside of the other submarines in the tender's nest. Fortunately, my experience at handling the S-48 in the Thames River currents paid off, and I probably made the best landing of my life.

Chapter 20
DECEMBER 1943
THE *RYUHO'S* LAST STAND
BY JOHN M. GOOD

> John Good sailed with Commander R. E. M. Ward in *Sailfish* (SS-192) and watched as his cunning captain out-witted the Japanese.

Early in December 1943, *Sailfish* (SS-192), under the command of Cdr. R.E.M. Ward made her tenth patrol. We were alerted by a radio message that a Japanese Task Group would possibly cross our path within the next twenty-four hours. Ward ordered relaxed battle stations, which meant to us in the forward torpedo room that we could rest, but had to be ready at a moment's notice.

The boat buzzed with excitement. Hours went by slowly as we circled the suspect area. The sky became ominously dark the barometer dropped steadily as mountainous waves tossed the boat about like a rubber ball. In the forward room, we were tossed from side to side and when the boat slid down one side of a wave it was like being on a roller-coaster. The skipper ordered the lookouts below, leaving himself, the executive officer and Tonton, the quartermaster, on the bridge to withstand the elements of nature. Hope of finding the task group was diminishing as the weather deteriorated. Our only hope left was to scan the area by radar.

After a full battery charge was completed, the captain ordered the main engines secured, using only the dinky to maintain steerageway. Another twenty-four hours dragged by with no abatement from the furious storm. We stayed in our bunks when not on watch. I was *woozie* from the pitching and yawing.

It was not until the third day that the context of our radioman's message bore fruit. Sighting a hazy image through the periscope, the skipper ordered battle stations. The tracking party was summoned to control while the skipper, exec and the OD remained on the bridge. A light flashed on and off along the starboard quarter. Blurry images appeared in the distance. The skipper strained to distinguish between mountainous waves and ships. This fast group of men-o-war appeared to be about 9,000 yards distant. The tracking party worked furiously to determine the target's course and speed. Two large ships and two escorts made up the task group. The nearest of the two largest ships was selected as the target. Diving to forty feet, the skipper decided to depend on radar alone.

We sweated it out forward. All our tubes were ready. The order came to open outer doors. I pulled the levers on tubes two, three, four and five. The hydraulics operated the muzzle doors to the tubes and the sliding side doors on the superstructure in one motion. There were five dull thuds as the tubes were opened to the sea. Word came from conn to set running depth at twelve feet. One by one each tube was fired from the conning tower. We watched the clock's second hand. Fifty seconds later we heard a resounding explosion through the hull, followed by a second hit several seconds later.

Depth charges began exploding, but none were very close. Going deep to evade, silent running was not imposed due to heavy sea conditions making sonar detection almost impossible. During the next hour and a half nineteen depth charges were randomly dropped, indicating that the escorts had not located *Sailfish*. We worked furiously to reload the expended tubes with warheads.

Surfacing at 0158, *Sailfish* commenced running up the target's track to intercept a possible cripple. By 0530 the rain had diminished to a steady downpour. Dawn was rapidly improving visibility. A radar image portrayed a slow moving target, obviously damaged, but of undetermined seriousness. Now, it was up to the skipper to keep the wounded ship from making a dash or freedom.

At 0552 *Sailfish* surfaced in subdued morning daylight and again we lined up to shoot. On orders from the bridge I opened the outer doors on tubes one, two and three. My buddy was on the tube-ready panel and as each tube was fired from conn. I pushed the duplicate firing button on the respective tube and he switched to the next ready tube. All were fired at a range of 3,500 yards. As *Sailfish* veered to the right, it heeled over in the heavy sea. The forward torpedo room gang glued our eyes on the clock, counting the seconds as they ticked away. Fifty seconds elapsed, finally we heard another boom. It was a solid hit! We grinned in the knowledge that we had done our jobs well.

The diving alarm sounded and the rhythmic beating of waves against the forward room hull slowly diminished then disappeared as the boat descended into the depths. As we went down, another terrific explosion indicated a second hit. Depth charges from an aroused enemy recommenced.

The fact that there had been ships scurrying to and fro topside, with no sounds of a breaking-up target, allowed room for conjecture about its size. Four torpedo hits would normally sink most men-a-war, but this wounded ship was putting up a real fight. Depth charges continued, but sea conditions, plus reverberations from the depth charges made it nearly impossible to locate us. Still, the very sound of the explosions sent chills up and down the spine.

In the forward torpedo room we again pushed and pulled with block and tackle the remaining torpedoes into the empty tubes. A few not otherwise engaged sat quietly on deck, or rested in their bunks. Although the air was hot, it was not yet fouled for lack of oxygen.

Deviation from normal behavior was to be expected during times of real stress. Strangeness lies in the type of deviation. One man busied himself eating everything he could find in the crew's mess.

Time dragged by until 0800 when periscope surveillance revealed the nature of the target in the morning light. A huge aircraft carrier lay listing to port, wallowing in huge swells. A lone destroyer stood by. Lining up for a stern shot, three more torpedoes were fired. Two terrific explosions shook the boat, quickly followed by the snapping and cracking of a ship breaking up. In the forward room we could relax a bit. We listened and acknowledged that finally the ship, whatever it was, was on its way down. Periscope observation revealed planes sliding off the carrier's deck like matchsticks as the big carrier slowly sank out of sight. The captain announced the sight over the I MC and smiles broke out in the men around me who had done their share in the effort. The time was 0940, Dec. 4, 1943.

After observing the carrier disappear into the depth, the skipper turned his attention to the destroyer. Instead of a destroyer, a cruiser was observed, crossing over the spot where the carrier went down. In an attempt to get a set-up on the cruiser, the skipper ordered a depth of fifty-nine feet. After vainly trying to ease the boat up to the ordered depth in the rolling swells, the diving officer lost depth control and the boat broached, exposing the conning tower.

A last fleeting periscope observation showed the cruiser heading directly toward *Sailfish*. Flooding negative and going ahead full, *Sailfish* quickly descended into the depths only moments before the fast charging cruiser passed overhead, laying down a terrific depth charge barrage as she went. But that Japanese cruiser didn't linger long within the range of this sharp-shooting persistent Yankee submarine. Soon the thunderous bursts subsided and the soundman reported that screw noises were slowly fading astern. Upon surfacing, the skipper ordered four main engines on the line in anticipation of tracking down the cruiser. Almost as soon as the chase began, the number two main engine began heating up and had to be shut down. The boat again made its way into the depths. Sailors buzzed excitedly about how the engine fouled-up their potential cruiser killing. One commented, "It's just as well. We'd have a hell a time with that baby on our hands."

There was an air of levity that came from a successful attack. It was as though each one had watched the battle through the captain's eyes. We all played a personal role in the action. Also, we were that much closer to going home.

PART THREE

Late-War Stories (1944–1945)

Chapter 21

FEBRUARY 1944

SUBMARINE ON THE LOOSE

BY WILLIAM DREHER

> While tied up in port with three other submarines Quartermaster Bill Dreher was immobilized by the sight of the outboard submarine being washed into an admiral's gig, crushing it to kindling.

As a member of the commissioning crew of the USS *Boarfish* (SS-327), I was the leading quartermaster. We had completed our first patrol and had been directed to go to Fremantle, Australia for supplies and repairs. We arrived on 15 February 1944. After arriving, two-thirds of the crew went for rest and relaxation and I was in the duty section that remained on the submarine to accomplish ship's work. At that time there were three other submarines tied up to the pier; two were inboard of us and one was outboard of us. The submarine tender *Euryale* (AS-22) was tied up in front of us and between the tender and us was a thirty foot launch called an admirals gig. It was tied up to the side of the pier. While standing topside watch at about 0400 the inboard submarine notified me that it was preparing to go to sea and that we would have to handle lines. I knew that it would be a bit more than just handling lines, because we would have to haul our boat alongside the inboard boat while still being abreast of the outboard boat. I notified the duty officer and he had the duty section awakened. Some guys fell in topside awaiting orders from the bridge to handle lines while an electrician stood by in maneuvering room. I asked the duty officer if we should notify the outboard submarine of the departure and he said, "No. Let them sleep. I can handle it."

When the inboard submarine was ready to depart, we took in all lines except for the bow line that we slacked to let the departing boat slide by us. After that we would breast in on the bow line, or so I thought. After the departing submarine backed out of the nest the duty officer, who now was the conning officer, ordered an ahead one third bell as we tightened the bow line. When we arrived in position, he ordered a back bell to stop us.

We came to a stop, but the outboard submarine kept moving forward and the singled-up lines that held it to our side slipped their cleats, then finally slipped free. The outboard boat moved slowly forward with no one on deck except the topside watch. Its 1,700 tons moved it inexorably toward the admiral's gig.

The boat's flustered topside watch, a young seaman, frantically called the duty officer who then was able to get a few men on station. But before they could get control of the submarine it slowly sliced into the side of the admiral's gig and stopped with its bow close to the pier. The gig was a mass of splinters and sunk by the stern alongside the pier.

The only remark I heard from our duty officer was, "I guess that's the end of my next promotion." The outboard submarine tossed our guys some heavies and we winched the boat back alongside us. After ten minutes the submarines in the nest were as ship-shape as if nothing had happened, except, of course, the gig was no longer there.

I left the next day for my rest period and I never found out the outcome of the gig episode. I have never seen an official report on this accident and I do not know if the outboard submarine got credit for sinking one more ship.

Chapter 22
APRIL 1944
USS *RAY*'S GREAT CONNING TOWER FLOOD
BY HAL MOYER

Hal Moyer survived a disastrous dive that flooded the conning tower and nearly cost the lives of *Ray*'s (SS-271) crew.

One dark night in the spring of 1944 while on her sixth war patrol, the *Ray*, (SS-271) under the command of W.T. Kinsella, was loafing along on the surface, charging batteries after an uneventful day of submerged patrolling. We were just off Island Passage and close to the entrance of Manila Bay.

Because we were near enemy shorelines and in water that might be expected at any time to spring to life with enemy activity, both the captain and the executive officer were on the bridge. This was out of the ordinary unless we were at battle stations, which we were not. The fact that the night was Friday, April 13th probably made the captain a bit uneasy. I was due to go on watch as officer-of-the-deck, and had been awakened and handed my red night-vision goggles. Being now fully dressed and ready for action in a pair of tattered shorts and submarine sandals, I was strolling the short distance to the control room when the diving alarm sounded. This was nothing unusual—probably a radar contact of an enemy plane.

I stood in the control room watching the lookouts come jumping down from the bridge and through the conning tower to take their control room stations operating the bow and stern planes for diving. The officer-of-the-deck, C.A. Hill, Jr., was close behind. On diving he became the diving officer. Something about Lt. Hill's action and expression told me that things were not quite right. At that instant water exploded down through the open hatch from the conning tower into the control room. I at once gave the order to blow main ballast tanks, but in the terrible noise and confusion I'm pretty sure I was not heard by either the chief-of-the-watch, who must close the vents, or by the auxiliaryman on duty who normally would open the high pressure air valve. The chief of the watch, on the hydraulic manifold didn't have to be told what to do. He saw the shaft of water and instantly shut the vent valves on the ballast tanks.

Chief Dick Weber was in his bunk, awake, in the after battery compartment when the alarm sounded. Sensing possible trouble he came forward into the control room just as the deluge hit. He instantly seized the air valve wrench and blew everything in sight.

Meanwhile, we were still going down. I couldn't see the depth gauges through the torrent of water, but I wasn't thinking about that. The thing I was desperate to accomplish was to get the hatch from the conning tower into the control room closed. If we couldn't get that hatch shut we were all dead.

When the water started coming down I was standing only about six or seven feet from the ladder which went from the control room up to the conning tower hatch. The hatch was only about eight feet above the control room deck.

By this time the water was coming down with such force that it was utterly impossible to stand up against it. I started pulling myself hand over hand on the outside of the ladder's stainless steel rail. I had to get that hatch closed before the pump room completely flooded. My feet were trailing straight out behind me. The force of the water was so great it tore both tightly strapped sandals off my feet. As I slowly neared the lanyard that I must pull to close the hatch, I realized that both the captain and the exec were up in the conning tower and once that hatch was closed they both might drown, even if we were to ultimately save the boat. And if that happened, I, as third ranking officer, would be in command of whatever might be left. Not a very pleasant thought.

Just as I reached the ladder top and was groping for the lanyard, a big pair of legs started dropping down through the opening in the midst of the water fall. It was the captain, and he was able to pull the hatch closed over his head. At least momentarily we were saved. The captain later said he was pretty much sucked through the open hatch and was fortunate to grab the lanyard as he went through.

With ballast tanks blown, *Ray* rose to the surface, heavy and unstable. All the watertight doors leading both fore and aft from the control room were shut and dogged, so that none of the seawater could get into the battery rooms. We were on the surface, but we were completely helpless. Most of the water in the control room by now had drained down into the pump room. The pump room was nearly full of water, which meant the motors that drove our pumps, compressors, hydraulic system, periscopes, etc., were knocked out. The conning tower was completely flooded. We could not yet know the fate of the two officers and six crewmen who were stuck in the conning tower. Hopefully they were not drowned and were now out of the flooded conning tower and up on the bridge.

I suggested to the captain that to find out the safety of our men and to learn the general situation topside that I should go up the engine room hatch so that I could go forward on the superstructure deck to the bridge area. He said, "Yes, do that."

The engine room hatch opens up to the superstructure deck, which is not much above water level when the sub is surfaced normally. With all the extra water on board, the *Ray* was a lot lower in the water than usual. I can still feel the deck planking under my bare feet. The boat was rolling in the water like the proverbial drunken sailor, because it was top-heavy from the conning-tower being full of water. I walked forward in a crouch to keep from losing balance and falling overboard. There were no railings or lines to clutch. I reached the bridge area and climbed up on the bridge afterdeck. The men were sitting or standing like a bunch of zombies. Nobody said a thing at first. After the life and death experience they had just been through, they were numb. Soon the exec, Lt. Leonard Erb responded to my questions and indicated that everybody seemed to be OK. Just enough air had been trapped in the top of the conning tower to keep them from drowning. It was agreed that they would stay on the bridge until we got the conning tower drained. I don't think they could have safely gone below by way of the engine room hatch. Their legs weren't all that steady.

It was fortunate that the airplane of the radar contact that caused us to make a "routine" evasive dive either never detected us or was not carrying bombs. So we were able to wallow helplessly in the water for a couple of hours or more without coming under attack. The captain wisely decided not to try getting under way until we were capable of maneuvering the ship. The primary helm was in the conning tower, so control shifted to the alternate steering station in control. The captain gave us a course that would keep our nose into the sea. We went ahead at one third speed, just enough to keep headway.

We finally got the conning tower drained down into the pump room, our topside people restored to the questionable safety of the control room, and access to the bridge restored. At this point, because of flooding damage, we had no periscopes, radar, sound detection gear, radio communication, compass, normal steering control, or hydraulic power, which meant, among other things, that we couldn't dive normally in case of any enemy contact. So the *Ray* limped seaward, away from the coast, where, at a reasonably safe distance we submerged, very carefully, using hand controls to open and close vents. We stayed there for two days or more, submerged in daytime, making such repairs as were possible to enable us to proceed.

By restoring radio we received orders to proceed to Biak, an island in the neck of the New Guinea bird, where an advance base submarine tender, AS *Orion*, had just been emplaced. Running on the surface at night we transited the area and made our way south to Biak.

During our run south we put together the events that lead to the flooding. Our young quartermaster's role on diving was to crank the bridge hatch dogging wheel and seal the hatch shut as the captain pulled with his weight on the hatch lanyard. It was a matter of timing. The hatch had first to be shut by the captain then the dogging wheel was to be turned. When the quartermaster spun the dogging wheel before the hatch was shut it only opened the space between the hatch cover and its rim. Becoming flustered he was not able to instantly see his mistake and reverse the spin. The result was a ton of water pouring into the conning tower before any corrective action could be taken by anyone. The event illustrated how one weak link in a precision crew could lead to disaster. The quartermaster was transferred to the surface fleet.

Chapter 23

April 1944

AMBUSH ON BORNEO

by Ken Harrington

> Ken Harrington went ashore from *Redfin* (SS-272) to rescue stranded people on Borneo. His rash volunteer adventure nearly cost him his life.

On 21 April 1944, orders were received to reverse course to conduct a special mission off the northwest coast of Borneo. Two other submarines had reconnoitered this situation and determined it to be too dangerous. Their opinion was due to changing currents and rugged coastal shoals. A powerboat would be needed and no submarine was equipped with one. This didn't seem to make any difference to our captain. USS *Redfin* (SS-272) had already sunk five ships and damaged two on this patrol, so we had complete confidence in our ability to accomplish the mission; specially, if the captain deemed it so. However, my gut feeling was saying, "Concur with the other two submarines that turned this little chore down."

A rendezvous was made via radio. *Redfin* submerged off the rendezvous point early in the morning of 22 April to observe any activities on the beach. A small steam launch was sighted near the pickup point and a white sheet was seen stretched between two poles at the point where the launch was to enter the water. This was the security signal. The entire setup looked good. We expected the party to come out in their launch. *Redfin* submerged to periscope depth to wait and observe. No boat appeared in the next three hours.

At 2200 we received word from ComTaskFor-71 that the party was in position, but had no boat. This seemed strange as we had observed a party go ashore in a launch. This could be an attempt to capture an American submarine. *Redfin* was ready and rigged for the mission.

The rubber boat was broken out and made ready by Torpedoman Dagwood, who remarked to me at the time, "You must be some kind of a liberty hound." Of course, I was completely oblivious of his remark at the time. Maybe he was giving me a morale booster or going into one of his many sea stories. I was informed that the captain wanted to see me. He informed me that, due to my previous Marine Corps background and being expendable, I would take part in this mission. His quaint sense of humor about my Marine Corps days was a flip of the coin to me. I never knew when he was kidding or really serious. But, he sounded serious when he used the word, "expendable."

"You'll be one of the four volunteers," he said, without even a hint of a smile. The skipper didn't know that I had enlisted in the USMC on the recruiter's ruse that my joining the Marines would help me get into submarines. That incident with that Marine sergeant recruiter seemed a lifetime ago. From here on out this ex-Marine business was going to be my secret. I hoped the skipper would never discover how gullible I had been in my quest to get into submarines. Now, eight years later, since I was truly a combat submariner and qualified, making use of my prior experience seemed appropriate.

The three volunteers were Ensign E.R. Helz, gunners mate George E. Carrinder and radioman striker Robert E. Kahler. I thought that all ensigns were considered expendable our little party's loss would not drastically affect the efficiency of *Redfin*. After taking leave from the skipper I spent as much time as possible with my eye glued to the periscope to familiarize myself with the coastline and to keep busy and adapt myself to the skipper's orders. I was still in hopes that the launch would bring them out and I could take it from there. Machinist mate 1/c Paul Grant fabricated two extra paddles from some shoring. "Just in case," he said. We were well armed, especially myself. Since I had qualified as a Browning Automatic Rifleman while in the Marines, I selected a BAR as my weapon of choice. I had ten fully loaded magazines with 20 rounds to a magazine stuck in my pockets plus my life jacket.

I truly felt like a battle-rigged Marine prepared for a landing assault. I was anxious to go. Although I had participated in such landings in the Marine Corps on maneuvers this would be the real thing. When we slid into the water in our crowded rubber boat it was black, overcast night. We had about three miles of paddle pushing to reach our designated rendez-vous point on shore. So, I mentally resigned myself to do my best and act like a Marine.

The low, irregular coastline could be seen. We soon became aware that the strong current and wind were taking us north of our pick-up point and our paddling was not sufficient to correct the drift. By my Marine Corps thumbnail navigation, I estimated we would land about three miles from the rendezvous point. And we did.

Immediately upon landing, a searchlight was turned on and something like a challenge shouted by someone on the beach with barking dogs. I had eased off the stern of the rubber boat and was in water just above my knees. I assumed this was not a friendly spotlight. Fortunately, I had not been spotted and shot the searchlight out with a short burst from my BAR. A uniformed Jap, judging from his seemingly wrapped leggings and cap, came charging at Gunner Carrinder. He came at full speed with rifle and fixed bayonet. Kahler was directly in front of me, about ten yards ahead, and Ensign Helz was about the same distance on my right flank. With the searchlight out of commission, I shifted my position and directed my fire to take care of the Jap charging Carrinder, who seemed to be close enough for hand-to-hand combat. As I commenced firing I breathed a silent prayer that I wouldn't hit Gunner. It would be close and Carrinder was never the forgiving type. When I saw tracers from my fire tear into the enemy I felt relieved.

Later Carrinder told me he felt the bullets pass, and the collar of his life jacket bore such evidence. I reloaded. About the same time five or six

Japs ran charging in straight for Kahler. I shouted for him to hit the deck and commenced firing. I didn't even wait to see if Kahler had heard me. Evidently he did as he was eating dirt. With the help of Gunner Carrinder, we killed all the Japs in sight. All this happened within five minutes after landing. I continued shooting in the direction of the barking dogs while the party made a hasty retreat to the rubber boat. In the confusion, Carrinder ended up with one of the Jap's rifles in place of his own. Ensign Helz, our leader, lost or dropped his .45 automatic pistol, and radioman striker Kahler had a muddy face.

Military commentaries probably would not judge this a good defense position. We didn't either, but it was the only place available at the time. We didn't have the firepower to establish a beachhead. Charging in, we could have faced stronger opposition. Also bare in mind this was a first for all of us and perhaps instinctively we wanted to run home to our skipper for protection. We all made the boat in record time and got out about 500 yards in the bay when flares were shot from shore. It seemed bright enough to read small print. About the same time, large caliber guns opened up from the beach. Judging by the sound and the red-boiled projectiles soaring through the air; it had to be at least five-inch. Our mixed-up landing party silently breathed a sigh of relief when all the Japanese shells landed far from us. Monday morning quarterbacks later ascertained that we had been mistaken for an invasion instead of four amateur sailors. I think I could add confused, as we surely were.

Ensign Helz put his 190 pounds behind our one paddle and the rest of us used rifle butts and hands to get as much speed as possible with as little noise as possible. We seemed to be standing still. We did clear the bay while the big guns continued their firepower. This firing from shore made it almost a sure bet that *Redfin* would not come in to meet us. The depth of the water and rocky shoals, even without the blasting guns, would discourage any submarine skipper to attempt a pick-up; surely not a skipper with his first submarine command.

We agreed to make for open sea and take a chance on being picked up by a friendly submarine. One thing we all agreed on: Not to be taken prisoners. The Japs were more than anxious for the scalp of any submariner. We had no choice. Go for the deep waters. We knew the USS *Cod* was operating in this vicinity. And, too, mother *Redfin* would be searching and be reporting our absence on fox. This was our hope and security blanket. We had to keep going. First light was due within the hour and unless we made tracks, the Japs would have patrol planes out at the crack of dawn.

So far we had suffered no casualties, except to our nerves. We had left several dead or injured Japs on the beach and probably a few dead dogs. The British reconnaissance party, the object of our mission, had been completely forgotten by us. Our only objective now was to make contact with *Redfin* or *Cod.*

At sunrise we sighted the *Redfin.* She had her stern flooded down and her bow awash, just high enough for the gun crew to man the deck gun. We pulled aboard the decks awash with the help of eager deck hands pulling us up. Dagwood, our ever-jovial torpedoman, commenced slicing the rubber boat with his knife to sink it, saying, "It's about time you got back. We all had to wait breakfast for you."

The rubber boat was taking on water almost before we had completely disembarked. I patted Dagwood on the shoulder and headed for the bridge. The captain was peering down from the bridge and was smiling. That good old skipper Cy Austin. I could have kissed him. To me he was the hero in the white hat. Needless to say, we were happy to be back aboard. I didn't give it a thought how the skipper would get the submarine out to safe water. I just assumed he would. I'm sure we all felt as if we had been snatched out of the jaws of a shark. We were beat, sapped, to say the least. My arms felt as heavy as lead. But the cook had held up breakfast for us and so we ate our fill then stretched out in our bunks while others on *Redfin* took us into safer water. I suppose, our mission had been a failure, but it sure felt good to have killed a few Japs.

The S-class of submarines was laid down between 1917 and 1921 for the U.S. Navy. It was an era of submarine innovation; each submarine class being an improvement over its predecessor. The S-boats replaced the sixteen submarines of the O-class and twenty-seven submarines of the R-class that were built between 1918 and 1919. Pictured is an early S-boat surfacing with water spewing from the boat's limber holes.
—*Naval Historical Center*

Some S-boat engines were built by American firms under license from a German firm. The boat's two engines developed a total of about 2,000 BHP. When on the surface, a clutch transferred power from the diesel engine to the battery when diving. Pictured is the starboard engine of an S-boat. The U.S. Navy took fifty-one S-boats into service.—*Naval Historical Center*

Most S-boats were built by Electric Boat Company in Groton, Connecticut and Portsmouth Naval Shipyard in New Hampshire. They had riveted hulls with over-lapped hull plate abutments. Although they were designed to accompany the navy's Atlantic fleet in an era when the battleship dominated naval doctrine, they proved inadequate both in terms of surface speed and range. Pictured is S-13 with its radio antenna and three-inch deck gun.—*Naval Historical Center*

Above: The S-boat was a scaled up version of earlier R-boats and was to be an oceangoing weapon with a range of eight thousand miles, however this design requirement was never achieved. As America's interests in the Pacific grew during the late 1920s and 30s, the S-boat's limited range needed to be increased and the navy began considering longer-ranged submarines. Pictured is S-26, commissioned into service in October 1923. Sadly, this S-boat was accidentally rammed and sunk on January 24, 1942 by a navy surface vessel.
—*Naval Historical Center*

Left: The S-20 series had raised bows for better surface operation. The boats were 222 feet in length and had a beam of roughly 23 feet and came with improved radios and sound detection gear. On the surface, the S-boats could obtain a top speed of about 15 knots. Pictured are three S-boats in a nest alongside their submarine tender at Coco Solo, Panama Canal Zone.—*Naval Historical Center*

Below: Early S-boats spent a great deal of time undergoing overhauls to install up-dated equipment. Twenty-one of the fifty-one S-boats built would go on to see service during World War II, accounting for fourteen Japanese ships during that conflict. Pictured are five S-boats in overhaul at Mare Island Naval Shipyard, California.—*Naval Historical Center*

Crewmen of the S-boat S-44 (SS-155) are shown painting a Japanese naval flag on the conning tower of their submarine after sinking the Imperial Japanese Navy heavy cruiser *Kako* on August 10, 1942. The other two Japanese flags painted on the conning tower represent Japanese merchant ships sunk previously by the submarine. —*National Archives*

The early V-boats (V-1 through V-7) had some design problems, however, the U.S. Navy was happy with the configuration of the V-8 and V-9 submarines and used them as a template to refine the design with some follow-on classes of submarines. These included the ten nearly-identical boats of the fleet-type Sargo-class. Pictured is the Sargo-class submarine USS *Seadragon* (SS-194).—*Naval Historical Center*

Above: The fleet-type submarine was intended to replace the S-boat design in response to the need for a truly ocean-going submarine capable of long-range, independent patrols in the vast expanse of the Pacific Ocean. The first group of fleet-type submarines was designated the V-boats and were a group of nine experimental submarines laid down between 1921 and 1931. Pictured is the V-5, named the *Narwhal*, which was 370 feet long and powered by two diesel engines.—*National Archives*

Left: After refining the Sargo-class design, the navy commissioned the twelve boats of the Tambor-class fleet-type submarine. This in turn led to the seventy-three boats of the Gato-class fleet type submarine. Pictured is the launch of the USS *Pompon* (SS-267), a Gato-class submarine, at Manitowoc on the Great Lakes.—*Edward Crawfoot Collection*

Below: The Gato-class fleet-type submarines were followed in production by a near-identical, but improved version that was designated the Balao-class fleet-type submarine. The biggest improvement to the Balao-class over the Gato-class was the adoption of thicker and stronger steel for the pressure hull, which meant their test depth was four hundred feet. The Gato-class submarine had a test depth of only three hundred feet. This postwar picture shows the USS *Ranquil* (SS-396) of the Balao-class.—*National Archives*

Right: The launching of the fleet type submarine USS *Wahoo* (SS-238) on February 14, 1942 at Mare Island Naval Shipyard, located in the San Francisco Bay area. She was a *Gato*-class submarine and would go on seven war patrols and sink nineteen Japanese ships in the process. The *Wahoo* was lost with all hands sometime in October 1943 on her seventh war patrol.—*Naval Historical Center*

Below: The USS *Herring* (SS-233) is pictured ready for launching on January 15, 1942. It was a fleet-type submarine of the Gato-class and was a near duplicate of all the other boats in its class. The similarity of design allowed crew members to transfer from one submarine to another with a thorough knowledge of each boat's equipment. World War II fleet-type submarines were named after fish, with the result that some names bordered on the humorous. —*National Archives*

Above: The U.S. Navy never stopped trying to improve its fleet-type submarine design during World War II, the final configuration being the late-war Tench-class. This class of submarine combined the best of many preceding designs, such as the Gato- and Balao-class, into a first-class transoceanic weapon. Pictured is the USS *Thornback* (SS-418) a Tench-class submarine. —*National Archives*

Left: Fleet-type submarines often carried a three-inch gun forward of the conning tower fairwater. Elevated above the walking deck were two gun platforms. The forward of which often supported a 40mm anti-aircraft gun, with the rear gun platform supporting either a single or twin barrel 20mm antiaircraft gun or another 40mm antiaircraft gun. These weapons were sometimes employed on seaborne targets that did not warrant a torpedo. —*National Archives*

Right: This postwar photograph taken aboard the Balao-class fleet-type submarine USS *Sterlet* (SS-392) shows the captain looking through one of the two periscopes on the boat. One periscope on a typical fleet-type submarine had a fairly wide field of view and was employed for general observation. The other periscope was known as the attack scope and had a much higher magnification, narrower field of view, and a built-in rangefinder and stadimeter to determine the range to a target.—*National Archives*

Fleet-type submarines normally had six or seven officers assigned, which included the captain, executive officer, operations officer, engineer, weapons officer, electronics officer and supply/commissary officer. Officers were housed in the forward battery compartment which had a small wardroom for eating and conducting business. Pictured are the officers of the USS Bowfin (SS-287), a Balao-class submarine, during its commissioning on May 1, 1943.—*National Archives*

Right: U.S. Navy submarines in World War II boasted a number of sensors, including various types of radars. These included both air-search and surface-search radars. Despite these electronic sensors it was the keen eyes of the lookouts that often spotted potential targets or incoming threats, such as enemy aircraft, when the submarine ran on the surface.
—*National Archives*

Below: The conning tower of the USS *Pampanito* (SS-383), which is a Balao-class fleet-type submarine, shows the late-war configuration of many boats during World War II. Visible are the two periscope shears and directly behind them the pole mast supports the SJ surface-search radar antenna. The large tower behind the periscope shears is for the SV air-search radar. The broom attached to the periscope shears represents completing a successful war patrol (a "clean sweep"). The USS *Pampanito* is on display as a museum boat at Fishermen's Wharf in San Francisco.
—*Michael Green*

The control room of the fleet-type submarine was the nerve center of the boat. Two large wheels, which visually dominated the port side with shallow depth gauges above them, hydraulically controlled the bow and stern planes. Also seen are inclinometers, plane position indicators, deep depth gauge, and the master compass in the lower right of picture.—*NavPers 16160, with permission*

It was up to the submarine's planesman to keep the boat at the required depth. To accomplish this goal trim tanks at the extreme ends of the submarine were flooded and pumped at his command to obtain an accurate fore and aft balance, while the overall weight of the submarine was balanced with the weight of its displaced water by flooding and pumping the auxiliary tanks located at the center of the boat. Pictured is a bow planesman relaxing for a moment.—*Submarine Research Center*

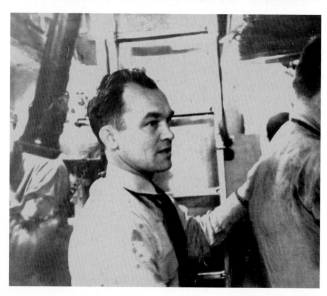

When a submarine dove the officer of the deck, while the boat was on the surface, became the diving officer as the boat went under. The role of diving officer was normally that of a commissioned officer other than the captain, executive officer or operations officer. In some submarines the senior chief petty officers stood diving officer watches. Pictured is Chief Sigmon of USS *Sirago* (SS-485), a Tench-class submarine, who watches the depth gauge of the bow planesman as the boat goes to periscope depth.—*Submarine Research Center*

Taken inside the control room of a Balao-class fleet-type submarine is this photograph of the boat's hull opening indicator panel. This panel was best known by its popular nickname as the "Christmas Tree" due to its red and green lights that represented every opening in the pressure hull. When all the lights on the panel were green it meant all the pressure hull openings were closed and it was safe to submerge the submarine. A red light on the panel meant there was an unsealed pressure hull opening.
—*Michael Green*

This is a partial view of the starboard side of the control room on a Balao-class fleet-type submarine. Visible are the various handles and knobs that controlled the boat's compressed air system, which was used for a variety of purposes including firing the torpedoes and blowing the main ballast tanks. Submarines referred to this side of the control room as the "dry side."
—*Michael Green*

Taken inside a Balao-class fleet type submarine is a picture of the upper portion of two of its four large diesel engines, in this case built by Fairbanks-Morse (F-M). Each of the submarine's four diesel engines was connected to a 1,100 kilowatt electrical generator that charged the onboard 252 batteries when running on the surface or to drive the electric motors that turned the boat's propellers on the surface. Top speed for the Gato/Balao/Tench-class boats was about twenty-two knots on the surface and nine knots submerged.
—*Michael Green*

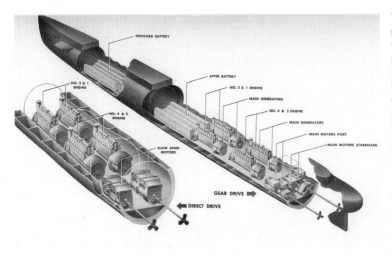

This navy diagram of a fleet-type submarine shows the location of the boat's four diesel engines and the two battery compartments. Electricians in the maneuvering room, aft of the engine rooms, controlled current and voltage going to the propulsion motors. These motors initially had reduction gears, but later in the war low speed induction motors were installed. Electricians answered forward and back bells, charged batteries when on the surface, and switched power from engines to battery when diving.—*NavPers 16160, with permission*

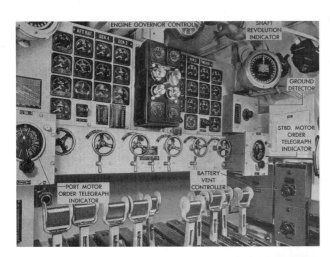

The maneuvering room main power control board was another crucial station in the fleet-type submarine. Engine speed was controlled from this control board by electricians using the four knobs seen in the upper center of the photo. Field and armature voltage were controlled by the small wheels and the "sticks" in the lower part of the picture, which controlled the flow of electrical power from generators and batteries to the main propulsion motors. —*U.S. Navy*

Beginning with the Tambor-class, fleet-type submarines had six torpedo tubes forward and four aft. The torpedo rooms also providing berthing for some of the crew who had bunks amidst the torpedoes and high in the overhead. Torpedo tubes had breech and muzzle doors with an interlock that prevented both doors from being opened simultaneously. Pictured is one of the forward torpedo tubes in a Balao-class boat. —*Michael Green*

Left: The fleet-type submarine had four toilets, or "heads." Two were located at the aft end of the after battery compartment. The officers' head was located on the starboard-aft side of the forward torpedo room. These three heads emptied into a storage tank in the submarine. The fourth head was in the after torpedo room and was an expulsion-type toilet that emptied outside the hull. An example is seen here with its water pressure gauge, hull stop valve, charging lever and expulsion handle. Only qualified submariners were allowed to use this head, since a mistake could be both embarrassing and dangerous.—*U.S. Navy*

Right: Visible in this picture taken inside a Balao-class fleet-type submarine forward engine room are the two evaporative stills used for producing fresh water from sea water. The two stills together could only produce 750 gallons of fresh water a day under optimum operating conditions. This output barely provided enough fresh water for the boat's engine's and batteries, leaving very little for the crew's hygienic needs and drinking water. World War II submarines were sometimes referred to as "sewer pipes" for a reason.
—*Michael Green*

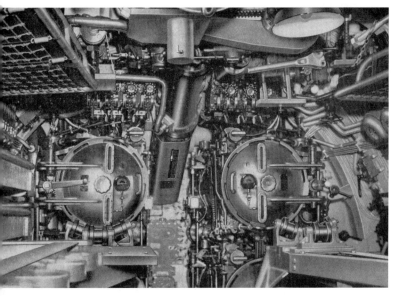

Left: World War II-era torpedoes required continuous maintenance and were loaded and withdrawn from tubes on a regular basis. Above the tubes is the blow and vent manifold and between the tubes is the stern plane ram. Torpedo skids are on both sides of the narrow walking platform. Pictured are tubes seven and eight in the after torpedo room.
—*U.S. Navy*

The pressure hull of fleet-type submarines was cylindrical in shape to withstand the pressure at great depths and the walking deck was free flooding and welded to it. Pictured is the USS *Pogy* (SS-266), a Gato-class boat, with its open stern torpedo tubes visible above water as the boat's fuel ballast tanks are empty.—*Edward Crawfoot collection*

Every submariner had to "qualify in submarines." Essentially, this meant that every crew member had to know every other crew member's job. Only by knowing the submarine thoroughly could a crew member be relied upon to step into an emergency and take the correct action. Pictured is a torpedoman on USS *Sirago* (SS-485), a Tench-class boat, instructing young submariners in the workings of a torpedo tube. —*Submarine Research Center*

Each submarine had a battle flag that displayed its emblem, usually a savage-looking fish, the number of war patrols, and small Japanese flags, one for each ship sunk. Pictured is the battle flag of the USS *Peto* (SS-265), a Gato-class fleet-type submarine, which was hung on the conning tower fairwater when the boat was in Australia.—*Edward Crawfoot Collection*

Submariners enjoyed the best and the worst food the U.S. Navy could offer. No expense was spared to provide submariners with the highest quality foods which were consumed until toward the end of a long war patrol fresh and frozen food would have run out. The crew was then obliged to eat powdered eggs and milk, canned vegetables, bread, spaghetti, and potatoes. Pictured is Chief Cook Norman O. Thomas on the USS *Bream* (SS-243) preparing a roast in his cramped galley.—*Mrs. Norman O. Thomas Collection*

A fleet-type submarine's mess space could accommodate about thirty men at a serving. It was cramped and men of all noncommissioned and enlisted ranks ate together. When meals were not being served in the mess space it became a place for the crew to study or have a little recreational time playing card games.—*National Archives*

This picture taken aboard a Balao-class fleet-type submarine shows one of the watertight doors that separated the nine watertight compartments that comprised the interior of the Gato, Balao, and Tench-class boats. The nine compartments of these boats consisted of the forward torpedo room, forward battery compartment, control room, conning tower, after battery compartment, forward and after engine rooms, maneuvering/motor room, and the after torpedo room.
—Michael Green

Onboard a Balao-class fleet-type submarine is an unheard luxury among the submarines of other nations during World War II, a washing machine with manually-operated dryer. With so little fresh water being produced by the boat's evaporative stills there was seldom enough water to use the washing machine and many submarines went to sea without them.
—Michael Green

The after battery compartment is the main crew berthing area in addition to the crew's mess. Thirty-six men sleep in this space with three bunks to a tier. A man's bunk is his only personal space. Wash towels and toilet item bags hang from the bunk's rail. Often the crew out-numbers the bunks, in which case the two least-senior men share a bunk. When one man is on watch the other man sleeps. Chief petty officers have a small room in the forward battery compartment which is known as the "Goat Locker." —*Submarine Research Center*

Until late 1944 American submarines were based in Brisbane on Australia's eastern seaboard and in Fremantle, on the western seaboard. Submarine tenders provided repair facilities. Pictured is a typical scene in 1943 Fremantle with *Blower* (SS-325), *Bluefish* (SS-222), and *Besugo* (SS-321) in a nest alongside the pier while in the background is another nest of submarines tied up to their tender.—*Edward Crawfoot Collection*

Japanese prisoners of war (POWs) walk off fleet-type submarine USS *Spadefish* (SS-411), a Balao-class boat, on August 14, 1945. American submarines played a key role during the war in the Pacific. Their actions against Japanese shipping led to the destruction of more than two thousand of their merchant ships and almost seven hundred of their warships. This success was not without cost as fifty-two American submarines were lost during World War II along with more than thirty-five hundred officers and men.— *National Archives*

One of the longest serving fleet-type submarines was the USS *Razorback* (SS- 394), which was a Portsmouth Navy Yard Balao-class boat built in 1943 that remained in U.S. Navy service until it was decommissioned in November 1970. The submarine is seen in its postwar modernized configuration. From December 1970 until August 2001 the *Razorback* served with the Turkish Navy as the TCG *Muratries*, after which, in 2004 she was transferred back to the United States where she is berthed in the Arkansas River and now serves as a museum boat at the Arkansas Inland Maritime Museum in North Little Rock.—*Naval Historical Center*

A wartime picture taken through the periscope of the USS *Drum* (SS-228) of a Japanese merchant ship the submarine had just torpedoed. The boat was credited with sinking fifteen enemy vessels during World War II. The periscope is the eye of the submarine and is made of corrosion-resistant stainless steel. The Type II attack periscope had an overall length of 41.5 feet and a tube diameter of 7.5 inches.—*National Archives*

Chapter 24
APRIL 1944
POGY'S STOWAWAY

BY W. E. BATTENFIELD

Bill Battenfield on USS *Pogy* (SS-266) was considered crazy by other crew members when he insisted a rat lived with a Japanese POW in the forward torpedo room.

The USS *Pogy* (SS-266) carried a stowaway rat as it left Pearl Harbor in 1944 on its sixth war patrol, Cdr. Ralph Metcalf, commanding. I'm not referring to the two-legged kind we sometimes meet in the human species. I'm talking about the four-legged furry rodent.

"How can that happen?" I hear you ask knowing the customary fumigation procedure prior to every submarine patrol. The "Brass" knew all too well the dangers of epidemics breaking out in the close quarters of submarine life. They did a thorough job of making our quarters hospital clean. So as we left Pearl Harbor April 7, 1944 I pondered how it was that a rat could have survived the fumigation. Unfortunately, I was to be the sole submariner to catch sight of the furry creature until near the end of our patrol.

Anxiety from fear of being hit by an enemy's depth charge plus conditions conducive to claustrophobia cause a small percent of submariners to go over the brink of sanity. I feared that my sighting of a rat might be interpreted as slipping over the brink. Only a fellow submariner can imagine the ribbing I took after announcing my first sighting. Crew members agreed that only borderline lunatics could sight rats on a submarine.

It was a hectic patrol for the *Pogy*. We left Pearl Harbor with the usual amount of fuel, torpedoes, and provisions plus a load of tame rabbits and rabbit food to be delivered at Midway Island. Four days later the rabbits and food were unloaded for the test laboratory at Midway's Hospital.

Two days later we were told we would be patrolling off the coast of Japan. We reached our station on April 21. The air was full of Japanese planes. On the second day we were spotted while surfacing. I was on watch in the forward torpedo room when the diving alarm sounded. We dived, and I caught sight of movement under the inboard torpedo skid, but couldn't tell what it was. Five days later, after dark on April 28, we surfaced and caught sight of a Japanese submarine that was also surfaced. We ran ahead so we could get a battery charge. Soon after midnight on the 29th, we fired three torpedoes and sank the enemy submarine.

Later as we reloaded torpedoes, I again saw the rat. He was bigger now, a real monster. Probably ate some of the rabbit food. I pointed and yelled, "There's that rat!" As luck would have it, no other torpedoman saw it. They looked at me skeptically, even suspiciously. About a week later we were patrolling off Kobie, Japan. We spied a Japanese merchant ship. We manned battle stations, submerged, shot three torpedoes and scored a hit. We were forced down deeper and deeper to avoid thirty-one depth charges that followed. As depth charges rocked and rattled our submarine, the rat panicked. He ran across the deck plates from port to starboard and back. Despite being under orders for silent running, I yelled, "There he goes!" Again no one saw him. The crew began staring at me with strange looks. The after torpedo room called and sarcastically asked if my rat was brown or white and did he have long rabbit ears. It was obvious my shipmates feared I was over the brink from battle fatigue. My situation was becoming serious. It was only a matter of time before one of my fellow torpedomen reported my aberrations to the executive officer. If I couldn't prove the existence of the rat I was in trouble.

I resolved to catch that rat and prove that I still had all my marbles. I reverted to the old bird trapping method of boyhood. I found a small square metal box, propped it up on a stick on one side and placed cheese bait underneath. I tied a cord to the stick. As I stood my four-hour watches, I held the cord in my hand, eyes glued on the trap, ready to yank the cord and entrap my elusive rodent. No rat showed, but plenty of crew members came to the torpedo room door to watch my fruitless efforts. As I sat hunched over my string I could hear snickers behind me. After three or four watches, I gave up.

It was worse in the crew's mess. While I ate I had to endure the comments of my shipmates who were merciless in their sarcasm.

On May 9 we went to battle stations on a Japanese tanker. As we were making our approach, a plane dropped a couple of depth charges. Again I saw my rat. As the charges shook the submarine, the rat hurriedly changed his hiding place. Again I yelled, "There's the rat!" I should have known better. No one else saw it. Now everyone was sure I was pressure happy.

A week later we sank another Japanese ship and took five prisoners aboard. Three were placed in the forward torpedo room and two in the after torpedo room. We made bunks for them in the empty torpedo skids.

Our prisoners of war broke our routine on *Pogy*. At first the men refused to eat, probably fearing poisoning. I took a bite from the food being offered, smiled at them, indicating it was safe. They too ate and by the time we turned them over to the Marines at Pearl Harbor each had gained about ten pounds. But that's getting ahead of things.

One Japanese prisoner lost his glasses and had difficulty seeing. I gave him my magnifying glass and a white hat. He followed me wherever I went. He went along when I stood watch. He used the magnifying glass and looked at magazines while I was on duty. One night the rat came in full view. I punched the Japanese companion and pointed. He, too, saw the rodent. At last I had confirmation. I was happy until I realized that our language barrier made it impossible for him to be a witness.

I gave up. I kind of felt sorry for the little guy. After all, he was suffering depth charge attacks right along with the rest of us. So I put food and water out for the stowaway.

My Japanese friend admired his hat. I taught him to salute and say, "Tojo barks at the moon." He saluted right and left as was convenient, repeating his English words. This lasted only until a fellow prisoner put a stop to my English lessons. The other prisoner had been in San Francisco and knew far more English than he pretended.

Chief Torpedoman Prinskie had problems with regularity. Every Monday morning while doing maintenance checks on torpedoes, he'd mix a little coffee and torpedo juice. Torpedo juice is 180 proof alcohol which the Navy mixed with croton oil to prevent men from drinking it. The croton oil was a severe laxative. A Japanese prisoner watched and asked, "Sake?" I nodded yes and repeated, "Sake." I fixed him a good drink. He wanted more. After four or five he was so happy he began singing. I made him get in his bunk fearing an officer might come forward and see him. After thirty or forty-five minutes in the rack he came out of it like a cat with turpentine on his tail. He ran screaming what I understood to be, *"Banzi, banzi,"* the Japanese word for, "Charge!"

While standing watch in the forward torpedo room with our prisoners we were armed with a Colt .45 automatic. I was standing by the wash basin in the after part of the compartment when this screaming Japanese headed straight for me. Before I could get out my .45, he ran right by me and into the forward battery. I called to another torpedoman to follow him. The prisoner ran through the forward battery, control, crew's mess and berthing. He was running straight for the head. My shipmate who had followed him later said the poor Jap would sit a while, then heave a while. He was really yelling, *"Benjo,"* the Japanese word for "toilet." I now knew two words in Japanese. When Chief Prinskie prepared his next coffee royal, I offered some to the Japanese. He didn't want any.

On May 19 we went to battle stations and surfaced on a Japanese patrol boat. Torpedoman Carbonary and I were alone in the forward room with the prisoners. We ordered them into their bunks. The others were topside on the guns. Carbonary was armed with a twenty-four inch pipe wrench. I had the .45. I was wearing the battle phone headset and was giving Carbonary a blow by blow description of the topside action. Every time our five-inch [deck gun] fired, the rat would change hiding places. Carbonary pointed and yelled, "Rat!" At last another crew member had seen the little guy. In the crew's mess I had Carbonary inform the rest of the crew there really was a rat. For me it was a moment of great satisfaction. There was much conversation regarding the best way of killing our rat, but by now I had grown attached to him. I put up an eloquent defense on behalf of the rodent, but in the end I had to admit that a submarine wasn't a good environment for a rat.

At Pearl Harbor we turned the prisoners over to the Marines. Some were reluctant to leave, wishing to stay with us. Our orders were to proceed to San Francisco for overhaul at Hunters Point. On our trip to the states I saw the rat from time to time, but didn't bother to inform anyone. At Hunter's Point we turned the submarine over to the yard workers. I was in the first leave party. When I returned to the boat I checked on the rat, but he was nowhere to be seen. Apparently he took a bit of shore leave himself. I imagined him enjoying stateside duty after the harrowing experience on a fighting submarine. He was probably out there romancing some girl rat at the local garbage dump. He sure had some great sea stories to tell his girlfriend about his ride on the *Pogy*.

Chapter 25

JUNE 1944

THE BATTLE OF THE PHILIPPINE SEA

BY ERNEST J. ZELLMER

> Ernest Zellmer was an officer aboard *Cavalla* (SS-244) as the boat sank a Japanese
> aircraft carrier and participated in the Battle of the Philippine Sea, also known as the
> Great Marianas Turkey Shoot.

Cavalla (SS-244) left Midway the beginning of June of 1944 and headed for its assigned station at San Bernardino Strait. We were to relieve *Flying Fish* (SS-229) whose patrol had already been extended. We would take over her mission to watch for the Japanese Fleet which was expected to come through the strait from Tawi Tawi, west of the Philippines. The U.S. [Navy] Fleet was about to invade Saipan, Tinian, and Guam in the Mariana Islands. Task Force 58 under command of Admiral Raymond A. Spruance needed to know the location of the Japanese Fleet.

Our course took us south of Marcus Island (held by the Japanese) and north of the Marianas, then south-west to the eastern shore of the Philippines and our station.

Before we started south-west, a typhoon engulfed us and the wind and sea became fierce. We couldn't make much speed and fell well behind our schedule. We knew that *Flying Fish* was low on fuel, and so we tried to make as much speed as we could. In that typhoon about five knots was all we could do as we pounded into the sea. I was the Junior Officer of the Deck positioned at the after end of the bridge deck. I stood inside of a pipe ring on which I could rest my arms as I held the binoculars and searched the sea and sky from the starboard beam, through the stern, and around to the port beam. When *Cavalla* was in a trough, I had to look up to see the tops of the waves on each side of the boat. A mountainous wave came over the bow, and over the top of the bridge. It swept my feet out from under me. I was hanging there suspended by the pipe ring with my arms, shoulders and head above the ring and my torso and legs below. I was in a U shape with arms and legs flapping aft of the ring, swept by the crashing wave. I had never before thought of that ring as a life saver, but it was.

Even the gooney birds didn't like the weather. A large albatross with its long wings and webbed feet sought relief from the buffeting wind and landed on the SD [air-search] radar antenna just over my head. The antenna was in its lowered position just a few feet above me. The bird clung with its feet and steadied itself by flapping its partially extending wings as the ship rolled and pitched. It was too much for the bird who puked his stale fish onto the bridge. The revolting slug was quickly washed overboard by the next wave, but I lost interest in mother-nature. As the boat pitched upward the great bird took to the air.

And then there came a huge wave; I had never seen anything like it. It rose up on both sides of the ship. It must have been at least forty feet high. We rolled more than *Cavalla* had ever rolled; I later learned that the inclinometer showed a roll of over fifty-six degrees. If we had gone much farther, we would have capsized. As it was, we were lucky that the battery acid did not spill all over the battery well. It was a very difficult time. Later during my watch, the captain decided that we weren't making more than three or four knots on the surface, and that we could do as well submerged. He considered diving to have a quiet meal. The question was how to get down.

A submarine couldn't dive moving into a mountainous sea where the waves hold the bow up. On the down-slide the stern would be pitched up and then the boat would take a large down angle. Trying to dive with the submarine moving at right angles to the wave motion was dangerous as the submarine rolled most violently on such a course. When the boat was submerging and the ballast tanks were about eighty percent filled with sea water, the free surface effect of the water in the ballast tanks caused the metacentric height to drop to zero and then become negative. At that point, which lasts only a few seconds, if the submarine was heeled far over (60-70 degrees), there would be no righting moment to bring her back. In fact, the sloshing sea water in the tanks would flow to the low side and make her heel even farther.

To dive safely, the boat must be headed slightly across the wave motion into a trough and then submerge when the boat is not heeling over. Our dive was safely made and every one enjoyed a peaceful meal. I did feel sorry for the albatross who had to stay in the air to avoid the violent waves.

For several hours before we dove, we had tried to send a radio message to ComSubPac to alert the fleet of the typhoon in the area of Saipan, where Task Force 58 was operating. Marines were scheduled to land the next day, the 15th of June. The bombardment of the islands had already begun on the 11th.

The waves were so high that salt water was continuously sweeping over the after deck and splashing high and grounding our radio antenna, which was about eight feet above the deck. We never were able to get a message out to say, "Hey, don't come this way for a few days."

After we surfaced later in the day, the wind began to abate and the storm continued to move north away from the Marianas. *Cavalla* continued its course toward the San Bernardino Strait and the *Flying Fish.*

By the 13th of June, Admiral Ozawa with his fleet west of the Philippines at Tawi Tawi, finally decided that the U.S. [Navy] attack was going to be in the Mariana's, not at Palau. He had been poised to head for Palau. He waited an extra day to be certain of where we were going. Part of his force then steamed through San Bernardino Strait and *Flying Fish* reported his passage on 15 June. We envied *Flying Fish* and wished that we had been able to relieve her before Ozawa passed by.

On 10 June 1944, part of Ozawa's fleet designated the *"Kon"* force, had been sent toward Biak to repel a landing there by MacArthur's forces. The *Kon* force was turned around when Ozawa decided that the Marianas were the point of attack. It was to join Ozawa east of the Philippines. *Seahorse* (SS-304) which was 200 miles east of Surigao Strait, detected and reported the position of the *Kon* Force as it steamed north.

As the Japanese fleet joined forces and moved toward the Marianas, it became essential that Admiral Spruance know their location and composition. He was concerned that the Japanese might split their force and try to get around Task Force 58 to attack the ships supporting the landings.

Cavalla was proceeding toward San Bernardino Strait when, just before midnight on the 16th, a convoy of two tankers and two destroyers was detected. *Cavalla* moved into position to make a submerged attack. She avoided the first destroyer, but a few minutes from her firing position, the second destroyer increased speed and headed directly for *Cavalla*. Captain Kossler went deep to avoid the destroyer. It passed directly over *Cavalla's* stern and then turned and went down the starboard side. She did not drop any depth charges, but remained in the vicinity for about a half hour as the convoy headed away. When clear, *Cavalla* surfaced, reported the contact, and headed for *Flying Fish*.

ComSubPac believed the convoy was going to refuel Ozawa's force and directed *Cavalla* to chase. The convoy had been making twenty knots and that was *Cavalla*'s top speed. She chased the convoy for most of that day (the 17th) occasionally slowed by having to dive to avoid a plane. About 1800, ComSubPac assigned *Cavalla* a new station and she headed toward it. She and five other submarines were given stations between Ozawa's forces and the Marianas.

Barely two hours after heading for the new station, *Cavalla* had a radar contact at 30,000 yards. Cavalla headed toward the contact. When about 22,000 yards from the radar contact, *Cavalla* headed away to reduce the closure rate and to determine the course and speed of the ships. As the range decreased to 15,000 yards a large ship could be seen. As the range continued to close, *Cavalla* submerged to radar depth and then to periscope depth. Captain Kossler believed it imperative to report this force to our fleet, furthermore, the pre-patrol briefing to him had made it clear that he was to report first and shoot second. If he made an attack on any of the ships, *Cavalla* might not live to report. Reluctantly, Kossler ordered the sub to hundred feet and quietly let the Japanese pass by. Sonar continued to follow the targets as they passed and reported that there were at least fifteen ships in the group. By 2130, the main force had headed away, but two small ships, probably destroyers lingered behind and it was almost another hour before *Cavalla* could surface and send her report. She then started to chase the fast moving Japanese, but could not regain contact.

About 0100 on the 19th, *Cavalla* changed course and headed toward her recently assigned station. Scouting now became the province of the naval aviator, *Cavalla*, and the other submarines, received orders to shoot first and report later.

It was now the 19th of June and the Battle of Philippine Sea (The Great Marianas Turkey Shoot) was about to begin. Ozawa's force was formed into three elements with C Force, battleships, carriers, cruisers, and destroyers fifty miles ahead of the other two. The other two forces were also separated laterally from each other. At 0825, C Force initiated the first strike against Task Force 58.

At 0856, Ozawa ordered strike number two and by 1030, strikes three and four had been launched and all three elements of Ozawa's force had launched their planes. The Japanese planes had a longer range than the carrier planes of Task Force 58. Ozawa kept his ships beyond the range of TF 58 planes.

At about 0700, Jim Blanchard, in *Albacore* (SS-218), was forced down by a plane. An hour later, he saw a carrier and a cruiser and the tops of several smaller ships at about 13,000 yards. *Albacore* started turning to a normal attack course, but while still swinging, he saw another carrier, a cruiser, and several destroyers for which he was in a better position to make an attack. He shifted targets. As he closed and was about to fire, it became apparent that the torpedo data computer had a wrong solution. Blanchard decided he had to shoot by, "Seaman's Eye" and continued the attack firing a six torpedo spread at the carrier at 0909. One torpedo hit the *Taiho,* Japan's newest and largest carrier, and Admiral Ozawa's flagship. *Taiho* continued on with her force. Blanchard did not think that a single hit would sink the carrier and neither did Ozawa.

Blanchard did not have time to try to repair the TDC. He fired by eye calling out the bearings for the torpedoes as he tracked the carrier with the periscope. He shot a spread of six torpedoes and got one hit. He received a pasting of about twenty-five depth charges, but was not damaged. Blanchard was very discouraged by what had happened. He knew that one torpedo could not sink a carrier. Blanchard felt that he had missed the opportunity of a lifetime. He didn't report the attack until he submitted his report at the end of his patrol.

What Blanchard didn't know was that *Taiho*'s inept damage control and a very volatile fuel were to turn his single torpedo into a lethal weapon.

In an attempt to remove gasoline vapors, the ship's ventilation system was opened spreading the fumes throughout the ship. A series of explosions then doomed *Taiho* and she sank in a little over nine hours after being hit by the one torpedo.

Later that morning, *Cavalla* had a radar contact on a plane and dove to avoid detection. The Officer of the Deck, stationed in the conning tower, and using the periscope, saw several small planes circling in the distance. *Cavalla* headed that way. When searching in the direction of the aircraft, the low frequency sonar operator heard ship noises. *Cavalla* went to battle stations. My battle station was in the conning tower at the plotting desk in the after starboard corner. My job was to plot our track and that of the target using data from the captain's periscope observations. Then, in collaboration with Lieutenant Jug Casler on the torpedo data computer, we determined the course and speed of the target and its *zig zag*, plan if any.

Soon, *Cavalla* could see tops of several ships. Over the horizon came a carrier, two cruisers and a destroyer. *Cavalla* headed toward the targets. The carrier was taking on planes and a number could be seen stacked on the bow. The captain did not know where Task Force 58 was. It was imperative that this target be positively identified before shooting. He did not want to torpedo an American carrier. The recognition manual of Japanese ships was checked and rechecked, but the carrier could not be positively identified. The angle on the bow was small and the range still large. The executive officer and the fire control officer took looks through the scope, but uncertainty remained.

Cavalla was getting closer and the captain would soon have to make his decision. We avoided the destroyer between us and the carrier. Decision time was getting very close. Kossler raised the periscope. He was closer and the angle on the bow of the carrier was larger. Now he could see the Japanese ensign. It was positive identification! On the next observation, at 1109, *Cavalla* fired a six torpedo spread and heard three hits. (Post war information from Japanese survivors claimed that four torpedoes struck the *Shokaku*.) As Cavalla was firing the torpedoes, the Japanese destroyer turned and headed toward her. All that Kossler could see of her was a bit of bow above a large bow wave. He had the periscope lowered and ordered negative flooded. Cavalla started to go deep as torpedo five was being fired. Torpedo six hung up in the tube. It finally broke the stop bolt and left the tube. The destroyer dropped two series of depth charges as *Cavalla* was passing seventy-five feet. They were very close. Cavalla's main induction line was flooded, but the hull stop valves held. This made Cavalla about 12 tons heavy. A sticky valve allowed a tank to overflow into the forward torpedo room bilge making *Cavalla* even heavier and gave her an exaggerated down angle. She was descending faster than intended. Before *Cavalla*'s descent was stopped, she was about hundred feet below her test depth of 312 feet.

It had been necessary to increase speed (and noise) and maintain an up angle on the boat to check *Cavalla*'s dive and to hold her at 400 feet. *Cavalla* could not pump out any of the water. The pumps were noisy and would help the destroyers locate us. For three hours the destroyers sought *Cavalla;* 105 depth charges were dropped. About two hours after the attack, sonar reported large explosions and continuing noise for many seconds in the general direction of the attack. We interpreted those sounds as the death knell of the carrier, and we were right.

The morale on *Cavalla* soared from the depths to which it had sunk after failing on our first attack against the convoy and then had dropped further when the major Japanese force was allowed to pass directly over us without a torpedo being fired at it.

As the depth charging became more sporadic and seemed farther away, *Cavalla* slowly planed up toward periscope depth. When the last destroyer had departed, the water from the induction line and that in the forward torpedo room bilge was pumped out and the forward tubes were reloaded. The stop bolt in number six had to be replaced before we could put a fish in the tube. When all was clear and we were again ready for action, *Cavalla* surfaced and reported our encounter.

On 19 June, during this phase of the battle, the Japanese fleet kept beyond the range of TF [task force] 58's planes as they sent their strikes against TF 58. In addition to the greater range of his planes, Ozawa also had his so-called unsinkable carriers, the Japanese held islands with land-based planes under Admiral Kakuta. Those land-based planes played a much lesser role than Ozawa had planned. In the pre-invasion bombardment of Saipan, Tinian, and Guam, many of those planes were damaged or destroyed and the airfields were damaged as well.

By 1845 on the 19th, all four raids were over as were the attacks from Admiral Kakuta's land based aircraft. Ozawa had sent 374 of his 473 planes into battle. Only 130 returned. Admiral Kakuta lost another 50 aircraft. In addition, 22 planes went down with *Taiho* and *Shokaku*. All together, the Japanese lost 316 aircraft and two carriers on the 19th. U.S. [Navy] losses were 32 planes. *Bunker Hill* and *Wasp* [aircraft carriers] had minor damage, *South Dakota* and *Indiana* [battleships] took bomb and kamikaze hits respectively and *Minneapolis* [heavy cruiser] had bomb damage. The destroyer *Hudson* took some hits from friendly U.S. [Navy]

AA [antiaircraft] guns. All American ships remained in action.

After the battle *Cavalla* again headed towards San Bernardino Strait. She patrolled off San Bernardino for a while. One convoy was found. An end-around was started during the night, but the convoy *zigged* while out of contact. *Cavalla* never regained contact. Because *Cavalla* had been running all over the Philippine Sea at high speeds, she was running short of fuel. After a few more days she was recalled back to Midway and Pearl Harbor.

Editor's note: The Battle of Philippine Sea owed its huge success not only to the prowess of American submariners and aviators, but also to the invention of the VT proximity fuse. The acronym "VT" stood for variable time fuse. Developed at Johns-Hopkins in 1943 the VT fuse allowed Navy gunners to destroy Japanese aircraft at a ratio of about 400 shots to one kill. This stood in contrast to contact or timed exploders which required a ratio of about 4300 rounds to achieve a kill.

Chapter 26
JULY 1944
PENNY PICKED ME
BY BILL GLEASON

> Enlisted man Bill Gleason aboard *Gurnard* (SS-254) couldn't resist the sad face of a mutt named Penny. Hiding the dog in a submarine was a full time job.

It was July 8, 1944 and the *Gurnard* (SS-254) was the outboard ship preparing to get underway. After morning quarters we stationed the maneuvering watch, for which I had no station. I remained topside by the gangway talking to my torpedoman buddy, Bill Parks when a little black dog ran across the gangway right to Parks and me. I picked up the little pooch and placed it back on the gangway, heading it back where it came from.

Turning away, ready to go below, I started down the forward torpedo room hatch. With my feet on the escape trunk ladder rungs, I heard the engines starting and peeked over the deck rim to see the smoke they made when starting. The OD was on the bridge barking orders. I took one last look at the Fremantle shore and there in front of me, eyeball to eyeball, the dog was trying to get on my shoulder. Quickly looking at the bridge, then aft, seeing that no one was looking, I picked it up and put it in my jacket and went below, hiding it so as not to give my secret away. It was a spontaneous reaction in response to the dog's pleading eyes.

Up to my bunk we went, taking heed to prevent any unnecessary commotion. I didn't want to draw attention to my newly acquired shipmate. The 1MC came on and the starboard sea detail was set. We were underway and I had no idea what problems my new little friend might bring. I was in the port watch section. This gave me four hours to orient my new pal to his or her new home. A name was to be had, food, water and toilet arrangements figured out. The first three were comparatively easy, but the last presented a major problem. When one has a problem on a submarine it is best to share it with someone. This time I thought of Parks.

The dog I named Penny because, she, as I discovered, was just so much small change. She was sleeping when I left her to go forward to see Parks at his station at the torpedo tubes. I explained the best I could to him about my predicament. He was flabbergasted. We discussed the alternatives; there were none. Finally I convinced him to help me out. Bill was starboard watch, I was port. He would keep her in the forward torpedo room while I was on watch in the control room.

While we were talking, my eye caught Penny hopping through the water-tight door into forward battery, where she squatted and did her business. Both Parks and I gasped at her audacity, but she had the right instinct. If one has to go somewhere, where better than officers' quarters? Luckily no officer had noticed her. Those in the forward room who saw Penny thought they had the after-affects from too much Fremantle booze.

Parks and I came up with the solution. We would train her as if she were in any house. I went to the cook and asked for any cardboard he had left from food cartons stored in the lockers below the crew's mess.

After three days Penny was trained to go on a piece of cardboard in the forward torpedo room. When we were on the surface I would sneak her topside and she would do her business on the after cigarette deck on a valve plate. All seemed to be working well and Parks and I felt proud of our accomplishment. On our way to the operating area, we navigated the Indian Ocean and pulled into Darwin to top off our fuel tanks. I again took special precautions to hide Penny as well as the Gurnard would permit, but somehow everyone on board knew of my dog, except the skipper, Cdr. C.H. Andrews.

It had been rumored that Captain Andy was making his last patrol, for he had taken the Gumard on the previous five patrols and was due for a shore station. So it behooved me to prevent any problems that could thwart his ambitions, namely discovering Penny. All went well, we left Darwin and began steaming towards Lombok Strait.

Six days out of Fremantle, the captain hollered for the steward. I was standing the 0400 to 0800 watch in the control room, while Penny was with Parks in the forward torpedo room, or so I thought. We had just made the 0700 trim dive and I was at the high-pressure air manifold.

I heard the captain's voice, "Steward, what the hell did you spill on the deck?" His loud, clear tones came from the forward battery passageway outside his stateroom. I glanced through the water tight door into the forward battery passageway and heard the steward reply, "I didn't spill anything, captain."

"Then what is this on the deck?" demanded the skipper. I gathered that he had been barefoot and had stepped out of his cabin right into Penny's mess.

"Captain, it looks and smells like a dog mess to me," analyzed the steward.

"How in hell could there be a dog on this ship?" persisted the captain. The poor stewards mate was trapped. He had to tell. I jumped back to the high pressure blow valve and waited for the worst. Then it came.

"Gleason to the captain's cabin, on the double," barked the 1MC. I wanted to go down into the Pump Room and die. Instead, I got a relief for the air manifold and meekly reported to the captain.

"Reporting as ordered, sir," said I.

He just stood there, eyes drilling through mine. I thought that I would surely be disqualified. I saw myself on a puky destroyer for the duration. "Where is it, Gleason?" asked the captain.

"Sir, Parks has her, sir," I answered, telling the truth.

Parks was summoned with Penny. He looked more frightened than I. He handed me Penny, and was dismissed. The skipper's eyes never left the poor dog. I could see the twinkle begin to radiate from them, and hoped for salvation.

"As you know," the skipper slowly started. "It is against submarine regulations to have an animal aboard ship during a war patrol."

"Yes sir, but I couldn't help it, I just couldn't throw her overboard, could I, sir?" I pleaded. It was all I could think of to say. At the same time, explaining the best I could how I tried to put her ashore.

"What kind is she?" asked the captain as he took Penny from my arms.

"I have no idea, sir. She only weighs four and a half pounds. Must be a rare breed," I embellished. He had to be a dog lover. He accepted her with grace.

"Although it's very unusual," he said, "I'm going to let you keep her aboard, but only for this patrol, when we get back to Perth, you put her ashore. After all, I can't very well throw her overboard, now can I?"

"Yes sir, thank you sir," I responded, taking Penny from his arms and saluting sharply.

From that moment on, Penny stood watches with me and accompanied me everywhere I went, even at battle stations, submerged. Penny was elevated to the status of mascot to ship's company. She stayed on board for four war patrols on Gurnard, earning her combat pin with one star. After her discovery by the captain and her acceptance by him, she presented no more problems. The only minor event was while relaxing at Perth between the seventh and eighth patrol runs. We were billeted at the Ocean Beach Hotel. One of the crew gave Penny to his Aussie girlfriend, but at the time her disappearance was a mystery. We searched high and low, made signs, placed ads in the paper, and even had printed notices on movie screens. Taxi drivers made a few pounds from Park and my-self, driving us around Perth and its outskirts looking for Penny. Time was of the essence. We had only a day left, so we decided to go up to Kings College and inquire. Sure enough it led us right to Penny.

The reunion was great, we forgave the girl friend, but I never forgave the chief electrician's mate who gave Penny away. I found out later, his sudden transfer was because, our new skipper, Cdr. N.D. Gage went for Penny also.

During our eighth patrol, something happened that convinced me Penny had had enough of sea duty. It happened during a more than usual depth charge attack. I was at the trim manifold near the chart desk over the master gyro, where Penny would lie on a small blanket. The Japanese dropped a close one. The boat shook, violently. The lights went out and cork flew. The lamp over the chart desk exploded and fell onto the chart table.

Penny cleared the chart table and was gone. I couldn't leave my watch station. The emergency lights came on. Penny was nowhere to be seen.

I yelled, "Anybody see Penny?"

None had and we didn't secure from battle stations for another two hours, at which time I started searching for her. Usually Penny would stay put or at least head for her bunk. Continuing to look for her, we finally found her in the captain's cabin, shivering and trying to hide under his desk. I knew then, Penny had had enough sea duty. I'm sure she went there to request a transfer, from the only one aboard who could honor that request.

I swore then, to myself that as soon as we were ashore, I would find a home for her and retire her from active duty in submarines.

Then the news came that we were setting course for Mare Island for a major refit and thirty days leave. We berthed at Mare Island on May 18, 1945. Parks and Studebaker, another close friend, were flying home and convinced me to go that way also. I was uneasy because I didn't know whether Penny would be allowed to go on the plane with me, but by then I knew how to hide Penny in my P-coat. She had learned how not to make trouble when the chips were down. We flew all the way home without incident.

When my mother saw Penny she couldn't resist her any more than Parks or the skipper. Penny was at last home, after having served honorably on the old *Gurnard*. She had earned a rest. At my house and under my mother's care that's what Penny got. At a ripe old age, Penny died in her sleep while in my mother's arms. She was seventeen years old according to the vet who examined her. She had become a local heroine, making front-page news, in the Ohio papers. She is buried under my old bedroom window.

Chapter 27

AUGUST 1944
STORY OF THE USS *FLIER* SECOND PATROL AND ITS SURVIVORS

BY ALVIN E. JACOBSON

> Al Jacobson tells the now-famous story of the sinking of the USS *Flier* (SS-250) and how he and a handful of its crew managed to survive.

August 4, 1944, USS *Flier* (SS-250) left Fremantle, Australia to start its second patrol. The officers and crew were, with a few exceptions, the same as were on the first patrol. The officers were Commander J. C. Crowley, captain; Lieutenant J. W. Liddell, executive officer; Lieutenant Paul Knappe, engineering officer, Lieutenant Edward Casey, gunnery and torpedo officer; Lieutenant junior grade Bill Reynolds, communication officer; Ensign Herbert Baehr, assistant engineering officer; Ensign Herb Monor, communications officer; Ensign Philip Mayer, under instruction, and myself with commissary, assistant gunnery and torpedo and assistant navigator.

After a night training period, we left Fremantle and late the next afternoon put in at Exmouth Gulf to refuel. We stayed there that night, leaving early the next morning. On our way out of the Gulf, we had target practice on a ship that had run aground several years before. This ship has the distinction of being shot at by more submarines than any other ship in the world. Every sub that passed it would fire at it.

We headed for Lombock Strait, which was our passage through the Indonesian chain of islands. When we were about twelve hours from Lombock Strait, we had an engine explosion, which we at first thought would force us to turn around and go back. However, Herb, the assistant engineering officer, said he thought he could and did fix everything.

Our passage through Lombock was the usual kind. This is where we were chased by two sub chasers, but with our radar we were able to outmaneuver both of them.

We passed through Makassar Strait, the Celebes Sea and the Sibutu

Passage into the Sulu Sea. We would stay on the surface at night and during the day until a plane would drive us down.

On Sunday, August 13, we received a dispatch saying there was a Jap convoy going down the West Coast of Palawan. This meant that to catch it we would have to make the passage through Balabac Strait. Our assigned area was off the coast of French Indo China with the special assignment of trying to get four supply submarines that were operating out of Saigon and supplying Jap outposts. So, rather than going north of Palawan through Mindoro Strait, we started through the Balabac strait to try and intercept the convoy. The route through Balabac Strait was given in an annex to the operation order.

At 2045 I relieved Ensign "Teddy" Bear as Junior Officer of the Deck and he relieved me at plot in the control room. My station was on the after-cigarette deck. Lt. Ed Casey was the Officer of the Deck. At 2130 the Captain called battle stations for the conning tower and also had Lt. Bill Reynolds and Ensign Phil Mayer come on the bridge as additional officer lookouts. Thus, we had four officers, four lookouts and the captain on the bridge.

About 2150, radar reported Camiran Island 7,800 yards, bearing 174 true. At about 2200 with Camiran Island bearing 190T and 6,700 yards, I was admiring the mountainous silhouettes on three sides of us, when suddenly a terrific gush of air came out of the conning tower hatch. Bill Reynolds was blown back to me and complained of a side ache.

I thought, at the time, that it was only an air bank that had let loose, so I told him to lie down; but before he had a chance, the boat started to go under. As I was talking to Bill, I remember seeing Phil dive over the side. As we went under, I was sucked down about fifteen to twenty feet. My first impulse was to struggle to the surface, because I could picture the screws coming by me. Upon reaching the surface, it dawned on me that I was shipwrecked. After looking around I had it impressed upon me that it was serious because I could not see any land or stars in any direction. The water was warm with about one-foot waves. There was an oil slick on the surface which made opening the eyes or mouth unpleasant. It wasn't long before I heard some shouting; so I swam towards the noise and found the rest of the group. At this time, remembering my lifesaving instructions about taking off your clothes in such an emergency, I did, all except for my trunks and t-shirt. This I later found out to be a very grave mistake. Before discarding my pants, I took out my knife. However, I had no way of carrying it, and soon lost it. I kept the binoculars I had while standing my watch. They were on a strap around my neck and almost floated, so they did not bother me much. When I joined the group, the main topics of discussion were; what had happened, where we were, and how to get the rest of the fellows together. It wasn't long before we were all in one group. As far as I can figure and know, there were fifteen people who got off the sub and started the swim. The Chief of the watch was the only man who was able to get out from below the conning tower and he was in such bad shape that he was not able to stay afloat for any length of time. A quartermaster was not able to get out of the conning tower.

To give you an idea of the extent of the power of the explosion, Jim Liddell, who at the time was standing in the conning tower hatch talking to the captain, had his shirt taken off by the gush of air and it lifted him up to the bridge. He weighed over 200 pounds. The captain said he was blown aft to the cigarette deck and before he could get back to sound the collision alarm, the boat went under. The men at the TDC and sonar could only remember pulling for all they were worth on the periscopes to get in the gush of air from the control room, and the next thing they were out of the ship and in the water. Several of the people coming out of the conning tower were caught in the guardrail of the signal bridge.

After the group was assembled, the question naturally arose as to what to do next. Jim, being the navigator, told us that there was land around us on three sides, the distances varying from fourteen to thirty miles. He said we could possibly try to swim to Camiran Island, which was only about two miles away, but it was so small that the chance of missing it was too great. However, it made little difference if we tried to plan where to swim, because there were no stars and we could not see any land, therefore, we had no means for direction. About three or four times during the night, we saw flashes of lightening, which showed up a mountain peak that was about 30 miles away. We knew we didn't want to swim in that direction. A few minutes after the lightening you completely lost your sense of direction again. Also, a couple of times you could see a group of stars which Jim said were the false cross. I'll never forget swimming the side stroke and looking back at them.

We decided that we would try to keep swimming at least in some direction, because we would probably be a little better off that way than if we just stayed where we were. It was finally decided that we would, as nearly as possible, keep the waves slapping us on the left cheek. However, this was a problem, because you rolled up and down with the waves. During the night, we tried to keep together in a group as much as possible. I do not know what type of course we swam, and I will not say we swam a straight course either, because I remember crossing the oil streak at least three times. The only things that came up from the boat, other than the oil, were pieces of cork about the size of a baseball. These few pieces were of no value because no one had a way to use them.

After about two hours of swimming, Chief Pope called over to Jim and asked how far he thought we would have to swim. Jim, trying to be encouraging, said, "About nine miles."

Pope replied, "To hell with this." He stopped swimming. This was the same man that when *Flier* ran aground at Midway and the waves were breaking over the deck, they tied a line to him and he crawled out to the bow to fasten a tow line.

Jim was troubled several times with a cramp in his leg; but, by taking the muscle and pinching it as hard as we could, it seemed to go away. This was an extremely painful procedure but it must have worked. I had a second chance to get a knife when I helped Ed Casey take his pants off and I got his knife out of his pocket. However, I lost it, because there was not a way to carry it.

We all agreed upon the policy that it would have to be every man for him-self. This was because the distance to swim was unknown and it would be unfair to anyone to ask assistance of them. This policy was willingly agreed upon by everyone, and to my knowledge was carried out by everyone. To give an example of how this was carried out, the explosion blinded Ed Casey so that he could not see the rest of us. At the same time, he, for some reason could not swim on his stomach. This made it hard for him to keep up with the group. He would often start swimming off to one side and we would have to call him back; once he went quite a way off and I went over to help him back. When I reached him and told him to rest a minute and I would push him back, he refused and said; "remember that we agreed that every man was for himself," thus he would not let me help him. As we were swimming back, he would joke about the parties we had previously planned to have when we got back to Perth, Australia. It was not more than ten minutes later that we saw no more of Ed Casey.

This, to me, was one of the greatest signs of courage that any man could show. I remember when Paul Knappe swam to one side and never came back to the group. I didn't realize why he swam away until he didn't return. This type of courage was also demonstrated by all seven fellows who were lost while swimming, because, to my knowledge, none of them in any way asked for help. When they figured that their time had come, and they could swim no more, they simply swam to one side without saying anything.

About 0300 the moon rose to help us hold a direction to an unknown destination. It was not until daylight, approximately 0500, that we were able to see any kind of land. At daylight, we picked out what we thought to be the closest island and agreed to swim to it at each person's own pace. I stayed with Howell and Baumgart. Russo immediately swam ahead and was the first to hit the beach.

During the afternoon, about 1300, a Jap patrol plane passed over us, but the pilot did not change his course, so we felt he had not seen anything. About two miles off the beach, we saw what we thought might possibly be a native boat, but, after trying to signal it, we decided it would be better to avoid it, and swim straight for our island. As we approached it, we found that it was only a floating palm tree; but we were thankful to find even that and climbed up on it to look around for the other fellows. We saw the captain and Jim and waved to them to come over and join us. The captain said he was just about ready to give up when he saw us but then decided to try to reach us. Later we saw Tremaine and hollered at him and he hollered and waved back at us but avoided us. This we couldn't figure out until later when he told us he didn't hear us and thought we were native fisherman. But if they weren't friendly enough to pick him up he wasn't going to chance coming to them. So, the five of us hung on to the palm tree the rest of the way in.

As we approached the island, we began to imagine seeing houses, etc., but, as we came closer, we could see that there was only one beach of about seventy-five yards that we would be able to lay down upon. Therefore, we headed for that. We were able to touch bottom about a block from the beach.

At 1530 in the afternoon, by the captain's and my watch, we sat down on the good earth, which made about seventeen hours of swimming. This island was Byan Island, we did not know about it then, but I have checked the charts since coming home.

The strange thing I found about the swim was that I had to fight with myself to keep from going to sleep. Also, I found that the breaststroke was my best stroke. I could not use one stroke very long, because I would tire too much that way, so I used three different strokes, mainly the side stroke, back stroke, and breast stroke. I do not remember thinking about anything special except I do remember repeating the 23rd Psalm, which surprised me. Also, I believe as a result of my experience anybody who can swim for a couple of hours should be able to swim for a good deal longer if they do not give up or get panicky.

All the fellows who went down did so in the first two or three hours, with the exception of one, who became panicky just before sunrise, and that was the last we saw of him.

We all stopped at the sandy beach, and Jim walked around the end of the island, to see if he could find any of the others fellows. He found Tremaine there. Russo had swum ahead and was waiting for us at the beach. He arrived ten minutes before we did. Thus, there were seven of us together at that time. They were: Commander J. D. Crowley, our Captain; Lieutenant J. W. Liddell, Executive Officer; Ensign A. E. Jacobson, Jr.; Chief Gibson Howell, CRT; D. P. Tremaine, FCR and; J. D. Russo, second class quartermaster; and E. Baumgart, third class motor machinist.

While walking toward the sandy beach, we found one drifted coconut that sounded as though it might be good, so, after making a poor excuse for a lean-to, we opened the coconut and got about two tablespoons of coconut milk and a piece of coconut about an inch and half square each for supper. However, none of us could hold it down and we lost it right away. We then lay down and tried to get some sleep.

After trying to build a lean-to and open the coconut with our hands, we realized how much we were going to miss a knife of some kind. We huddled together as we slept, trying to keep a little warmer. We didn't think it was wise to try to build a fire, because it might attract attention from the Japanese city, which we knew to be on another island. However, tired as we were, little sleep was gained, because of the sunburn we had, which gave us a fever. Every time we moved to try to get into a more comfortable position, the sand would rub against the sunburn and it would be mighty uncomfortable. I spent most of the night lying and wishing, more than anything, that daylight would come so that I could get warm and stop shaking.

We rose at sunrise and decided we had better look around the island for some food and water. By this time, we had made enough of a search of our end of the island to know that there was no water which we could drink around there. Jim and the Captain were to go around one way to the other side while Baumgard and I were to go around the other way. Howell, Tremaine and Russo were to stay and try to improve the lean-to and also watch the spot where the boat had gone down. Howell had wrenched his knee while leaving the boat, which made walking difficult.

The men who stayed at the camp had noticed water dripping from the coral and thought that it was fresh. It was only seawater that had splashed up there at high tide. But, as they had gathered about two shells full, we were satisfied to believe that it was fresh and so each took about three tea spoonful's. We used a little shell about the size of a teaspoon to dish it out to each of us.

At about 1815, as we were sitting and looking out to where the ship had gone down, we noticed a large geyser of water come up. Shortly afterwards we heard an explosion. We have no idea what caused the explosion. It may have been a mine going off, or something from the ship. Another plane had passed over in the afternoon without deviating from its course.

Before lying down at night we laid out about twenty large shells to collect rainwater if it rained. You could possibly trace our path through the island by just looking where we had laid out shells. The sleep that night for me was not better than the first night—we again rose at sunrise.

The captain and Jim had worked out the plan that was agreed upon. There were only two courses open for us to follow: one was to follow the chain of islands that led toward the Japanese town, which was the only sign of civilization; and the other was to follow the chain of islands in the opposite direction. That would lead to another main island where we didn't know what to expect. The latter course was chosen, because we did not want to turn ourselves over to the Japanese at this stage of the game.

We started to walk around the end of the island so we could find the closest place from which to start swimming to the next island. We knew that we could not start to the next island until late afternoon, because of the Japanese air patrol that came over at 9:00 in the morning and 1500 in the afternoon. Also, the Jap launch patrol might come by and spot us. Another reason was that we had to wait until slack tide. There was about a six knot current that flowed between the islands and we could not hope to buck that. While walking around the end of the island I found a small piece of canvas, which I thought would work well for a pair of shoes. However, I couldn't find any way to wrap the cloth around my feet without it rubbing on the sores and make it more painful than being bare foot.

We spent the day building a raft and resting, also keeping out of the sun. The raft was constructed out of bamboo about four inches in diameter, which we picked up on the beach and tied together with vines that we pulled off the trees. The captain made two paddles by splitting a bamboo pole part way up and then putting small pieces in crossway, then tying it with vines. We also found two long sticks for polling. The raft was big enough to hold two people. We did not dare build it any larger because it would be too easy to see.

At about 1430 we started to swim to the island number two, now known as Gabung. About half way across it started to rain. However, we could not catch any of it. We just hoped that someone had left a lot of shells spread out on the island to which we were going as we had done on the island we just left.

We were able to pole about a quarter of the way across. The rest of the way we had to swim and tow the raft. The captain rode on the raft and paddled. The rest of us took turns riding the raft and paddling. When we were about one-third of the way a patrol plane came over and we all ducked under the raft. When we were about three quarters of the way across, the tide started to change and the current started to get strong. There were several times that we didn't think that we were making progress. Finally, we were carried into the lee of the island. From here we were able to swim to the island.

We reached the island about 1900 or four and a half hours later, which was after dark. We found a sandy beach and all were satisfied to lie down wherever there was room. Again we became very cold, and so to keep warm, we buried ourselves in the sand. This however, was of little use, because after about ten minutes, we would start to get the shakes and shake all the sand off. What I did was to lie down for about half to three quarters of an hour and then when I started shaking too much, I would get up and walk around until I settled down. Jim and I even tried burying ourselves together but we just couldn't shake in unison so that the sand came off twice as fast.

I believe there is nothing that I have ever wished for or ever hope to wish for, more than I did hope for daylight at this time. Daylight meant warmth.

The first thing we did after sunrise was to plan our next move. We decided to take the long way around the island, because we couldn't start for the next island until about 1500, after Japanese patrol and the tide current was lowest and we could more likely find some coconuts or something to drink that way. By now, our feet were pretty well cut up by the coral and so walking was getting harder all the time. We walked in the shallow water because the coral was grown over with weeds and was easier on our feet. The disadvantage of walking in the shallow water, however, was that you were in the sun, and we were already more sunburned than we wanted to be.

We reached the far side of the island about 1330 and did not find any edible coconuts, food, or water of any kind. Again we opened several coconuts by hand, only to find that they were no good.

After the 1500 air patrol passed, we again started for the island number three. The water here was a little shallower in places and we were able to wade part of the way. This greatly eased the strain.

It was between these islands that we saw the fins of a couple of sharks. These were the only ones we saw during our entire trip—something for which we were very thankful. By this time, we had assumed an attitude of, let come what may, what comes, just comes, and what doesn't is O.K.

We arrived at island number three, now known as APO, about 1800, only about a three-hour swim and were again able to find a sandy beach. We spent the night there in the same manner as we had the previous nights that is, spending most of the night wishing for daylight.

It was the fifth day and the third island. We started about 8:00 to circle the island to the seaward which was the long way again and pushing the raft ahead of us. This island was the same in form as the other islands, except that it was a little more round. We found on this island an abandoned dugout, but it proved of no use to us, because it was full of holes.

Baumgard and I became inquisitive about one of the trails leading in to the center of the island; but, after walking on the customary hard coral for about three blocks, our curiosity was satisfied that there were only monkeys on the island.

About 1100 we found a coconut, making the second one we had found so far that was edible.

Upon rounding the furthest point, we saw on the next island, island number four, now known as Bugsuk Island, what we thought to be houses. Naturally, our hopes reached an all-time high. It was agreed that we would eat our coconut and then start for the next island, planning to get there just before sunset. We found that eating the coconut was harder than it was worth. We could down only about a square inch of the meat and there was no milk in it.

At 1400 we started for the island number four, Bugsuk. The water was fairly shallow, so we could pole a lot of the way and we were able to hang on to the raft. As planned, we were there just before sunset and also to come on to the island about a mile and one-half down from the houses. This was around a point, which should have blocked the view of anybody who might be in the houses. We reached the shore about 1730 and landed where we wanted to land. We rounded the point very cautiously and saw that the houses were abandoned. On the way to the houses, we passed a coconut grove, plus indications of a small native village, so Baumgard and I stayed and rounded up about twelve good coconuts. Upon reaching the house, we found in the rear a cistern that was filled with rainwater. Needless to say, we wanted a feast that night, eating fresh coconut and drinking fresh water, this being the first food and water we had for five days.

We found that the work of getting one coconut open with our bare hands was enough to discourage us from eating any more. We found a sharp rock and by pounding the coconut on it we could gradually work the outer shell off. Once this was off, it was easy to pound out the eye and drain the milk out of the coconut and then crush the hard shell. All of us, except Howell, drank sparingly of the water, as the captain had advised us to do.

By this time it was dark and we proceeded to find places to lie down and rest. I found a bamboo door that made a very good mattress and so slept comparatively well that night. Before going to bed, we had looked around the house and decided that at one time it had belonged to a wealthy landowner. However, someone had attempted to wreck the house.

There were several discarded receipts for the purchase of cattle and the sale of lumber, indicating that the owner had a prosperous business.

In the front of the house was a launch about thirty-eight feet in length, heavily constructed, which showed signs of having been purposely destroyed. There was another launch of about the same size that had apparently been in the process of being built. There were several large clearings around the house, which indicated that they had been used for vegetable gardens. Also, there was a stream in which we could see many fish that could easily be caught or netted. Thus, plans for the next day were very cheerful.

During the night, Howell became very sick, and we believed that it was due to the fact that he drank so much water.

We arose at sunrise and had another coconut for breakfast. We were just getting organized as to who would build the fire; do the fishing; go on the scouting trips, and gather coconuts; for we were getting set to spend several days here and recuperate a little. Then, from the jungle, came what appeared to be two small native boys. Knowing that they had, undoubtedly, seen us already, we did not try to avoid them, but rather went down to meet them. The captain spoke to them and asked them, "Americans or Japanese?" One boy said, "Americanos" and smiled. He then said, "Japanese," and motioned as though he was cutting his throat. This relieved us considerably. Next, the boy pointed to the cistern and said, "Don't drink water." This puzzled us, but remembering our policy of letting come and go what may, we disregarded his statement, and asked him if he had any food. He patted his stomach and said, "Rice." He then motioned for us to follow him back along the path into the woods.

This we did, and shortly after we started along the path, the native boys ran ahead and picked up their poles and the small packs on poles in which they carried their food. As we walked along, we passed an abandoned sugar cane field. They took us into it and motioned for us to sit down while they cut each of us a piece of sugar cane about three feet long. We spent at least a half-hour chewing on this. The only reason we did not eat more of it was because we were too tired to chew anymore.

We then continued along this path about two blocks and came to a clearing where we found a deserted schoolhouse. It consisted of a raised platform with a roof over it and had several school benches on it. There was about a hundred yard clearing around it.

They motioned to us to sit down and faster than I could start a fire using matches, they had whittled themselves a spindle and had started a fire by spinning the spindle in a notched block. It was like we did in Boy Scouts, except that they did not use the draw bow, but rather spun the spindle by rubbing it between their hands. As soon as they had this fire going, they brought out a small pan about five inches round and deep. They filled this with water from a nearby stream and poured some rice into it. While the rice was boiling, they cut down some banana leaves and laid them out to make plates for us. They then brought us some water, which we were to drink. It was as muddy and dirty as you could find. However, they assured us it was all right by drinking some of it themselves. We were not in a position to seriously doubt it.

As soon as the rice was cooked, they laid it on the banana leaf plates and also laid out some dried fish, which they had brought along with them. There were about three fish and they looked like bluegills.

We had no more than started to dig into the rice when from across the clearing we saw ten men; three armed with guns and six with blowguns and bolos. Our spirits naturally dropped to the lowest ebb, until one man who seemed to be leading the group hollered out, "Hello." He spoke very good English and ran up to us, grasping our hands and introducing himself. He was Mr. Pedro Sarmiento, leader of the Bolo Battalion of the Bugsuk Island and a former school teacher who had been educated in Manila and was overseer of the abandoned plantation during peacetime. The other men who were with him, he explained were the natives of the island who had organized into the local Bolo Battalion.

After identifying himself, we asked him what the native boys meant when they told us not to drink the water back at the house. He told us that the man who owned the house had, when the Japanese at the beginning of the war chased him out of it, filled the cistern with arsenic, to kill any Japanese that might drink the water. We believe that this is the reason why Howell became ill that night. We were very fortunate that more of us did not become ill.

We asked him how he knew we were in the house. He said that at all times they had several points around the island, where native look-outs watched for Japanese coming to make an inspection of their island. It was one of these lookouts that had spotted us swimming to the island. He immediately notified Pedro about the swimmers.

As Pedro did not know whether we were Japanese or Allies, he sent out word during the night to the several surrounding islands to bring in guerrillas. They then had the house surrounded in the morning, and were going to attack us if we were Japanese, or to help us out if we were Allies. The native boys were sent in as scouts to find out whom we were. If we had been Japanese, they were to pretend that they were going to the coconut grove, and if we were Allies, we were to be brought back to the schoolhouse.

Pedro then explained his plan. He had been instructed that any Allied survivors found were to be sent to the main guerilla headquarters on the southern coast of Palawan at Cape Ballilugan. We were to walk across Bug-suk Island, which was eight kilometers, or about five miles. There he had a native boat called a *kumpit*. He said that it was very important that we get started walking right away, because the routine Japanese patrol was to land at the house either that morning or by the afternoon. They would make their formal inspection and spend the night in the house. He said that if we could get a mile back into the island, we would be safe, because the Japanese were afraid to go that far into the island. With this in mind, we accepted his plan without any hesitation.

In fact, we were willing to start before eating, but he said that he wanted to send the boys back to the house and see that we did not leave anything indicating that we had been there. The only thing that we could have left, which was all we had, was the magnifying glass we had taken from my binoculars. This turned out to be a very welcome gift for Pedro as he used it to light his pipe. We ate while the natives went back. Then after finishing the dinner we started marching.

The ground was made up of coral. Up until now, we had not realized the extent of our fatigue, or the condition of our feet. There is no doubt that there has seldom been a sorrier looking bunch of hikers starting a walk. They stationed native guerrillas ahead and behind us, and the rest cut the path for us. We had hoped to make it to the other side of the island by nightfall, but after walking for about an hour and a half, it became quite apparent that this was an idle dream. So, it was agreed that we would go half way that day and continue the trip the next day.

It wasn't until 1700 that afternoon that we reached the native village at the center of the island. It meant that we had walked for eight hours to gain a total of two and half miles, which was certainly a good day's work. Upon reaching the village, we were taken to the leading man's hut, and he had bamboo mats laid out for us. We were there probably only 15 minutes before we were all asleep.

While we were asleep, the captain had brought to his attention the fact that as long as you are in the navy, you can never be free from paperwork; for while he was sleeping he was awakened by Pedro who wanted to have all our names and where we were stationed, so he could make his formal report. Writing paper was one of the scarcest items on the island, but, still, he had to make a formal report to his guerilla leader

We were awakened about 1830 to find that they had killed one of their very few chickens to make a chicken broth for us. The chicken was so thin and run-down that in the United States, you probably couldn't have even given it away. However, here it was a great sacrifice to kill it. Thus, we felt very honored and were glad to taste something besides rice and coconut. We had wild honey for dessert, which was good.

After eating, we went back to sleep again. Pedro had assured us that there were guards posted all around us to warn if any Japanese should come. The next thing I knew, it was morning and we were told we would have to get started. Water here was taken from a stream that was about four inches deep and ten inches wide, also very muddy. The water was carried in hollowed out bamboo poles about five inches in diameter and five feet long. However, it was the only water around and the natives drank it all the time, so we assumed it was all right.

Our next objective was the next village, which was half way to the other side of the island. The plan was to have a noon meal. We started out and after walking for about three hours we began to wonder how much further it was to this native village. It was then that Pedro started to tell us that it was just another kilometer. I believe that about every 20 minutes somebody would ask him how much further it was and he would say, "Just another kilometer." Pretty soon this got to be a joke.

We reached the hut at about noon and were glad to get a chance to rest and eat. Here we were introduced to something new: blue rice. Even though it was all we ate, we were beginning to learn to enjoy rice. Again our dessert was more rice with wild honey, very tasty.

After resting for about an hour, we started our march again. The native owner of this hut donated a large basket of rice, which was all he could give and was a great sacrifice. This was to be brought to the guerilla headquarters as a donation to the guerrillas. That is an example of how the guerrillas were supplied with food.

Our pace was not improving very much. About 1530 we came across another native hut. As yet we were not very hungry, however, the native insisted that we stop and have something to eat with him. So we ate more rice. Again we started walking, and again we started asking how much farther it was, and again it was, "just another kilometer."

We finally reached the Bugsuk River and our boat. This was timed very well, for it just gave us time to get aboard the boat and have enough daylight to navigate down the river before sunset. Here we bade goodbye to the major part of our guard, but met one of the most interesting people we were to meet. His name was *LaHud* but we called him "The Sailor" because he very capably did all the sailing and navigating from here to Brooks Point, and was very capable at handling both.

We asked Pedro to come along with us to the next island because he was the only one who could speak English.

We also met *TomPong* who was to be with us for the remainder of our trip. The sailboat or kumpit as the natives call them was typical of the type used by the Moro tribe of natives. The Sailor was a Moro trader and they were the type of people who we were told to avoid meeting if we were ever shipwrecked.

This kumpit had a wooden hull about sixteen feet long, a six-foot beam, pointed bow, a four-foot wide square stern, and a smooth round bottom. The hull was flush decked over from the stern to the mast. Forward of the mast was just enough space for a jug of water and two native boys. It was from here that the native boys did the rowing. A split bamboo mat could be stretched overhead to give shade and hold off the rain. It had a large oversize gaff rig with a tiller and a detachable rudder. We sat on the decking. Below this was the cargo area of the sailboat where everything was carried: bags of rice, cooking utensils, a gun and everything else a person needed to live. For more storage space they had racks built out on both sides of the kumpit, which ran about three quarters of the length of the boat. It was surprising that the kumpit would even float when we had twelve people and all the stores in it, let alone make any speed under sail. However, with hardly any wind, we moved along at a fair speed.

About 1800 we shoved off and started down the river. The river was so narrow and sheltered that we were not able to sail. Therefore we took along two small boys who would do the rowing. We rowed down the river for about three miles and reached the mouth of the river just before dark. As we were leaving the river, the guide who was acting as lookout started to make a lot of noise and pointed towards the beach. They turned the kumpit towards the beach and we naturally began to worry. However, we were glad to find out that all he was pointing at was some kind of seaweed that a doctor had told them was a good medicine. So, whenever they found it, they would eat it. It tasted like a bitter sweet pickle and contained a form of iodine.

By now it was dark, which was what we wanted. It was only safe to sail at night and the next island was about twenty miles away. To get to it, we needed to pass through several reefs. The night was pitch black; but the Sailor and Kim-Jon knew the waters so well that they sailed in and out of the hidden reefs with very little strain, having to pole themselves away from the coral only a few times. The wind died down when we were about half way across, which made it necessary to row the rest of the way.

We arrived at Cape Ballilugan on the southern end of Palawan Island at about 0300. The members of the regular organized guerilla outpost greeted us. They had received word that we were coming, and were down in full force to greet us. They then took us to their hut and introduced themselves by showing us their official papers. This outpost was made up of Filipinos, all of whom had some kind of formal education. They were schoolteachers or the equivalent. They were full time guerrillas, and devoted their whole time to this outpost.

It was here that we met Sergeant Pasqual de la Cruz, USAFFE [United States Forces Far East], who was in charge of this outpost. Pedro turned us over to him. We then went to their barracks, and were given bunks, which were merely tables and were fed more rice and sugar cane.

The captain asked if they had any medicine. Sergeant Cruz went to the shelf and brought down a jar of white salve, full of bugs and dirt, so the captain politely refused the offer. The sergeant said that he was sorry, but that was all they had. So we continued to let Mother Nature heal our sores.

We talked for quite a while for these were the first people who understood English and could explain the situation to us. We now found out that we would have to go about seventy miles up the island to the main guerilla headquarters. It was also decided that we could sail only during the night, but we would leave that night, so we were to spend the day around there. We went to sleep, awakening at about 0930.

The guerillas rounded up enough clothing so that each of us had a pair of pants and some of the luckier ones were able to get a shirt. My shirt was about three sizes too small, but was very much welcomed.

Sergeant Cruz told the captain that about two weeks before the Japanese were transporting four prisoners from Balabac City to Puerto Princessa prison camp on Palawan. They were on a submarine that was sunk near Camiran Island, six got off and two were killed on the island. Sergeant Cruz wondered if we were off the same submarine. The captain told him we were sunk nine days ago, so they were not from our submarine.

That day we spent inspecting the outpost and talking with the guerillas. We had a real treat for dinner: caribou meat, cut so thin it was like paper. Even then you could just barely chew it. They had also fixed coconut in a new form; they made a spread out of coconut and honey that was great.

The outpost was made up of one bamboo building about 40 by 50 feet, built on stilts and six feet off the ground. Below and around the edge of this house were a series of trenches. The guerrillas could drop from the house into these trenches and repel any attack from the beach. Other things around the house were items we were later to find around all the settlements; a big pot to boil down salt water to get salt, a small clearing to raise sugar cane, a few skinny chickens and a cistern to collect rain water from the roof.

It was now the 10th day of our journey. The wind was favorable, so it would be safe to start sailing after the scheduled 1500 Japanese Patrol. So shortly after 1500 we set sail. The sergeant, the Sailor, Kim Jon, and the new member of our party, Kong, were with us. Kong helped Kim Jon do the rowing. Pedro departed to organize a search of the surrounding islands to see if anyone else had gotten off the submarine. He had previously sent people to all the islands but wanted to check again.

The wind and sea were favorable when we left and our hopes were so high that we thought we could make the seventy miles by next morning. It was about 1730, when we had settled down to a comfortable pace that the Sailor, without much warning, started to head for the beach and spoke to the sergeant in their native tongue. This aroused our suspicion, and after quizzing the sergeant, he pointed out towards the sea and told us, as we could see, that a Japanese patrol was passing by. We dropped our sail, which cut down our silhouette, so they could not see us. By this time the boat had gone by, it had become dark and the wind had died down. For the next few hours, the sergeant, the Sailor, Kim Jon and Kong took turns rowing. Later the wind came up again and the sailing became very pleasant. For supper that night, the Sailor had cooked us rice in his improvised galley. This galley consisted of a two-foot square sheet of steel, which he laid on the deck. On this steel he built an open fire. Then from a tripod arrangement he hung a pot to cook the rice.

About 0300 it was decided that we couldn't make the headquarters without traveling too much in daylight. So they rowed us about two miles up the Tuba River to the homes of natives. He and his wife and family accepted us very graciously and made room for us in their house. We slept there until the morning, and found when we awoke that our host had killed one of his pet chickens and was cooking it for our dinner. This met with great approval, but we were sorry to see that they had made such a sacrifice.

After the 1500 patrol we continued our journey. This time our party had grown. Our host's daughter had just married and he asked if it would be possible for the bride and groom to travel with us. Of course, after his hospitality, we had no choice. However, the party did not stop with just the newlyweds, they brought chicken, rice, and many other articles with them; so now our boat was loaded until it had about two inches of freeboard. In fact there was only sitting room for us with no room to move or stretch.

The Sailor did not leave with us, but instead ran ahead, and we were told he would join us later. We had become so fond of him that we were sorry to see him go. After a couple of hours, when we were a few miles off shore, we saw a man swimming in the water out to us. It turned out to be the Sailor, who, we were told, had stopped off to see his family. He brought back with him a new way of fixing rice in the form of pancakes. Shortly after joining us again, he cooked our evening meal and resumed his duties. The Sailor's duties included about everything in the book and he would do them all at the same time. For example, he would be handling the tiller with one foot, rowing with the other foot, handling the sheet with his teeth, sewing up a hole in Baumgart's pants and cooking our meal, all at the same time.

At 0600 we noticed several boats ahead of us, and as we approached we saw that they were *boncas* with natives diving for fish and spearing them under water. A *bonca* is basically an outrigger type of canoe with a sail. They turned out to be friends of the sailor's and they gave us some fish. Later on the sailor cooked an eel and two other types of fish. The eel, after it was skinned, was very tasty.

The wind was favorable but not very strong. We were sailing along when there began a lot of shouting. Our sails were immediately dropped, and we were amazed when another boat came alongside. It seems that this boat belonged to a friend of the sergeant and the Sailor, who had just come from where we were heading. The sergeant was anxious to know if there were any signs of the enemy ahead. They reported that there were none and departed.

While we were sailing, Kong would roll a cigarette and smoke it. Russo and Baumgart decided that they would like a smoke, so Kong rolled them one out of native tobacco and split Napa leaf for the paper. They claimed the cigarette was so strong it felt like hot tar going down the throat. It gave them a tobacco cure for a while.

The whole time we were sailing, we were going among reefs and hidden rocks, and it was very satisfying to see the way the Sailor seemed to know where each one was located. About 0530 we rounded the point that formed the bay where the headquarters stood. After much shouting by the sergeant the guerilla lookout was awakened, and told to notify their captain that we were coming. About 0800 we landed the boat and were greeted by an army of guerrillas and their captain. Their captain identified himself as Captain Nazario B Mayor USAFFE, Acting Commanding Officer of Section D of Sixth Military District, and invited us to his home, which was about two blocks off the beach.

Captain Mayor was a native Filipino who had graduated from the University of Kansas where he had received a commission in the U.S. Army through the ROTC. We later found out that the house on Bugsuk Island, where we had first landed, was his home. He had been running a profitable lumbering business when the war started. When the Japanese came, he had to hide his tractors and equipment in the jungle, abandon his home, and destroy all his records and escape to the jungle.

We were still unable to walk very well and must have appeared a very disappointing sight to the guerrillas as examples of American soldiers. It was not only our sores that disabled us but also we had been so crowded together and unable to move while we sat on the hard wood deck of the sailboat that we were stiff

On the way to Captain Mayor's home, we met Mr. T. H. Edwards, whom we were later to know as a great friend. Mr. T. H. Edwards, an American citizen, was in business at Brook's Point before the war and now in evacuation. We reached the house and met Mrs. Mayor and the rest of the family, plus many natives. They invited us to wash up and started to prepare a good meal. The captain's wife spoke English and had a formal education.

We were not at their home very long when Sergeant Amado S. Corpus, who was in charge of the U.S. Army Signal Corps Coast Watcher Unit stationed there, introduced himself He was a great sight for he was an American born Filipino and this was the first time that we could feel completely relaxed. No matter how assuring the natives were, "you still had a doubt about where their loyalties lay".

We now found out that there would be a chance to contact Australia and ask for help. Our first worry was to get news to ComTask Force Seventy-One to warn him not to send any more ships through Balabac Strait. Mrs. Mayor now had dinner ready and we sat down to a meal that was served in a crude form but showed signs of fashion.

It was decided that because of our poor physical condition and the fact that it would be unsafe for us should the Japanese come around that we were to go to the home of Mr. Edwards, which was about three miles inland. The coast watcher had a radio there to contact Australia. After dinner captain Mayor arranged for two caribou carts to carry us back to the home of Mr. Edwards. This trip proved very amusing. The caribou that was hitched to the cart that drew the captain and four of us was an older bull. It was during the hot afternoon that we made the trip and unfortunately it had rained the day before. So about every hundred yards there was a mud wallow in which the caribou would lie down. The native boy would hit him and kick him as much as he could but the bull would not move until he wanted to do so. Thus, the trip took us all afternoon and we didn't reach Mr. Edward's house until 1700.

As we came up to a stream, we saw the house, and saw Mr. Edwards working on the rice mill. He greeted us very cheerfully and sent his native boy to the house to make it ready for us. When we arrived, we were greeted by Mrs. Edwards and the rest of the Signal Corps Group, plus Bill Wigfield and George Marquez of the U.S. Army, Chuck Watkins S1C U.S. Navy Air (they were Japanese prisoners that had escaped and now lived in the area), as well as Henry Garretson, a U.S. Citizen. The house was made of bamboo and built on stilts and as native as almost any of the houses we had been in, except that it was larger and had chairs and other indications of civilization. Next to the house was a house built by Captain Mayor as a retreat for his family in case the Japanese landed. However, due to the Malaria around there, Captain Mayor kept his family down at the beach.

There was room for only three of us in Mr. Edward's home so the officers stayed there and the other men stayed with the coast-watcher group in Captain Mayor's home.

The coast-watcher group brought out their medicine kit and we were finally able to get sulfa and other medicine on our cuts. We also received cigarettes, soap and some clothes. In fact, we even had some coffee, and cheese and crackers. These were the emergency rations of the coast-watchers. Our first task was to send a message back to Australia, so the captain made out a message and gave it to the coast-watchers to send.

We were fed a good meal of coconut sprouts, rice, *kalamayhatii*, and a fruit similar to grapefruit. After dinner, Mr. Edwards brought out the news reports for the last few days, the reports being those that the coast-watchers received over the radio every night and typed up for the people around the area. This brought us up to date with the outside world. We also realized what an important factor these news reports were for the guerrillas. That night we slept as peacefully as any person could.

The next few days were spent lying around and recuperating, talking to the natives, the coast-watchers, and Charlie, Bill, and George. Of course, our main project was communicating with Australia and arranging to be picked up.

Our first day there, Mr. A.M. Sutherland, A Scottish Missionary, came to visit us. He was a fine person. At the captain's request, the next morning we held a church service, which was very impressive. The Edward's being very religious people, further helped to make this service as fine as could be. Shortly after we had arrived, Mr. Edwards had dispatched a native to get a native doctor who was a short ways away. The following day he came with what little medicine he had. However, we had more faith in our medical care; but, to humor him, we let him change our dressings. The primary medical care that we had was atabrine, from the coast-watchers' supplies and we started taking it faithfully every day.

It was decided that haircuts would improve our appearance, so the coast-watchers got the native lady that they had trained to give us all haircuts. It had been arranged before we arrived that the native girls from the village would give the coast-watcher boys a party. This meant tuba for all of them. Tuba is a white sap that they drain from coconut blossoms and is about as strong as beer. So the boys dressed up in their best suits of coveralls and started out for the party.

Sergeant Corpus, however, did not leave at the same time as the rest of the boys, and before they had gotten a half-mile away, they heard a shot; and when they returned to investigate, they found that Sergeant Corpus had shot himself. Immediately we called off the party. They managed to scrape together enough boards to make a coffin, but the wood was so scarce that they made a close fitting box. It was later revealed that Sergeant Corpus felt it was his fault that we were sunk. He felt that he should have known that Balabac Strait was mined and reported the fact to Australia.

At a later date we did get a chance to taste the 'tuba'. I wouldn't want it as my choice for a drink.

We had one scare while waiting around. One afternoon we heard an explosion that sounded like gunfire down on the beach. This brought us all to our feet and we ran to the top of the nearby hill to see if any landing boats had come into the bay. To our delight there was nothing around to cause alarm. We didn't find out what it was. It must have been some native activity. From the house we were in, we could see Japanese coastal boats sail by all day long, which was the only indication that there was still an enemy around. I amused myself during this time by reading six-year-old copies of Reader's Digest, and making cribbage boards and other things out of bamboo. I was not, however successful in making a comfortable pair of sandals that did not rub on some of the sores on my feet; so I was still bare footed. One of the days when I was tired of sitting around, I decided to go hunting wild boar with George Marquez. We borrowed a carbine from the coast-watchers, but, though we saw several boars, we were unable to hit one. They moved so fast and the underbrush was so thick. We did, however, get one bird.

The only thing of merit that I really accomplished during our stay at the Edwards' place was to fix a belt for Mr. Edwards' rice mill. Mr. Edwards was very grateful. This rice mill was driven by a diesel engine, which Mr. Edwards had managed to salvage from his previous home. The fuel for it was furnished by the Japanese through barrels of oil that had drifted up on the beach from sunken ships.

The arrangements for being picked up were made by Captain Crowley. After finding out that the District Dato had two large kumpits and an outboard motor, we sent a message to request the use of them. This would give us means of reaching any submarine that might come in.

We next had to decide where would be the best place to be picked up. We consulted some Japanese charts that had been taken from a Japanese supply boat that had run aground at the other end of the island. The charts were used by the people as paper for printing money, because there was no other paper like it here. The place we decided upon was right off where we were located. We also arranged a series of signal lights whereby the arriving submarine would know approximately where we would be. We arranged to have three large lanterns hung in a row on an abandoned radio tower down on the point. When all the arrangements were made, we were sent a message saying that USS *Redfin* would be there to meet us about 2000 the following night.

Ever since we arrived at Mr. Edwards' place, we had heard about Mr. Vans Trivo Kierson, a citizen of Finland who was a seaman, diver, and engineer. They hoped he would be back in time to leave with us. The night before we were to leave he arrived and we met him. He is one of the most interesting people I've ever met. He had just returned from visiting the native villages on the island to get enough rice to feed the guerrillas. This was a tough job, because most of the natives did not have enough rice for themselves. However, he came back with several kilos of rice and promises for enough to supply the guerrillas for the next six months. One of his approaches was to swap with the chiefs of the village's rice for some beer or whiskey that he had managed to salvage from a Japanese supply ship that had run aground on one part of the island. When the day for us to leave was finally known, we notified the non-native people in the area that we would be leaving the next day, and for them to dispose of their personal belongings in less than 12 hours. We arose early and started our walk back to Captain Mayor's at the beach. We were in much better shape by now and some of us were able to walk a good share of the distance.

On our way down to the coast we were not able to see the bay, and when we arrived at the captain's, we had a great surprise waiting for us. For the first time since the beginning of the war a Japanese *Maru* (coastal ship) had anchored off the spot where we were to be picked up. We immediately assumed that the Japanese knew we were there and were just waiting for the submarine to come in. Our spirits hit low ebb. However, we continued our plans and organized the party that was to leave with us. This party consisted of Mr. and Mrs. A.M. Sutherland, British missionaries and their two children who were six and three years old, Mr. Kierson, the Finnish engineer, George Marquez, William Wigfield, U.S. Army, Charles O. Watkins, U.S. Navy, and Henry Garretson, a U.S. citizen. This made for a total of eight *Flier* survivors and nine others for a total of seventeen people.

Chief Howell had not gone back to the Edwards' with us, but, rather stayed down on the coast to repair one of the coast-watchers' radios that was broken; he joined us at this time and reported that the transmitter radio was in working order now.

That afternoon, the captain and Jim Liddell went along the beach to investigate the Japanese coastal ship that was anchored. They decided that we wouldn't be able to show our signal lights, but we would try to go around the anchored ship and meet *Redfin*. The coast-watchers had two portable transmitter radios, one to be on the beach, and the other to go in the kumpit with us. Thus, we would be able to communicate between the beach, the kumpit and *Redfin*.

After dusk, at 2000 we began sending out our call to *Redfin*. We found out that the unit we had on the beach wouldn't work, so we started calling *Redfin* with the unit we had in the kumpit, but we did not get any reply from them. After trying for quite some time with no luck, we became discouraged because none of the plans we had made were working. We had no signal lights on the beach and after two hours of trying we were receiving no signals from the *Redfin*. We started out with the kumpit, which had the outboard motor towing the other kumpit. We went down the coast about three or four miles and made a big circle around the anchored Japanese ship. All this time we were turning the generator crank on the radio and calling the *Redfin* in every way we could, but we will had no reply.

After another hour and a half, at around 2330 we finally heard what we thought was a reply by *Redfin*. This boosted our hopes, but we could not locate them. They told us to use C.W. keying because the voice was too weak. We told *Redfin* that we would flash a light and ask them if they could see us. We did this several times, but still did not hear from them again or see them anywhere. We repeated this flashing several more times and by this time there were several people claiming that they could hear the submarine engines, but we thought this was only imagination as we couldn't see the sub. Then at 0053 we received the word to stop the flashing because they had spotted us. Soon after that we saw them!

At 0100 *Redfin* passed close and its skipper recognized Commander Crowley's voice, so they came along side of us. When somebody reached out their hand to pull me aboard, I didn't hesitate or ask permission to come aboard!

After much handshaking and other means of expression, we told the skipper of *Redfin* what we thought the guerrillas needed most, and he really gave them about everything he could spare aboard the submarine. This consisted of guns, ammunition, food, medicine, and clothing. A special item was a pair of size nine and a half shoes for Mr. Edwards. When the two kumpits left the side of the submarine they were loaded to the gunnels and the only worry was to keep them from capsizing.

As a parting gesture to the natives and coast-watchers we were to sink the Japanese ship and they could get the salvage supplies. Unfortunately we were unable to sink it.

The trip back to Australia was spent having the pharmacist's mate doctor our cuts and feed us quinine and atabrine. Tremaine started to get his attacks of malaria during the trip but the rest of us were quickly getting well. The morning of September 6, 1944 we saw the port of Darwin, Australia and then realized it was all over. We stayed in Darwin that day and night where we received some clothes from the army. The clothes were some that were to be sent to the guerrillas in the islands, so they told us to help ourselves.

The next day Admiral Christie's private plane flew up from Perth and flew us back to Perth. This was a twelve hour flight so we arrived there about 2300. Lt. Bob Hanson was the pilot and a very good one, too. We were met at the airport by the Chief of Staff and two captains. They personally drove us into town and there we split up. The captain went to the Admiral's home to stay; Jim and I had a suite of rooms in a BOQ [bachelors officer's quarters] and the rest of the men went to quarters in another part of town.

We were given two days to draw some pay, obtain a clothing allowance, purchase daily clothing and order uniforms. All of us, except the captain, were flown 300 miles inland to the town of Kalgoorlie. The admiral did not think it was a good idea for us to be around sailors who were going back out to sea.

Kalgoorlie was the gold mining town where President Herbert Hoover made his money and they were still mining gold. Jim and I stayed in the home of the mine manager. One day the manager suggested to me that I go to the mine at 0600 to witness the strength of the unions in Australia. At 0600 the union leader shouted "Are we going to work today?" A loud "no" was the response. The manager turned to me and said that his orders were to run the mine to full capacity. This same routine happened each morning for the remainder of the week. This was their annual race week with horse races every day. After ten days we were flown back to Perth. My uniforms were finished and pay records were completed. In two days I had my new orders so I was flown to the states in a China Clipper plane for a two-week vacation at home.

Chapter 28
SEPTEMBER 1944
LEFT ON THE BRIDGE
BY JOHN P. JONES

Despite his name Seaman John Paul Jones was less than a perfect lookout. His submarine, the *Bang* (SS-385), submerged while he was still on the bridge.

The year was 1944, there was a war, it was August and the sun was warm off the south coast of Oahu. Completing our exercises, we were standing by to surface. With three blasts from the klaxon, the USS *Bang* (SS-385) hesitated then came to the surface. White caps of foam skidded along on wind-whipped waves. A squall was coming out of the West. Soon darkness would fall. As I stood my lookout watch in the shears of the submarine, I could taste the sheets of salt brushing against my face. The weather continued to worsen with high winds churning the sea. This was typical of the changes in Pacific weather.

We had just finished our yard overhaul at Pearl and were operating fifty miles southeast of Oahu conducting exercises and tests. I would be relieved shortly and then I could go below. I relaxed, picturing the warmth and protection that awaited me in the crew's mess. It was near midnight and I was certain that we had secured for the night and would remain on surface until daylight.

Suddenly, with overwhelming awareness I heard a tremendous gushing and roaring of escaping air. I was thrown against the lookout support. I could hardly believe it, but the boat was diving out from under me. I looked for the other lookouts, but they were gone. I looked ahead and saw the bare outline of the bow planes rigging out. The boat had started to dip down into the waves. She started to go under, as the sea entered her tanks. Now with her bow almost under and the sea rising up, I was struck by wild panic. I dove from the platform to the deck of the bridge and I flung myself at the hatch, but it was shut tightly and dogged. I twisted and wrenched and struggled with the wheel. Finally, after what seemed forever, it started to turn, first, ever so slowly, then faster and faster until it was jammed.

As I un-dogged the hatch, the open-shut light on the, "Christmas Tree" panel in the control room fluttered from green to red. Although the hatch was still closed, the panel light indicated that it was open. As the boat dipped her bow again and started under, I could hear the vents being closed. In control they knew something had gone wrong with the dive.

As I squatted spread-eagle over the hatch I tried to use reason, but there seemed no escape from the water. Crashing and surging, coming at me from all directions the water closed in. It didn't seem to rise up, but to tower down as it would if I were in a waterfall. I was now lifted up, twisted and thrown from the bridge and along the sides of the conning tower. I was utterly helpless and as the sea closed around the submarine I was tossed up again and thrown into the roaring torrent.

Now I was only semi-conscious, striking parts of the shears, but without any sensation of doing so. Into this swirling mass I was rolled and sucked down. I tumbled end over end as the submarine passed beneath me. I was trapped and had the sensation of being near death; not knowing, not caring. Finally, I was released from the grip of the eddy. I could feel the pressures changing as I ascended. I finally broached and sucked in my first bit of air. As I started to breathe, I violently vomited large quantities of slime. The vomiting continued until my whole head seemed to give way. I was alive, barely alive. I wondered how much longer I'd be permitted to live. I was being drawn down into the trough of a swell with its great crests towering high above me.

The fifteen foot crests flattened out and I was pushed upward to the next one and then sucked down again into a great chasm. This rhythm of the sea sapped what little energy I had. My mind had started to clear. Maybe it was the pain that throbbed from within, or the quantities of blood and water in my mouth, or from the air, or just the sensation of being alive. I was a good swimmer and without fear, but here in the still of the night I was completely abandoned, and badly hurt.

Up to the crests once more and then down into the troughs. Again and again, this was repeated until I was barely aware of life at all. As consciousness filtered away I fought the battle for life. Then on the crest of an unusually long swell, I saw in the distance the bursting and boiling of the sea. Then the picture disappeared. I strained to see in the night. On the ridge of the next swell, my eyes cleared. There it was, yes there it was again. At first an image, then a dark shape, and now a ship, yes a ship, standing bold against the faint light of the moonrise, she had turned on a light and was slowly moving away.

At first, I couldn't believe this apparition. I started to cry, not from pain; not from joy; not from the ordeal; I just started to cry, and I started to pray. To whom or what, I didn't understand.

Again I was swallowed by the sea. I could only see the light while on the crests, and then only for a moment. The ship now appeared to be dead in the water with her light sweeping the sea. Another light was turned on aft of the first. I tried working my way toward the first light, but the sea resisted. It was running hard at my back and I was at least 200 yards out, but slowly, ever so slowly, I was closing. My only chance was to be spotted before the two lights gave up the search and went away. I struggled to keep my head above water. I ached all over and again I started swallowing more and more water.

I was swept down again and then upward. I was getting desperately tired, and on the next swell the lights stopped. When I saw the lights again they were still fixed in my direction. I tried to wave, but my attempts were feeble. My chest and ribs ached and in my mouth I could taste more blood. I was almost certain my foot and leg were broken, but this was of no importance. I treaded water frantically, pushing myself to the next crest, waving with both arms!

Both lights were simultaneously turned off and then on. My mind was still alert enough to register some hope. I was so desperately tired. My face, my body, my mind all were turning numb. I was still vomiting blood and water, and from the inside I could feel the final curtain starting to close. Neither my legs nor arms would respond anymore. I had given my best, but I was through, and I knew it.

My head dropped lower and lower as the sea was now full in my mouth and before I could spit it out it was in my nose. I was struggling for air, but I was getting heavier and could no longer fight the sea. An arm circled my neck and a familiar voice whispered, "Take it easy, we'll make it." I moved my head slightly and there was a man. He was a shipmate who had come to save me. In the grip of one hand he held a line and his other hand cupped my chin. It was Pearce R. Duffy, our quartermaster. It was he who had missed the bridge count when we dove. It was Duffy who now entered the cruel unknown of wind and sea to make up for his error.

With pain and struggle, I reached out, but Duffy easily pushed my arm away. He held my head above the sea and I started to throw up more and more, but between heaves, I sucked in small amounts of air. I was partially blinded by the ship's lights, but I could easily recognize her, for she now lay dead in the water. The *Bang* looked, as always, sinister, yet awesome, bold and beautiful.

A crewman on the after deck took up the slack in the life line. The sea now swept in and pounded us against the sub's hull again and again. This continued until I could feel my ribs cave in, and blood started to spread over Duffy's face. I was completely beaten and I knew the next wave would be my last. As the sea came roaring in, I put my hand on Duffy's head and pushed him under; using his head as a platform I raised up as far as I could and at the top of my surge, a crewman grabbed my arm and hauled me aboard. I was hustled below, but before I started down the ladder, I looked aft and saw Duffy being pulled aboard.

Shortly after being taken aboard and lowered below into the crew's mess *Bang* changed course to the northwest. Within an hour we broke out of the storm and the sea started to settle. I was carried into the torpedo room where I was near collapse, for I felt nothing but pain. I knew that I was badly busted, as my entire body trembled.

My clothes were cut away and I was handed a cup of brandy. I shook my head, no. I was trembling so badly that I couldn't even hold it. I tried again, this time it went halfway and then the blood came up. I dropped my head in despair and stared at the crimson mess. I was given a shot, patched up and slowly but painfully rolled over. I drifted into a world of half sleep.

Later, an ambulance was waiting on the pier when we slipped into Pearl. I was drained of all strength and had to be carried off. In the hospital, I was on the emergency table for over two hours. My chest was probed and the bleeding brought under control. My foot and ankle were both broken and placed in casts. My chest and shoulders taped and my head and face were bandaged. After two transfusions, I was put to bed.

My bed in the ward overlooked the submarine piers. One morning before the eastern light fully illuminated the sky, I rolled over and looked toward the piers and there was old *Bang* softly straining against her lines.

Even at this distance she looked as she was, a queen, long and majestic, yet awesome and deadly. The boat was ready for sea, ready to get underway.

As the streaks of first light rose slowly from the east my submarine started her diesels and with veils of gray smoke covering her afterdeck, her brow was pulled over. She slowly backed and eased gently astern into the channel. Bringing her bow about, she moved quietly ahead and within a few minutes she made her turn toward the sea and was gone.

In mid-September, a coded transmission was received by ComSubPac, Pearl regarding her ETA [estimated time of arrival] Midway. The message contained a request for SubDiv 42. It read, "Transfer Jones, John P., Torpedoman Third Class to SubDiv 201, Midway, for further assignment to USS *Bang* (SS-385).

Chapter 29

SEPTEMBER 1944

DYING FOR THE EMPEROR ON PALAU

BY NORMAN R. DIREY

> Norm DiRey was in the conning tower when *Tunny* (SS-282) chased the juiciest of prizes: a Japanese battleship. Torpedoes were fired, and an explosion was heard, but did that mean that *Tunny* had sunk the battleship?

During the Second World War, Palau was a major Japanese naval base, captured by the U.S. in 1944. In preparation for the attack, Admiral Nimitz decided in that summer that a softening-up air strike on Palau was needed. The usual flotilla of carriers and supporting ships were assembled and sent to carry out the strike. Before the carriers left Pearl Harbor the submarine, *Tunny* (SS-282) was dispatched to patrol outside the harbor.

The Japanese command intelligence was excellent. They quickly learned that an air strike was in the making and knew that their ships in the harbor of Babelthuap would be at risk. *Tunny*'s job was to patrol outside the harbor and intercept any ships that would be flushed out when the strike took place.

I was a chief radioman on board as we headed for Palau. We had a scare while running on the surface to our destination. Since our skipper, Cdr. Scott was anxious to reach our designated station well before the strike. We made maximum speed by remaining on the surface even though we ran the risk of being spotted by Japanese aircraft. We must have been out about a week, and actually in range of enemy patrol aircraft, when the radar operator reported a blip on the SD radar. We dove promptly, but no bombs were dropped. However, the captain was perplexed and suspected a malfunctioning radar. He called me to the conning tower and read the riot act. "I want you to test every resistor and capacitor in that radar," he insisted. Since I was the radio-radar-sonar technician, as well as radio operator, I had to act. I climbed down into the control room and commenced my inspection. I knew that the SD was functioning properly, but in response to the captain's order, I had to do something. I wiggled the tubes in their sockets of the receiver and checked every component in the transmitter. I then reported to the officer of the deck that the testing was completed and that all was in order.

We surfaced and I turned on the SD as soon as the antenna was out of the water. Watching the radar screen, I was startled to note the tiny aberrations in the sweep, indicating an approaching aircraft. I reported this to the bridge and we submerged immediately. We could not have been down more than fifty feet when we felt a close-aboard bomb explosion. It had hit just about where our fantail had been moments before. Needless to say, the captain retired to his stateroom and nothing more was said about the testing. We remained submerged until dusk then continued toward our patrol station. When we arrived on station we set up our patrol schedule. Two days later SubPac notified us that the carriers were to be on station in another two days.

I suppose the Japanese patrol aircraft had detected the approach of the carriers as one afternoon the conning officer, while making a periscope sweep, detected several small Japanese ships leaving the harbor. The captain was not interested in these, nor even the large oil tanker that came out of the harbor that mid-afternoon.

Finally, when the sun was setting and we surfaced, the lookouts detected a very large ship steaming at high speed in our general direction. The captain submerged the boat, made a periscope sweep then exclaimed to the engineering officer in a surprised tone, "My God, it looks like a battleship."

I detected the steady beat of the battleship's screws while standing my sonar watch next to the captain in the conning tower. Making a full periscope sweep, the captain noted that there was one destroyer accompanying the larger ship. Due to the high speed of the target and our slow speed submerged, the captain was having trouble getting a satisfactory setup. He finally seemed satisfied and ordered the outer doors forward opened and gave the order to fire. We all waited with high expectation for about a minute, then the assistant approach officer said, "You made one hit, captain."

Cdr. Scott was perfectly happy to have such a report, even though he may have had reservations about the probability of a hit. I was on the sound gear, and I heard no explosion indicating a hit. However, I didn't contradict the officer. The next day the American carriers launched their planes. The Japanese installations were damaged, small ships sunk, and many aircraft were shot down. In a day or so the transport ships would bring the landing force and the invasion would be on in earnest.

A few days later I was in the conning tower with a mustang lieutenant. I told him about the officer telling the captain that he had made a hit on the battleship, but that I had not detected anything on sonar. The mustang officer, quite a salty old sea-dog, said, "If the captain said that he was going down to his cabin and soak his head, he'd say, 'Me too.'" I chuckled and the issue was forgotten.

Our mission now was to remain submerged and be available to rescue any downed pilots. We stayed at periscope depth and the captain and watch conning officer made periscope searches during the action. Shortly before darkness we surfaced to charge batteries. It was only a few minutes later that a lookout reported a Japanese fighter plane being shot down, the pilot ejected and parachuted down, landing in the water about four or five miles from our position. Tunny was only about six miles from the beach. In an attempt to rescue the pilot, we cruised for about an hour, then lowered the bow planes and had a man, with a line attached, jump down on the port bow plane and attempt to haul in the pilot who now showed signs of extreme exhaustion. He turned his head and swam away when attempts were made to cast him a line. Finally the captain said, "Let the bastard go." I had to wonder about that guy. He would never make shore. Tunny was his only hope for survival, but he refused our hospitality. The mustang lieutenant read my mind and said, "The poor slob wants to die for his emperor."

Chapter 30

SEPTEMBER 1944

PICKING UP THE LEFT-OVERS OFF PALAUIG POINT

BY R.C. GILLETTE

R. Gillette was on *Lapon* (SS-260) when she was depth charged. Going deep she escaped the enemy's attack and upon coming to periscope depth found herself in the midst of a Japanese convoy.

The USS *Lapon* (SS-260) left Fremantle, Australia on its sixth war patrol under command of Lieutenant Commander Donald G. Baer, USN. I was the executive officer and navigator on this, my sixth *Lapon* patrol. I had put the boat in commission starting my submarine career as its most junior officer. Our course was set for the South China Sea and a patrol station off the West Coast of Luzon, not far from Manila.

Lapon proceeded north, passed through Lombok Strait on the surface at night and at full power, avoiding four patrol craft. She passed Mindoro and on 19 September 1944, arrived in her patrol area off the West Coast of Luzon, not far from Manila. The scene was now set for the Battle of Palauig Point.

After having charged batteries, *Lapon* submerged at 0500 on 21 September 1944 about eight miles off the coast of Luzon, close to Palauig Reef, and then headed slowly towards the beach. The diving point had been carefully selected to enable us to intercept any traffic from Manila rounding Palauig Point proceeding up or down the coast, either inside or outside the reef

Customers arrived early, starting at 0520 when the JP passive sonar picked up screws to the North. We determined later the range to be an amazing 16,000 yards; in excess of design standards for the JP. Later, as the sun came up, through the periscope we saw smoke to the North, and we immediately headed for the target. It was a large, modern, single ship, smoking heavily. It turned out to be a hospital ship, properly marked. We broke off the attack and returned to our patrol plan. This was the third hospital ship we had encountered during our patrols. All of them were heavy smokers. Two of the encounters had resulted in fruitless aborted attacks, which wasted a great deal of time and fuel—this appeared to be a good ploy by the Japanese.

At mid-day our return to Palauig Reef was interrupted by four single engine unidentified, fighter planes flying at about 1,000 feet. We leaped to attention on their sighting, as their presence suggested an aircraft carrier nearby. They were likely American and events confirmed the surprise location of several carriers. At about 1300 the periscope watch again reported smoke bearing 126 degrees true. We changed course to 090 degrees headed toward and called away the tracking party. An hour later we could make out two sets of masts and more smoke. We went to battle stations and increased speed to close the target track. The masts were small and heavy smoke was seen to the right of the masts. We decided that there was an advanced patrolling ASW search group followed by the main body of the convoy and that we were almost dead ahead of the main body.

It had to be a large convoy. At 1430 a series of explosions, similar to depth charges, were heard, but we couldn't believe that we had been sighted. We rigged for depth charge and continued towards the targets. Lapon then went to a shallower periscope depth and took a good look. What a sight! The sky was covered with antiaircraft bursts. Splashes surrounded the ships we were closing. The convoy was scattering in all directions. We watched seven dive-bombers attacking our target ships in the convoy's main body. We reasoned that our carriers were probably located east of Luzon. The planes had flown over the huge island and struck our convoy. Ships were being pounded all around us. Every time we closed in on a damaged target some aviator would sink it. With mixed emotions we watched the carnage. On one hand we wanted to sink some ships of our own, on the other it was satisfying to see the enemy being destroyed by our fellow countrymen.

The aviators left us with three damaged ships, all of good size. We should be able to get to them before dark. At about 1535 more explosions occurred. A look through the periscope revealed once again, massive anti-aircraft fire and many more dive-bombers. The second wave came down almost vertically and pulled out at masthead level. One of our prospective targets blew up close aboard. Another ship nearby was hit and exploded, shaking the *Lapon* violently. A destroyer was putting up rapid AA fire forward and aft. As fast as we selected a new target and headed in, it blew up in our faces.

Another destroyer target was hit by a bomb resulting in a sheet of yellow flames and the loudest explosion yet, again shaking *Lapon* and its crew. From the conning tower we could hear members of the crew in the after battery compartment cheering. It must have been his depth charges had blown sky high and rattled our boat.

He was still afloat and we hoped to close the damaged destroyer, sink her as well as the one standing by to rescue survivors. As we watched the destroyer standing by we noted that he began jettisoning his depth charges as the dive-bombers continued their attack. Try as we might we were coming in a dollar short. It was getting dark and the dive bombers were going after the last destroyer. We had been running submerged all day and needed to charge batteries. As a result, we decided to pull clear, surface, charge up the battery a bit, and have at the last damaged destroyer and escort on the surface at night. However, at about 1700, as we started to open out, four undamaged destroyers and an escort vessel appeared. They were all radar equipped and headed our way with bones in their teeth. We hoped to clear them and then settle down to a good night's destruction of damaged ships. It was not to be.

A close depth charge was heard. We went deep under a gradient and went to silent running again. Part of the formation passed right over us. We were at the center of a wheel of five ASW ships all pinging. We now attempted to crawl away under a temperature gradient and get behind the formation. At about 2030 all seemed clear so commenced easing up through the gradient. As we passed 125 feet on our way up through the gradient, pinging started and two sets of screws could be heard through the hull closing fast. One came from the starboard bow and one from the port quarter. One passed overhead, running fore and aft, but didn't drop as we could hear the Pearly Gates swinging quietly in the background, so we went back to 300 feet under the gradient and took stock of our situation. The boat was very hot and damp, and about a dozen of the crew were suffering headaches and nausea. We had been down over seventeen hours, mostly at silent running. The air was getting pretty foul so we put out some CO_2 absorbent to clean the air.

We lit the smoking lamp for five minutes to ease the crew's stress, but matches wouldn't light. At 2200 all was quiet, no pinging, so we again started up. At 200 feet the sonar operator could hear heavy rain, so we surfaced at 2300 in a blinding rainstorm with visibility zero.

We headed west on four main engines, lined up for a battery charge, aired the boat out and worked on the radar which had experienced a small fire while we were submerged. Our chances in this rain and zero visibility were as good as anybody else's. I set the section watch and told the radar technician to call me when he thought we could fight using radar to get range and bearings to targets. I wanted to be there looking at the PPI [plan position indicator] screen if we were to make an approach in solid rain.

At about midnight the radar was ready to light off. As the screen lit up we found ourselves in the middle of about twelve ships. We went back to battle stations and started an approach on one of the larger targets. Radar now showed three very large targets and at least three escorts. It was raining heavily with zero visibility so we turned away to let the rain squall pass and await better visibility while sorting out the targets. We were going to have to get in real close in order to pick up the targets on the bridge using the Target Bearing Transmitter. We closed to 2,000 yards, but still could not see the targets. We then circled around, hoping for better visibility. No luck, so we decided to fire on radar bearings. Slowing to two third speed, we commenced firing six bow tubes at 1,800 yards using radar firing bearings. The range, as the sixth torpedo went out, was 1,550 yards on 90-degree starboard track 0-degree torpedo gyro angle. It was a perfect set-up. At 0400 I was on the bridge and reported two hits on a large ship and possible third hit on an overlapping target. Suddenly the entire target area lit up from the flames of the exploding ship, which was a large tanker.

We commenced swinging right at full power to bring the stern tubes onto a target of opportunity. The range was now down to 900 yards, but the light from the tanker fire was blinding us. Although we knew one remaining target was out there, we couldn't pursue and attack.

So it was that we got a large tanker, our only score. But we had the satisfaction of seeing an entire convoy wiped out by a combination of our airmen and submariners. The following sinkings and damage were observed by periscope during the Battle of Palauig Point.

1. One destroyer (large) last seen with decks awash up to bridge and bow protruding from water at about 40 degrees.

2. One large transport hit by bombs and commenced burning at about 1430. The ship exploded at about 1545 and threw white smoke and debris about 400 feet in the air.

3. One large transport blew up at 1537 and smoke ceased almost immediately.

4. One large ship hit and straddled by many bombs. It continued to send up a large column of black smoke. Fire could be seen until 2313 finally disappearing about 2345.

5. One ship hit and straddled by bombs; last seen with dense black smoke rising.

Add to that our tanker and it turned out to be a pretty good day.

Chapter 31
OCTOBER 1944
A TOTAL LOSS

BY FARRELL STEARNS, with narrative augmentation by Bureau of Ships War Damage Report Number 58 entitled, "War Damage Report of the USS *Salmon* (SS-182)"

> Farrel Stearns wrote a report on the incredible near-destruction of the USS *Salmon* (SS-182), the most heavily damaged submarine of the World War II to survive a depth charge attack.

We put to sea on September 24, 1944 from Pearl Harbor in company with *Sterlet* (SS-392) and *Trigger* (SS237). It was *Salmon*'s eleventh patrol.

The submarines headed for waters around *Ryukyu*. The transit was normal for that stage of the war, but the Wolf-pack ran into a tanker with four destroyer escorts. While *Sterlet* fired the torpedo that eventually sank the tanker, one destroyer escort picked up *Salmon* and came after us. I was on board the night of the attack. The guys called me Red because of my red hair and I was only a seaman, but in the hours that ensued, every man was vital to the survival of our boat.

On the evening of October 30, 1944 we were in company with *Trigger* (SS-237). She attacked a Japanese tanker which was being protected by four destroyer escorts. We were on the surface and I watched the action from my high lookout perch. Our captain was Lcdr. Harley K. Nauman who pressed our own attack in spite of a squealing shaft which later hindered our chances of evading the destroyer escort. It was night and at first the Japanese couldn't find us, but a broaching torpedo gave us away. All the Japs had to do was follow the wake. And that's exactly what they did. They came after us at flank speed. The diving alarm sounded and the captain yelled to clear the bridge. I was an additional lookout and jumped down into the conning tower and then down the ladder into the control room. Seaman Adams who had been manning the .50 caliber machine gun came down right after me. I made my way to the stern room as the boat went to 310 feet at standard speed. We took two sets of depth charges, one of which struck very close above the engine rooms. A total of thirty depth charges were dropped. The Jap must have dumped his entire inventory on us.

William P. Gattis was a first class cook in the galley. He told me that he felt as though some giant had hit *Salmon* with a hammer. Cork dust was everywhere, choking the lungs. Bolts holding oxygen tanks in the overhead shook loose and the tanks were rolling around the deck of the crew's mess. He looked up at the main induction indicator. It was holding, but Gattis didn't know how it could stay shut under such a pounding.

The boat shook so violently that the captain in the conning tower bent his knees to absorb the shock. Damage within the boat was severe. Mechanical failures occurred in every compartment. Topside must have been a shambles. The flexural vibrations caused by the explosions put stresses on poor old *Salmon* that the designers never contemplated. There was extensive flooding in most compartments. As the pump room flooded,

Auxiliaryman Burton Block stayed in the cramped space, furiously turning valves to pump the sea water aft through the trim and drain system. Fear of producing an oil slick prevented pumping the bilges to sea. The boat remained with a thirty degree down angle and heavy forward, heavy overall condition in spite of our best efforts. The guys on the bow and stern planes shifted to hand operation, but there was little that could be done. The diving officer did his best to correct the loss of depth control, but he was stymied by the enormity of the damage.

I ran into the after torpedo room. Torpedomen Ragel, Page and Beaumont yelled for me to help them. They were trying to free the bent shaft to the stern planes. We put our backs into it, but nothing could be done. Torpedo tube impulse air had all leaked out and the after outer torpedo tube doors were jammed shut.

Those in control managed to stop most of the forward flooding, but back aft we were in bad shape. As flooding continued in our space the boat became heavy aft and heavy overall. The external main engine induction piping had collapsed from the beating and that weight was added to that of the three flooded deck access hatch trunks. The hatches to each of these trunks had been secured but the explosions had bounced them open despite their dogs. Profuse sea water leaking at various points along the pressure hull, and the displacement of about 7,000 gallons of fuel oil in FBT [forward ballast tank] number seven with heavier sea water through the ruptured vent riser of that tank added to our heavy aft condition. It was nightmare, but most of the damage was invisible to us at that time.

The stern planes had jammed at ten degrees dive. This had been caused by the separation of the planes from the warped tilting shaft. I was a member of the damage control party in the after torpedo room who fought to repair the damage to the planes. No amount of our sweat was able to unjam the planes.

We could see the structural deformation, particularly in the area of the forward and after engine rooms. It looked like an enormous sledge hammer had bashed in our pressure hull. It was a miracle the pressure hull held its integrity. Our excessive depth must have helped to cave in the pressure hull, back aft where we were. We all expected those moments to be our last.

The boat maintained its submerged power in spite of a few cells having been ruptured. Stephens was the senior electrician controllerman handling the sticks in maneuvering, answering bells as the boat struggled to stop the downward plunge. Ship's lighting failed, but the emergency lighting system took over.

The most serious leakage into the hull was that which occurred in both engine rooms through the fuel ballast tank riser inboard vent lines. Their hull stop valves were torn from the hull as their holding studs parted. The engine room bilges were rapidly flooding. Chief engineman Mollator was in the forward engine room and attempted to pump the bilges to sea. We had long since abandoned any idea of trying to hide. If oil was to surface then so be it. By this time the boat was in imminent danger of collapse from excessive depth. He was not successful since the trim and drain system was rendered useless by cork debris which fouled the strainers.

The diving officer asked for a full bell and was able to gain a 20 degree up angle on the boat despite the jammed stern planes. It was only accomplished by the heavy aft trim condition kept the stern down and the bow up. Strangely enough, the dive aspect of the stern planes helped to support the heavy aft end of the ship. The boat's twenty degree up angle was only maintained with a continuous full bell. The diving officer tried to slow to a two thirds bell. This caused *Salmon* to resume its downward plunge where it finally reached a depth of 578 feet, still holding the twenty degree up angle. The after torpedo room at this point was below 600 feet, well over twice the test depth of the submarine.

The captain ordered all main ballast tanks blown in spite of the escorts still being overhead. The air banks were nearly emptied because the high pressure air piping had been blown at more than one point. The boat surfaced at about 2030 in the evening. It was a half-moon night, but the escorts failed to detect us. The deck was awash and Salmon had a fifteen degree list. The ten pound blow was not operable. Men manned the deck guns in spite of their optics having been destroyed. Adams got back on the .50 caliber. A destroyer escort at 7,000 yards illuminated *Salmon* while, in the engine rooms, Mollator and the other enginemen fought frantically to get engines on propulsion. Only the number three main engine responded and *Salmon* turned away from the escort.

By 2050 both number three and four engines were on line, but the Japanese were now firing their three-inch guns at us. Fortunately, they were poor shots. The escort stayed at about 5,000 yards, continuing its ineffective shelling while the men in the forward engine room used a chain fall to open the engine air exhaust valve. At 2115 the number two engine was started. Number one engine had its Roots scavenging air blower drive damaged so that engine could not be started. Heading away at sixteen knots on three engines, with the list corrected and air in the ballast tanks producing a reasonable freeboard, *Salmon* headed for a rain squall. At 2130 she radioed *Silversides*, *Trigger* and *Sterlet* of her condition by using a jury rig antenna. In the conning tower John Stallings tried to get the periscopes back into operation, but the damage was too severe.

The escort then steamed ahead and attempted to prevent *Salmon* from getting into the squall. The captain changed course and headed directly at the Japanese. The two ships passed close aboard with all *Salmon* guns firing. The Japanese crew was raked by .50 caliber fire and the submarine's deck gun. The escort retreated and *Salmon* sneaked under the protection of the rain. Later it was joined by her sister submarines which gave it a safe haven to Saipan.

When tied up to the pier I looked at my old boat. The after part of the deck and superstructure had been torn away. The piping was a tangle of steel. I listened to the inspectors. They concluded that the mild steel used at the time of the boat's construction may have acted to save *Salmon*. The mildly tempered steel had compressed and yielded between frames up to two inches. The worst dishing occurred between the main ballast tanks above the engine rooms between frames ninety-five and one hundred seventy. Pressure hull frames within the same area were in some cases tilted or buckled. No frames tore free from the hull plating. Damage to the hull caused flaking and dusting of internal cork insulation which interfered with machinery close to the hull as well as extensive failure of lines and valves at hull openings.

After temporary repairs were made on Saipan, *Salmon* sailed via Eniwetok and Pearl Harbor to San Francisco. At Hunters Point [shipyard] we received more repairs after which we made our way through the Panama Canal to Portsmouth Navy Yard. It was determined that her hull and equipment had suffered so much damage that repair was impossible. We were all sad at the demise of our boat which had held together under the worst pounding of the war.

There were many medals earned for heroism as we said good-by to our ship. I and nearly every other man were assigned to the new fleet-type boat, the USS *Stickleback*.

Salmon was awarded the Presidential Unit Citation for extraordinary heroism against enemy surface vessels during her eleventh war patrol in restricted, enemy-held waters of the Pacific. She was assigned as a training vessel for the Atlantic Fleet, then was decommissioned on 24 September, 1946 and scrapped on 4 April, 1947.

Chapter 32

NOVEMBER 1944

THE SAPE STRAIT SHOOTING INCIDENT OF NOVEMBER, 1944

BY H.E. MILLER

> Ed Miller wrote of trying to catch Japanese cruisers that went by so fast there was no time to take aim. Finally, *Besugo* (SS-321) sank one of the ships. It was a bittersweet victory, because a strange event blemished *Besugo's* reputation.

The Japanese light cruiser *Isuzu* and her screen of escorts churned the waters of Sape Strait as they *zig-zagged* to avoid submarines. I commanded USS *Besugo* (SS-321), the center boat in a three-boat wolf pack as this small task group came toward us, heading east. They lucked out, going exactly halfway between the adjacent boat to the south and us. Neither submarine got close enough to shoot.

We pursued the Japanese ships, but were unable to get close enough to the cruiser to inflict any damage. We did sink an escort destroyer, but couldn't claim it. The rules were that a submarine had to identify the ship and see it sink. Real confirmation could also be achieved by taking a Japanese survivor as prisoner. Accordingly, Admiral Fife ordered all the boats to pick up a survivor from each ship sunk.

We went back to the south end of Sape Strait to wait for any traffic going north. The other two boats guarded the north end to catch any that got by us. There was a large deep bay at the south end of Sape; a nice, straight channel about two miles wide. There was a lighthouse above us on the big island to the west, so we took up a periscope search, raising the scope every fifteen minutes. We were surprised to spot the same cruiser, steaming north, back through the strait. She came up doing twenty-two knots right for us. She was moving so fast we had to make a ninety-degree turn to shoot up her tail. We didn't get her, but one of the boats at the north end hit her. She went behind the island and anchored to make repairs. The next day she came out and was sunk by the third boat in our group. That took care of the cruiser. The staff at Fremantle was pleased that the Japanese captain had been rescued, but he committed hari-kari as soon as he was ashore.

Back in *Besugo* we waited to see if any more of the Jap warships had survived. In the afternoon, a big minelayer, converted to anti-sub duty, steamed by at fourteen knots. She was an easy target. We got two hits, both into her bow, but she didn't sink. She broke in two at the bridge, the bow section sinking immediately, but the main part of the ship stood dead in the water, down just a little by the bow.

We had one torpedo left in the after room. It had a flooded gyro. Our torpedomen worked frantically to overhaul it before what was left of the minelayer got away. We remained submerged and watched her. Men swarmed over the after portion of the deck, but we couldn't make out what was going on. They had a machine gun set up on their port quarter and every time they saw our periscope they fired at it. After a short while, no one appeared topside anymore.

After two hours the torpedo was ready. Then came the problem of getting our stern pointed at the target at the right range with the full beam of the target to shoot at. We didn't trust the gyro and so wanted a straight shot with no gyro angle. Finally, at dusk, everything lined up. We let the torpedo go, set to run on the surface. It hit the forward part of the engine room. She up-ended and sank quickly. With her stern in the air it was quite evident why she hadn't maneuvered out of there. There was no rudder or screw. One of our torpedoes had blown them off without doing much damage topside other than breaking the bolts on the depth charge racks causing all of the depth charges to roll off the stern.

Admiral Fife's order to pick up a prisoner came to mind. She was the last ship so we surfaced to pick one up. I gave the gun crews orders not to shoot unless fired upon. There was a nice American-style raft, with empty oil drum floats under it.

Of the two army officers on the float, one wore the best tailor made summer-weight wool uniform, while the other was dressed in the standard Jap cotton summer uniform, freshly laundered and perfectly pressed. They hadn't even gotten their feet wet. In the water all around them were about 75 soldiers, each with a pink water wing sticking out under each arm. There were no sailors. We tried to figure this unusual situation out. The army commander on board must have retaliated against the ship's crew for getting them into their present predicament. It seemed strange to us, but there was no other explanation. Our theory was corroborated by the appearance of the two officers in the raft. They looked like they were capable of such an outrage. Also, we thought of their abandon-ship scenario. The engineering spaces appeared to have been undamaged. Personnel aft of the bridge and many on the stern, who hadn't sustained broken bones in the torpedoing, had had three hours to prepare for abandoning ship. There should have been twenty to thirty sailors in the water, but there was none. The army field machine gun, manned by soldiers, disappeared from the after deck after the first hour.

From the bridge, I watched the Japanese soldiers in the water and the two officers on the raft.

Several of our men were out on deck following my directions. The chief of the boat, with a heaving line, and my executive officer, Don Kable, with a Jap language booklet in his rear pocket, went out on the bow to get a survivor. He looked into his book and shouted, "Hands up" in Japanese. All the men in the water faced us and raised one hand. The two officers on the raft belligerently turned their backs to us. The one in the fancy uniform shouted out an order, and all the men in the water turned away. Don shouted again and they all stopped, faced us and raised one hand. The Jap officer gave them another order which made them swim away from *Besugo*. When the Jap officers had contradicted Don's order four times, all the swimmers were farther away than the raft, so I yelled to Don that we'd try to get one officer off the raft as I maneuvered *Besugo* up to it.

The starboard lookout called my attention to a thick red book barely afloat near the starboard bow. It looked like a codebook. Just then, firing from small arms broke out among the men in the water. I told the gun crews to find and silence the shooter. I looked up at the bow and told Don to go into the water and retrieve the code book. Just then I saw blood squirt from both ears of the officer in the fancy uniform. The men on *Besugo*'s deck shrugged their shoulders. The chief had thrown a heaving line right over the shoulder of this officer, but he had reached up ceremoniously and threw it aside. He must have committed suicide right after that. Meanwhile, Don was preparing to go over the side to get the code book. He did everything left-handed because he had lost half of his right hand in the Jap attack on Pearl Harbor.

The other Japanese officer had gotten down into the water on our side of the raft facing us as though he was willing to be rescued. Before I got him to stop, Don got off a shot. It landed in the water a couple feet short of the man in the water.

The chief tied the heaving line around the waste of the executive officer as he went into the water to retrieve the red book. Before he could get to it, the propeller wash from our backing down to stop at the raft, hit the book and sank it.

The lookout spotted a Jap plane ten miles north of us, flying east to west. I yelled for Don to get back aboard. The plane was obviously searching the channel for survivors. We got Don back aboard as quickly as possible and dove. He had picked up a red bordered chart; it was a chart of the sightings of U.S. Submarines for October 1944. It was dusk and getting dark.

During the first two days on our way to Fremantle we received messages of congratulations from seven layers of command, including General MacArthur, but for what we weren't quite sure.

When we got to Fremantle things had changed. Adm. Fife had moved to Subic, leaving Chief of Staff Captain Brown in charge of the base.

Sugi, our mascot dog, did his usual round of the deck and then sat beside me as I waited for some visitors that were scheduled to come aboard. Instead of the usual group of intelligence people, Captain Brown came alone. He was obviously in a bad mood and Sugi bit him in the leg. Captain Brown was not amused. He said, "You load up and get out of here and don't come back until you have taken the shooting out of your patrol report." I was speechless, because we hadn't shot anyone and there was no mention in our patrol report of any shooting.

The few days we were there, my name was mud with the staff people. The Japs had started a month-long propaganda campaign about us shooting the ship's crew in the water, which, of course, we hadn't. They had the body of the army commander who was really responsible for the missing crew members as though that were some sort of proof.

Later, after our next patrol had ended, we headed into Subic Bay, rather than Fremantle, Australia. After the standard group interrogation, Admiral Fife took me aside and said, "If you want to shoot Japs in the water, do it on my responsibility, not yours." It was useless to explain what had happened. The Japanese version of events was more convincing than ours.

That was not the end of it, except that when our medal recommendation got to the awards board they absolutely refused to award a medal to *Besugo* because of the Jap propaganda about shooting survivors in the water. We just chalked it up to the vagaries of war.

Chapter 33

DECEMBER 1944

FROM THE PERSPECTIVE OF AN AVIATOR

BY C.B. SMITH, US ARMY AIR CORPS

Charlie Smith, a B-29 Superfortress flight engineer, described his rescue by USS *Spearfish* (SS-190) and how he learned to love the boat and its crew.

Early on the morning of Dec. 18, 1944, our B-29 crew, along with several other crews in the 500th Bomb Group, 73rd Bomb Wing were called to a briefing on the bombing targets in Nagoya, Japan. This would be our first mission to Japan and the first time with such a heavy load of gasoline, bombs, oil and ammunition. We were scarcely airborne by the time we reached the end of Saipan's 9,000-foot runway.

After eight hours in the air and covering 1,500 miles, we arrived over the target area and began our bomb run at 31,000 feet. Black puffs of anti-aircraft fire began to break around us, shortly followed by fighters. Fortunately, speed enabled us to outrun the fighters and prevent their making a second pass, although several crews were lost in that brief period over the target.

I was the engineer and upon leaving the coastline, I asked the pilot to reduce the power setting in accordance with our reduced weight in order to achieve maximum fuel efficiency. Shortly thereafter, it was discovered that our number three propeller governor had been hit and could not be reduced. Other troubles soon developed and our pilot got on the VHF [radio] and told our story to another B-29 in the squadron. We threw out everything loose that might act as a battering ram, and secured our emergency kits to our flight suits. I was very apprehensive and it seemed quite appropriate that maybe this would be a good time to pray. I did, promising that I would be a better person.

I was the first one out when the plane hit the water. Soon other heads popped up. We released the life rafts and began picking up the other crewmembers. We wound up with three men on our raft and four on the other one. We lashed the rafts together and prepared for the night. It was soon dark and I never spent such a cold, wet night in my life. I never before got so close to another man to keep warm enough to survive.

At dawn the wind and sea became a bit calmer. The sun came out and we began to dry out and get a bit warmer. We could see the island of Kota Iwo, and the current was bringing us closer to it. The Japs had a 2,000 man radar and radio group stationed there. In the afternoon we saw a plane in the distance and fired a parachute flare. This was the B-29 sent to search for us, and when they spotted the flare, they turned and came directly towards us. They dropped a parachute message, "Dolly Folly will be here at 1700." We speculated as to what this message meant, and as 1700 came and went we didn't know what to think.

At dusk we heard a rumbling noise and looked into the sky for the answer. Debating whether to fire another flare for fear of attracting Japanese, we decided to go ahead and risk it. A few minutes later we saw a ship bearing down on us at high speed. Never having seen a submarine at sea before, we at first thought it was a small Japanese warship, so those of us who had a .45 [pistol] put a shell in the chamber. It was so near dark that we couldn't make out its nationality until one of the sailors on deck called out, "Can you handle a line?"

The USS *Spearfish* (SS-190) crew quickly hustled the seven of us aboard and immediately submerged. We wondered why such a rush until later it was explained that radar indicated that planes from Iwo Jima were expected momentarily.

The injured among us were immediately taken care of by the corpsman. Many stitches were required to close the many wounds. Fortunately for me, I had only a small cut on my index finger. Shortly after being brought on board, we were offered some sort of medicinal whiskey. The executive officer offered me a large tumbler of whiskey. I was flustered. My high school and college coaches never allowed drinking, so I said, "Sir, I don't drink." With that, this worldly old officer said, "Don't want this to go to waste." He drank the whole tumbler in one swig.

We were given some underwear and various kinds of clothing by kind and generous crewmembers. Commander Cole, Spearfish's captain, gave me a couple sets of navy shorts and I was assigned a temporary place to sleep. Mine was a top bunk behind the crew's mess where I slept like a log. Evidently the sub had been on the surface charging batteries through the night. Then, I heard this loud klaxon sound like the horn on a Model T Ford. Not realizing where I was, I raised up suddenly, whacking my head on a steel beam. The crew evidently figured I wasn't smart enough to sleep in a top bunk, so they moved me to the bench in the wardroom. A disadvantage here was that I had to wait until everyone cleared out of the wardroom before I could turn in. But an advantage was that I got to be a good friend of the steward.

He asked me, "Lieutenant Smith, would you like some peaches before going to bed?" Assuming he had some left over from the evening meal, I nodded my head. I watched him in the pantry as he opened a gallon can of peaches. He then topped the dish with ice cream and sat it before me.

I gained fifteen pounds before leaving *Spearfish*. Our Saipan food kept us alive, but it was mostly Australian mutton. Instead of returning to Saipan we headed north toward Japan. Captain Cole had his orders to complete a war patrol and that's what he would do in spite of the extra passengers. Realizing that it would be difficult to keep the airmen bottled up inside the submarine for any length of time, the captain offered us the opportunity to stand lookout watches while the boat was on the surface. I took advantage of this offer and marveled at the excellent navy binoculars.

A day or so later we ran into bad weather. Trying to find optimum speed and course through this storm was difficult. The heavy sea flooded the main induction and drenched the galley. Eventually Captain Cole found the elusive speed and heading where water intake was tolerable. It was one wild ride, particularly for those of us on the bridge.

Battle stations sounded a few days later when the lookouts spotted a small boat, thought to be a Japanese supply boat. The decision was to destroy it by gunfire and take the Japs aboard as prisoners. When the boat surfaced the gun action crew pumped 40mm shells into the small vessel and it went down rather quickly. A Japanese sailor swam to the submarine and was lifted aboard. He seemed genuinely happy to be in an American submarine rather than the sure death of swimming in the Pacific Ocean.

I visited him in the after torpedo room. He kept himself amused by laying out his yen on the deck plates and slowly counting them in English. I thought that the man must be a pragmatist; taking the opportunity to improve his limited English. I asked him what he did for a living when not being a sailor. He replied that he was from Kagoshima and had been a truck driver. He seemed respectful and not the least put out that his fortunes were at such a low ebb.

We proceeded toward our destination, Tokyo Bay. Cruising on the surface at night we were occasionally forced to dive due to radar contacts or radar interference, indicating that another radar was in operation somewhere in our vicinity.

Christmas day we celebrated just sixty miles from Tokyo. We took the day off and the cooks really outdid themselves in preparing our Christmas dinner. We had turkey, strawberry shortcake and all the rest. Following Christmas dinner we had a movie, "Tarzan in New York." It wasn't much of a movie, but it was a little bit of home and for that reason I watched it in rapture.

Captain Cole informed us that he had received orders to take us to Saipan on the boat's return trip to Pearl Harbor. When we tied up alongside the pier I was sad to say good-bye to crew members I had made as friends. Captain Cole shook our hands as we left the boat.

We were interviewed by the 73rd Bomb Wing Commander, as we were the first crew ever to be picked up by a submarine. Later we were flown to Hickam Air Field where we were accommodated in a temporary billet. I found out that *Spearfish* would be arriving in a few days. I hiked over to the submarine base and met the *Spearfish* as she arrived in Pearl in late January. As close as I was to the members of my flight crew I never forgot the men of the *Spearfish*. Those submariners were special and whenever I heard that the boat was in Pearl I made sure I was on the dock to meet her.

Chapter 34

DECEMBER 1944

A SUBMARINE HOME

BY MYRON ALEXANDER

> Myron Alexander was aboard S-47 when it took out a few VIP guests on a day cruise. On the demonstration dive, depth control was lost and it took some convincing acting by the crew to maintain the illusion that all was well when hull rivets were popping around them.

About mid-morning of December 12, 1944, a shore boat pulled alongside the submarine tender, USS *Pelias*. Next to her were three submarines. After reporting to the squadron office, I walked across the brows of the two inboard boats and onto the deck of my new home, the US S-47. I stepped onto the deck with a minimum of ceremony. She looked her age, old, tired, and small, but I was easily the happiest ensign in the Navy.

The gangway watch, a Motor Machinist Mate 2/C, welcomed me aboard, helped with my luggage, and called down to the executive officer who took my orders, noting that I had been expected. At lunch, I met the commanding officer. He was also new aboard, having just been given his first command. His former assignments included a number of war patrols as executive officer aboard the USS *Tautog* (SS-199), an older fleet-type submarine. Our executive officer was a reservist lieutenant, who was a peacetime high school history teacher. He would prove to be my mentor aboard the S-47, and a lifetime friend. I was assigned duties as first lieutenant and commissary officer.

It's obvious what the commissary officer did. Actually, on the S-47 I just stayed out of the way and let the number one cook and the yeoman administer the food department. Our meals were never better. We all ate from the same mess, officers in the wardroom in the forward battery compartment, and the crew in the after battery compartment.

The first lieutenant was the shipboard officer responsible for the maintenance, operation, and record keeping of all electrical and mechanical equipment not located in the engine rooms. My small group of skilled men took care of our air compressors, periscopes, winches, anchor, mooring equipment, rudders, diving planes, trim pumps, etc. This was a great job for me and I worked hard to learn all the gear and men in charge. The icebox and air conditioning equipment were high priority items.

The 47 boat was alongside the tender, on her port side. She had just returned from her last patrol, a special mission that had landed and retrieved a small group of Australian commandos. They landed on an unspecified island in the Borneo area, seeking information about a radar/radio installation. They learned that it had been closed down and the enemy technicians moved elsewhere. We provisioned, fueled, and watered from the USS *Pelias* and had the tender perform some minor repairs and a few alterations. I had to learn the ship from stem to stern and from keel to periscope top. I spent all my time with the senior ratings, torpedo men, motor machinists, sonar ratings, radiomen, quartermasters, signalmen, cooks, electricians, etc. For the most part, they were pleased and anxious to tell me about their role in the operation of the submarine. It didn't matter whether they liked me or not. I was now a family member and they fully understood my need to know everything. We all had to know everything. We had to count on each other to know our own jobs and our neighbor's too. It was a great feeling for me and I worked like a tiger. The executive officer, and the chief-of-the-boat, (our senior enlisted man), made sure I learned correctly. They watched me like a hawk. I had to measure up or it would be back to the relief crew.

In order for me to qualify as a true submarine officer and to earn the right to wear the gold dolphin insignia on my uniform, I had to jump over a number of hurdles. I needed to know every man's job I had to make a diagram of each air, water, hydraulic, drain and flood, mechanical and electrical system in the boat. This was the "Officer's Notebook," and must be submitted to the commanding officer for his approval. I needed to be able to stop and start the main engines and motors. I had to be a whiz about charging our two main batteries. I should be familiar with the handling, loading, and firing of our Mark-10 torpedoes. I had to be able to take charge of the three-inch deck gun during a surface action exercise.

I would gain proficiency at mooring, maneuvering, getting underway, and coming alongside. All officers took a turn at these exercises, which were the most fun of all. The intense learning took place alongside my performing regular officer of the deck (OD) duties. My background, experience, and training on surface ships made OD watches easy.

On my third or fourth day aboard, we received our first assignment to train with a destroyer (DD) and two destroyer escorts (DE) for the day. In this exercise we would assume the role of an enemy submarine. Our surface ships were to locate and destroy us. For their attack, they would toss a hand grenade over the side to simulate a depth charge and we could tell with our sound gear just how close to us they were. We could communicate with them using Morse code on our sonar while we also towed a buoy for safety. We always enjoyed these exercises and were able, more often than not, to escape safely from their attack. We were very good at maneuvering the submarine.

On this first occasion, almost the last dive for all of us, the captain had invited several young officers from the Torpedo Boat Squadron, stationed at Mios Woendi, to accompany us on the daylong exercise. We had been alongside the tender for some days, and weights within the submarine had changed significantly. Food and fuel came aboard, torpedoes were sent over to the tender torpedo shop for testing and charging. One of the officers had the job to calculate and compensate the boat for all these weight changes. Seawater would be flooded or pumped from the trim tanks at either end of the boat, plus a big tank in the middle of the S-47. These were our variable ballast or trim tanks and were used during every dive to maintain a neutral buoyancy condition. The chief-of-the-boat followed the compensation instructions in flooding and pumping the various tanks to the calculated values. Soon, in the middle of a beautiful morning, we were ready and backed away from the tender.

Along with our escort, we headed for the designated practice area, I would guess some 15-20 miles south of Mios Woendi. On station, we rigged the buoy and prepared to dive. The captain ordered a running dive rather than a standing dive, indicating complete confidence in the trim calculations. As the klaxon horn sounded two blasts, and the OD shouted, "Dive, Dive" it became immediately apparent to the executive officer and chief-of-the-boat that something was terribly wrong. The S-47 was heading for the bottom of the Pacific Ocean like a fire engine horse heading for a blaze. Our PT-boat officers and I had no previous experience with S-boat diving characteristics, so we were fascinated and comfortable in our ignorance. Not so with the chief and the exec. The exec immediately took over the dive. Orders and actions in the control room came at a frenzied pace. "Surface, Surface, Surface!" screamed the exec, as he sounded the alarm three times. "Blow main ballast, blow safety, blow negative, hard rise on bow planes, hard rise on stern planes, all back emergency," all came in rapid succession.

The orders and the instant reactions were fast and exact. All eyes were on the exec. The chief pushed me away from the air manifold and quickly opened the high-pressure air blow valves to all our main ballast tanks. Suddenly, I realized the severity of the situation. We had a large, down angle on the boat and she was sinking like a rock. We passed ninety feet (our normal operating depth) like a runaway train going down a steep hill; hundred feet, 125 feet, one hundred and fifty feet, 175 feet (test depth), two hundred feet.

Almost imperceptibly, our descent slowed. We poured air into our bow buoyancy tank; we opened our 2,000 psi air valves to the main ballast tanks, all the way. We engaged the trim pump to pump from the amidships trim tank to sea. Main propulsion motors were backing emergency as the dive slowed and the bow began to rise. We prayed silently.

The torpedo boat officers continued to show great interest, thinking we did this all the time, or that we were putting on a show just for them. When the dive started, the captain knew we were experiencing a problem, as he manned the periscope, his normal position on a dive. It "dunked" almost before we could close the hatch and report, "green board, pressure in the boat." Our old girl, built just a little too late for World War I, shuddered and slowly, ever so slowly, began to rise. The depth gauges told the story. She shot up, some 200 feet. Our executive officer and chief-of-the-boat saved the submarine and all our lives by being cool and taking the correct action with not a second to spare. The bridge hatch was opened, and we all drew a deep breath.

The PT officers were white-faced when they learned how close we came to visiting the bottom of the Pacific forever. We pumped much ballast over the side and made a slow, standing dive with negative tank and safety tank flooded. We obtained a good trim fore and aft with overall neutral buoyancy. Our exercises proceeded normally. The first dive of the day was never logged. I don't think anyone on the tender ever formally knew what had occurred that day.

Chapter 35

DECEMBER 1944

MY FIRST WAR PATROL

BY JOSEPH CORNEAU

> Joe Corneau described the sights, smells and sounds of his first war patrol. The famous *Flasher* (SS-249) was commanded by Commander George Grider and Joe watched as the captain sank ship after ship.

The evening meal is over. The garbage will be bagged, weighted down and inspected by the disposal officer before being thrown overboard. *Flasher* (SS-249) is deep in enemy waters and when it submerges again at dawn, no trace of its passage must be left. The crew's mess now becomes an entertainment center and library. The cribbage boards come out; letters get written and old ones re-read. Photos of loved ones are held so that the light may somehow bring them to life. The record player in the ward room is piped in to the crew's mess tonight, and as on many previous nights it will play, "Mexically Rose, Chattanooga Choo Choo, and the Wabash Cannonball." The month is December, and out there in the real world, Christmas is coming.

It is approaching midnight and the midnight to 0400 watch is getting ready to relieve the 2000 to midnight watch. We are on the surface and a few young seamen are on their way to the bridge to stand lookout watches. The smell of freshly baked bread and coffee helps the on-going watch to wake up before going to their various stations in different compartments of the ship. A few pleasantries, are exchanged when the off-coming watch standers come into the mess. And again the mess tables fill up; this time with tired and tense looking men. Some are very young and look exhausted, some are older, also tired looking, but pensive and preoccupied. Here's the chief auxiliaryman; he's the oldest person on the boat. He must be at least thirty-eight or thirty-nine, even older than the "Old Man," our captain, Cdr. George Grider, who is rumored to be thirty-six.

One by one the off-coming watch standers go to their respective sleeping quarters, some to the crew's quarters, some to the forward torpedo room, some to the after torpedo room. Soon there are only one or two men in the mess, reading, or maybe thinking of loved ones. It's quiet; deep in the night and men are left to their thoughts.

A new smell overtakes the after battery compartment. The baker, having completed baking the necessary loaves of bread for our new day, is now baking cinnamon rolls. Pretty soon the smell will be carried throughout the boat via air conditioning ducts just in time for the next change of watch.

Those men on the 0400 to 0800 watch will complete the battery charge and make preparations for diving the ship at first light of the new day. We are off the Indo China coast, looking for a convoy that has eluded us. The water is not very deep, but if we want to spot enemy shipping we must take the chance. It's our skipper's first command. He's a brave man, well trained, and a real patriot. During a discussion between several of the older crew members I heard one of them say that the old man was really gung-ho, but one of the other sailors reminded him that the old man was married to a beautiful woman and had two beautiful daughters, so he wouldn't do anything too crazy. He said the exec is the one you have to worry about. He's single and he really hates the Japs. He won't be afraid to put pressure on the old man to get in and sink ships.

The diving alarm goes off. I can hear the thumping of men jumping down into the control room to man the bow and stern planes. All the people on watch have a job to perform, and diving the boat is an orderly procedure. For a few seconds nothing seems to happen, but soon I feel the boat taking a down angle. The engines have stopped; all is very quiet except for a short blast of high-pressure air being released inside the boat. A voice in the control room reports, "Green board, pressure in the boat." Our depth is fifty-eight feet, speed one third, course 000. For the next fourteen hours, unless enemy aircraft, shipping, or patrol craft are sighted, we will cruise north and south at slow speed, five miles up and back looking for the convoy.

I hope we find them, not because I'm a real fighter, but because the sooner we send our torpedoes into enemy ships the sooner we'll get back to Australia. Suddenly, the General Quarters alarm goes off and a voice on the ship's 1MC calls out, "Now, battle stations torpedo, battle stations torpedo." The convoy has been sighted. The skipper maneuvers to intercept as I get up to the forward torpedo room. Soon we are in firing position, and six torpedoes are launched from the forward tubes, with four more from the after tubes. No sooner had the last torpedo left the tube, when the captain's voice comes over the 1MC, "Rig for silent running. Rig for depth charge."

Four loud explosions are heard, and the faces of my torpedomen buddies light up. Four of our torpedoes have hit their target. Soon four more explosions are heard. These are the torpedoes from the after torpedo room. I too am pleased. There's a lot of back slapping and muffled laughter. I'm a novice, but I know we've done something pretty special. And it all seems so simple.

Soon the smiles on the veterans disappear and apprehension appears. We are at "silent running." Then, loud and fast running propellers can be heard nearby through the hull, approaching rapidly. I look at the torpedomen around me for a signal that would lend comfort and hope, but I can find none. And then it comes; the "click" that old timers talk about. In about five seconds the depth charge goes off. It's like my head's in a bell and the clapper is pounding. It's a sharp, nasty bang that bounces us like we're a toy. Some light bulbs are broken, deck plates bounce, loose gear falls to the deck, and soon another goes off, even louder than the first. The noise is incredible. I want to look at the faces of men who have experienced this before hoping to be reassured by some sign or by eye contact where I could find some comfort, but what I see is fear, and even terror, in the faces of men whom I thought of as being brave and fearless.

Again the propeller noise comes, a little faster this time, and heavier, and a string of four charges go off closer and louder than the first two. And again they come louder, closer. It's six this time, and then again. Why do my skin and bones hurt? I'm not hit, so why the pain? The propeller noises go away and for a minute or so all is quiet. Then I hear a whole series of explosions in the distance. They are a rumbling and the boat rocks, but not violently. One of the old timers says in a soft voice, "Enemy ships exploding." He must have read the question in my eyes. He says, "We are okay now, unless the old man decides to go back in."

"No, he wouldn't do that," I think. "He has a beautiful wife and —." Before I can finish the thought, the order comes to reload the torpedo tubes. We're going back in. It seems to be just a few minutes ago we were under silent running, now we have ten men moving torpedoes with chain falls that can be heard in the next county. The job is completed quickly, only because the torpedomen are led by experienced men who have trained us well and often. Fear is a great motivator and under it all we are scared. Hard work takes my mind off what might lie ahead.

Now the word comes. "Torpedoes forward, conn. What is the status on the reload?"

I answer, "Conn, forward torpedo room. Reload is complete."

"Make all tubes ready for firing," orders corm.

"Tubes forward ready for firing," I answer.

It's the quartermaster's voice. He transmits the captain's order over the sound powered phones, "Very well, forward room. Stand by."

The same conversation is taking place with the after room, and a few moments later the ship's 1MC announcing system blares. "This is your captain. We are going back to the convoy to finish the job. Stay sharp and alert."

Now we can feel the up angle. We are heading toward periscope depth. Soon we'll be turning toward the convoy and the battle will begin again.

Most of these guys have gone through previous depth charge attacks.

I wonder if it's possible to get used to such things. I don't think so. But they were still here. I can't shake the thoughts. What about the guys who didn't make it back? How did they spend their last hours, their last moments? Did they die in a flooded compartment, gasping for air? Did their bodies get crushed by high pressure? Did they get blown to bits when the ship exploded? A chief once told me that when the hull goes there's nothing left inside. A person is smashed into tiny fragments and shoved into corners. It takes a pair of tweezers to pull out the stuff. I force my mind away from the morbid picture. The faces of the other torpedomen seem relaxed and I hope that mine doesn't tell of my dread. There is little conversation; only a few whispers. Is that why they call it the "Silent Service?"

The voice on the sound powered phones brings me back to reality.

"Stand by number one," says conn. "Fire one," comes the order.

"One fired electrically," I reply as the room rumbles with the release of compressed air and the torpedo leaving the tube. The stand-by light on the torpedo-ready panel is switched to green for tube number two. Again, the order, again the rumble, and again my report to conn. The scenario is played four more times until all six tubes have been fired.

By this time the temperature is very high in the compartment and so is the humidity. There seems to be a fog, and the air pressure is high from venting the tubes after each shot. Our voices and other familiar sounds seem to be distorted. I hear the slosh of water in our WRT [water round torpedo] tank below me. I think I can smell gunpowder. How can that be, I ask myself. How can I smell gunpowder? Am I cracking up?

The chief looks at his stopwatch and he is joined in the count by another sailor, "Thirty-eight, thirty-nine, forty, forty-one, forty-two." He is counting the seconds since the last torpedo was launched. He says, "All six torpedoes are running hot, straight, and normal. The escorts must have spotted the torpedoes and dodged them." Then I hear, Boom! . . . Bang! . . . Boom! Three hits. Must be the after room's torpedoes.

"Those Japs must be awfully angry up there," I say to myself. "And they'll be coming after us."

I can feel the angle on the boat now. We are going down deep, and going fast, and the order comes, "Rig for silent running. Rig for depth charge." I hold onto the port torpedo skid. The angle increases.

I look around the torpedo room and see scared men, tired, and sweating covered with cosmoline [rust preventative] we paint onto torpedoes to protect them from moisture and dirt. I look at my arms and they are black with the sticky stuff. It smells bad. Loud explosions can be heard all around us; enemy ships blowing up. But nobody smiles because we know that soon we'll pay the price.

Sure enough, I hear screw noises through the hull. They get louder. They are above us, and the click goes off, and now the charge itself. I tighten my grip on the skid. The boat is thrown sideways and I slam into the skid. Pain in my ribs is ignored as I spread my legs, waiting for the next explosions. More screws are coming, with no clicks this time, just another enormous bang, and another, and another, and on it goes. I'm hanging on with both hands. Dust is everywhere, cork and paint chips float down from the overhead. Now the sound of more propellers, this time I feel the noise rather than hear it. Then more depth charges, more explosions, and then suddenly a tremendous jolt. I know my grip on the torpedo skid is not enough. It's in slow motion. There's no sound, like a silent movie. The lights go out, and everything becomes quiet. I feel no pain. I look up and see the most brilliant, beautiful light. Inside the light I see human figures and they are singing, and calling my name.

Now I feel someone holding my head, and a voice says, "You're okay, kid. You got knocked off your feet and bumped your head. Stay still and I'll patch you up." It's the pharmacist's mate. I recognize his voice. I fall back to sleep.

I awaken and feel the boat rolling. Flasher is on the surface. The air is fresh. The man on watch looks at me and smiles.

"That's quite a bump you have," he says.

I look around and realize that I'm in my bunk in the after torpedo room. I feel my head. It doesn't hurt that much. I wonder how I got here and how long I've been unconscious. I can't ask, for fear that someone will say that I'm cracking up. But something happened during that depth charge attack that I can't explain, and I'm scared and puzzled. George, the veteran torpedoman on watch looks at me and says in a reassuring voice, "You'll be okay, kid. This is your first depth charge, isn't it?" Yes, I nod.

"Too bad your first one had to be such a bad one, but then the next one will probably be much easier on you," reassures George who goes back to reading from the stack of letters he keeps in an old shoebox. I get up, a little groggy, and slowly make my way through maneuvering, through the engine rooms with their thundering engines, and into the crew's head space where I look in the mirror. My face is streaked with grit and under it I am pale, like a snow-man pelted with coal dust. Then I go into crew's mess, hoping to get the answer to what had happened to me when I saw the bright lights and heard voices calling my name. I pour a cup of coffee and sit next to an auxiliaryman. He looks at me and asks, "How do you feel?"

"Good," I answer. "But, I'm curious. What happened to me there?"

"You slipped on the wet deck plates and knocked your head on the loading skid," he says. "You were out cold for a spell. I'm glad you're okay."

Pretty soon I'm alone at the mess tables, drinking coffee and trying to reconstruct the events that took place during that depth charge attack, when a thought occurs to me. This is a submarine and I'm a submariner. I can't go around asking questions about what happened to me. I take a last sip of coffee as the cook tells me he's got to set up for the noon meal. He smiles cheerfully and says, "Sure feels good to be heading back to the barn." I realize that I have endured my first war patrol.

Chapter 36

JANUARY 1945

BUCKET BRIGADE

BY HANK, "NATE" HENDERSON

> Electrician Hank Henderson told of *Pompon's* near demise following a severe depth charging. It took all hands to get the boat back under control.

Pompon was a great boat and I was always glad to be a crew member. I was regarded as sort of a plank owner since I had made all her patrols during the Second World War. I knew each man in the crew as if he were my brother. We had a couple of skippers and were lucky to have good, aggressive and quick-witted officers.

We had the secret SJ radar and after picking up the boat in New

Orleans we headed from the Panama Canal Zone directly to Brisbane, Australia. The transit was very difficult with stormy seas. The 20mm gun had its splinter shield wrapped around the barrel. The captain took every opportunity to train the crew. He knew that the war would not allow him to spend much time with drills. His assessment of the situation was correct, for upon arrival in Brisbane the boat headed north to the Truk area where we were nearly sunk by a Japanese submarine.

In 1944 we went back to San Francisco for refit and then headed back to sea. It was great to walk the streets of San Francisco, but it was also good to get back to sea. We left Pearl on December 13, 1944 and headed for our new operating area in Japanese home waters. In the area of Majuro, Marshall Islands we picked up a Hawaiian fisherman who had been adrift at sea for 42 days. He was in bad shape and it felt good to help a victim of the war.

On January 27th, 1945 we picked up a convoy and attempted to attack, but was forced down by an escort. We evaded the escort and his depth charges caused us no harm. That night *Pompon* went ahead full on the surface in an end-around attempt on the convoy. When in position far ahead of the Japanese ships, our skipper, Lcdr. Stephen H. Gimber dove the boat. It was to be the first trim dive of the day. No one noticed, but the dogs on the bridge hatch had been inadvertently turned slightly inward.

As sea water gushed over the bridge the conning tower hatch was fouled by the partially closed dogs. When the quartermaster spun the dogging wheel, without looking up, he only exaggerated the problem. The dogs spun further into the shut position while the hatch was cracked open. Water poured into the conning tower, and into the control room and from there into the pump room. The flooding was immediate and severe. At that point the boat had a huge negative buoyancy and plummeted downward out of control. Since the flooding was at the approximate center of longitudinal gravity it took only a small down angle as the shallow depth gauge needle swung passed one hundred feet.

The captain, executive officer, helmsman, quartermaster and pharmacist's mate, all of whom had been in the conning tower, jumped into the control room amid the water fall engulfing them. I had just entered control from the after battery when I saw a cascade of water hit the stern planesman. Not knowing the severity of the situation, I laughed out loud. It would be my last laugh for a long time as water continued to pour into control. Doc. Gray, the pharmacist's mate, came plummeting down into control as though going over Niagara Falls in a barrel. He was the last man out of conn and managed to get the lower hatch shut and dogged. Those in the forward and after battery compartments quickly shut the watertight doors. Sea water in a submarine's battery produced chlorine gas which could spell death to the boat.

The control room was chaotic. Water had completely flooded the pump room and I, in the control room had water up to my waist.

The captain quickly assessed the situation and reasoned that *Pompon*'s only chance for survival lay on the surface. We would have to take the chance of being spotted by the Japanese. He ordered all main ballast tanks to be blown as *Pompon* passed 200 feet on her way down. Sloshing through waist deep water, the auxiliaryman grabbed the air manifold handle, fitted it to the main ballast tank blow valve and opened wide the stop valve. *Pompon* was so heavy her downward moment came off sluggishly. At last she started to rise, still nearly horizontal. She broke the surface and rolled heavily in a moderate sea. Her center of gravity was so high that her righting moment was close to zero. Additionally, even with ballast tanks empty she had very little freeboard.

The free surface effect of the water in control meant that as *Pompon* rolled over to one side, the water in the compartment followed the roll. On a roll to starboard both the auxiliaryman and I were up to our necks in water. My laugh of only minutes before rang in my ears like the voice of the grim reaper.

We were in real trouble since most of the electrically driven pumping equipment was shorted from sea water incursion. The trim and drain system was submerged and its pump was useless. The bow and stern planes could not be manned. Water had put out of commission all the communication equipment in the radio shack except a high VFH [radio] set that escaped the flooding.

The captain began giving orders to restore *Pompon*'s buoyancy. The hatch to the after battery compartment was opened to decrease the water level in control. It poured into that compartment and into the lower spaces of the cool box and refrigerator. The galley, crew's mess and crew's berthing spaces were under several inches of water. Men drug a mattress onto the hatch leading to the after battery well and sat on it.

The ballast tank blow had expended the high pressure air banks and the air compressor motors had been flooded. She had a ten degree list and continued her slow and heavy roll. The captain could feel the boat's instability. He and every man in the crew felt that we were hanging on by the skin of our teeth.

Chief electrician Richard "Buster" Crab had been in maneuvering on the dive. He was summoned to control to see what could be done with all the electrical equipment damaged by sea water. The first thing to do was to get rid of the water within the pressure hull. With nearly all pumping equipment out of commission, the men formed a bucket brigade. The immediate chore would be to evacuate the after battery compartment. The line extended from the compartment's lower flats, up the after battery hatch by means of ropes, then over the side. There were four men stationed on the deck, topside to hoist the buckets. Two men hoisted and two men tossed the water overboard.

As the water level decreased the bucket line was extended into control and finally into the pump room. It took a day of constant work. I was one of the bucket handlers in line. We used every bucket in the boat. It was tedious and constant and we all prayed that the Japanese wouldn't spot us in our plight.

When the pump room had been cleared of sufficient water, the conning tower was drained into the pump room and water continued to be lifted, passed and dumped overboard. It was slow and backbreaking, but there was no alternative. Throughout the day the men worked below decks as lookouts, who had come onto the bridge from the after battery hatch, kept their eyes on the horizon.

At last the lower conning tower hatch was opened and the captain took stock of damage to the TDC, sonar, radar and helm. He then inspected the hatch to the bridge and it came as no surprise to find the hatch dogs in the shut position and the hatch partially open. He swung the hatch fully open and went out onto the bridge to greet his lookouts. They were smiling.

I stayed in control where I helped Chief Crab in the enormous task ahead of us. Essentially, each electric motor had to be opened up and drenched with fresh water to flush out the sea water. Then we had to blow down each part to remove any trace of water. Some of the equipment refused to work, so we had to bake electrical parts in the cook's oven to rid the parts of water. Electricians and auxiliarymen dried out the number two low pressure blower motor. This gave the boat some freeboard and corrected the list.

The master gyro was opened up and the men took turns damping water out of the compass with engine room toweling. They then blew out the remaining visible water and crossed their fingers. The gyro lit off and at first, seemed to be operational. Chief Crab shook hands with the quartermaster. Things were looking up. The biggest problem was high pressure air. It had been exhausted on the surfacing. The auxiliarymen and torpedomen transferred air from the torpedoes and torpedo air banks into the high pressure air banks. They would have enough for one more surface if we had to dive.

The electricians and enginemen cross connected the lube oil pump in the forward engine room with the trim and drain system. They were then able to rid the pump room and food storage spaces of the last sea water.

Electrician John Davison told Chief Crab that his mother had once mistakenly dumped a whole salt shaker into a stew. She threw a handful of raw potatoes into the stew and the potatoes drew off the salt by osmosis. They tried it. Into the cook's largest pot went numerous electric motor parts. They filled the pot with fresh water from the scullery and dumped in some potatoes. After a few hours they gave their parts a stir and waited another few hours. Then they rinsed the parts and blew them down with reduced twenty-two pound service air and put the parts in the cook's warming oven. Davison's mother had been right. Megger tests on the parts showed infinity.

As the electricians, torpedomen, auxiliarymen, enginemen and cooks all worked together to get *Pompon* in order below decks, the captain attempted to navigate the boat out of danger. The convoy which had looked so juicy the day before now came over the horizon together with escorts. But *Pompon* was toothless. The air in the torpedo banks had been used up. We were in no condition to do battle. We dove to a 100 feet and stayed there until the convoy had enough time to go by. We used up the last of the air banks in surfacing.

Our lookouts reported a submarine running on the surface. *Pompon* attempted to signal the boat with flares, but it disappeared over the horizon.

Since *Pompon* was without long range radio communication the decision was made to head directly for Midway. She sighted *Pogy* (SS-266) and communicated with her via flashing light. When *Pogy* understood Pompon's problem she got permission from ComSubPac to escort Pompon back to Midway on the surface.

Pompon pulled into Midway still with a healthy port list. The low pressure blower had again refused to work. The captain's report included the following: January 27, 1945—Dived for trim. Bridge tower hatch jammed open. Got back on surface with pump room completely full—a mess.

Learned new expression: *FUBAR* fouled up beyond all recognition.

Chapter 37

FEBRUARY 1945

THREE SUBMARINES IN THREE DAYS

BY HUGHSTON F. LOWDER

> H. Lowder tells the story of how *Batfish* (SS-310) managed to sink three Japanese submarines in three days, a feat that stands as a record to this day.

USS *Batfish* (SS-310), commanded by Cdr. John K. Fyfe, hit first and hardest when in February, 1945 operating in Luzon Straits on her sixth war patrol she encountered three of the enemy's five remaining submarines then operating in Philippine waters. Although under torpedo and bomb attack from both Japanese and American aircraft, *Batfish*, in a deadly three day underwater battle, relentlessly tracked down the enemy and in three separate, brilliantly executed attacks, launched her torpedoes with devastating speed and skill and demolished the Imperial Japanese Navy submarines RO-55, RO-112, and RO-113.

The official communication of the time used that phraseology, but, in fact, that's just what happened. Three submarines in three days was a pretty decent score. When the third enemy submarine went down on February

13, *Batfish* turned in a record that was equaled by no other submarine in history.

It started when we arrived on station on 6 February. Three days later at 2250, a radar contact was made at 11,000 yards. Captain Fyfe started tracking. In a few minutes our electronic counter-measuring equipment began to register strong signals on the Japanese air search radar frequency. Fyfe directed a surface approach using only radar bearings and ranges. At 2331, range 1,850 yards he fired four torpedoes at the target. All four missed.

The moonless night was unusually dark, and the target had not been sighted. Suddenly, the radar contact ceased. Fyfe instinctively guessed the target to be a submarine. Soon the radar contact reappeared. The Japanese submarine had again surfaced. The captain left the bridge and came into the conning tower to converse with the attack plot officer and me about the quality of information we had generating in the TDC. The plot officer said, "We had her speed wrong, captain." He pointed to the plot. "She's doing fourteen knots, not twelve." The captain nodded and I entered the correct target speed in the TDC.

We now pulled out to 5,000 yards off her track and began a high-speed end-around while making a bow reload. Still confident that our target was a submarine, we wanted to close to visual range for the next attack. The crew was beginning to react to our stalking one of the subs we'd been sent to kill. A tingle of excited anticipation was in the air, already taut from the miss on our first go around. At midnight we had closed to 1,500 yards and could see our target vaguely. At 1,020 yards she was clearly visible from the bridge. Her silhouette differed drastically from any of our own submarines. It was too dark to tell whether she was an I-boat or an R-boat, which differed primarily in size, but she was Japanese for sure. Binoculars in hand, Fyfe pressed the bridge intercom button. And said, "Japanese submarine in sight. Prepare to fire."

The word came down and went throughout the boat. Sweating, forward torpedomen silently awaited the final firing data to send their three Mark 18s on their way. Fyfe called down a swift stream of observations to me on the TDC and to the plotters. Then he yelled, "Clear the bridge." The lookouts scrambled below, leaving their night vision behind. Alone on the bridge, his eyes intent upon the enemy silhouette and transfixed on the TBT's crosshairs, he concentrated on the approach. We, in the conning tower, were confident we had a correct solution.

We closed to 900 yards without spooking her; we were indeed beautifully in position. On she came, in blissful ignorance, at fourteen knots. "Ready to fire, captain," the exec relayed to Fyfe. For another tense moment he trained the binoculars on the submarine in case she made a last-minute move.

"Final bearing and shoot," he called down. He pressed the TBT button to send the final bearing into my position keeper section of the TDC.

"Conn, bridge. Fire when ready," came the captain's voice over the 7MC. I checked the solution. All looked good. On the angle solver section of the TDC a light flashed that the bearing, speed and depth information had been transmitted to the forward tubes. I said, "Set." The assistant TDC operator on the angle solver said, "Shoot." The quartermaster pushed the red firing button. We expected the report to come from the forward room that the electric torpedo had left the tube.

"Hot run in the tube!" called a frantic voice over the sound powered phones. "Number one failed to fire!" The telephone talker in conn repeated the report in a loud voice so the captain on the bridge could hear.

Number one was stuck in its open flooded tube with its arming vane spinning. If *Batfish* traveled 350 yards with the torpedo in this position, it could arm itself, the vane aligning the detonator with the charge. Then the torpedo would explode on contact, but could also detonate at the instant of arming. We all froze. Confidence turned to apprehension in two seconds.

"Fire it again, manually!" Fyfe bellowed down to the phone talker. He didn't wait for number one to clear. Lose our setup, and we'd likely lose our target.

"Fire number two," he yelled. "Fire two," the exec repeated up the bridge hatch. Number two kicked out. If the target saw us and turned to attack, we'd have some problems evading with a "hot run" in the tube and the outer doors open. And we sure must have been in sight, should they have bothered to look.

Forward torpedomen wrestled to blast free the lodged torpedo with torpedo impulse air.

"Fire three," Fyfe roared. The solution still looked good. I nodded and the quartermaster hit the firing button after having switched the firing order panel to number three tube. Number three sprang from its tube with a jolt twelve seconds after number two.

"Three away," repeated the conn telephone talker.

Fyfe was torn between staring at the target and preoccupation with our jammed number one torpedo. The assistant attack officer was intent on his stopwatch, accounting for the two fish on their way. Sweating, holding his breath, he was waiting for an explosion.

"Number one fired manually," the talker shouted. But we had felt it before he yelled. That torpedo probably ran erratically, but at least it was clear of us.

"Helm, left full rudder, come left to two seven zero," Fyfe ordered. The course change would take us away from the target. As we began our swing, the blackness burst with flame; a column rocketing skyward at least a thousand feet.

Shock waves pummeled *Batfish* and the conning tower rolled. Those on the bridge saw flames sweeping out from the base of the explosion, for an instant silhouetting the stricken submarine. Her screws stopped. APR, our electronic counter measure equipment, reception ceased abruptly. I watched the radar PPI screen as the pip fragmented into smaller pips, each one extinguishing in quick succession.

The executive officer popped up to the bridge in a hurry to see if there was anything left to see. I and the others in conn relaxed and congratulated each other on making a good approach. It was all over so quickly. Several of the crew passed us in the conning tower as they asked the captain for permission to come on the bridge. Fyfe granted most of them, and smiles and handshakes made the rounds throughout the boat.

Coming down the hatch, Fyfe asked me, "How many hits did you count?"

"Just one hell of a big one," I responded. He grinned without looking up. "Number two from the sound of it must have blown her out of the water. Number three tracked dead on, but must have passed under or maybe through her. Number one unaccounted for," I added.

Within an hour after dawn, six plane contacts were made by radar. They were arriving to inspect the area. We were driven right back under by a single patrol plane, coming in low from the east. Despite heavy overcast, it was growing fairly light. Since the planes seemed determined to keep us under, we rolled with the punches and took a break in the concealing depths.

At 0947 *Batfish* was again patrolling at periscope depth. It was still too crowded upstairs for us to satisfy our wanting to search for survivors and souvenirs. The periscope spotted a group of five US Navy planes coming up from the mainland at a distance of four miles. A Black Cat torpedo bomber flew in low to investigate the oil slick. The other four fighter escorts kept their distance, some genuine US Navy planes for a change.

"High-speed propeller noise. Bearing zero nine zero," said the sonar operator. "Sounds like a torpedo, I could hear it splash!"

Fyfe roared, "Flood negative, take us deep."

At ninety feet the propeller spun passed directly overhead, then faded rapidly.

"Two hundred feet," Fyfe ordered. *Batfish* remained submerged for the remaining daylight hours. When we surfaced at 1054, the planes had fled, probably to find someone else to annoy. We dove to avoid a Japanese early bird and spent the day on submerged periscope patrol. At dusk, we resurfaced and shortly contacted two planes sporting radar at twelve miles. They disappeared without forcing us to dive. Little more than a half-hour later, APR reported radar interference at 158 megacycles. Weak at first, the signal increased steadily. Batfish swung in order to find its null and determine the source's approximate bearing. Cautiously keyed, our SJ radar probed the pitch-black void until we had a definite fix on the next suspected Japanese submarine. At 8,000 yards we found her bearing; she was on a 170 beeline for Luzon.

We went to battle stations and began tracking. This night was as dark as the last. We would make a surface attack if developments permitted it. Assuming radar capabilities equivalent to last night's target, we would attempt to close for visual identification before firing. Throughout the boat the clanging battle station alarm roused members of the off duty watch sections and sent them scurrying to their stations. Again, I was on the TDC and my shipmates were around me in the conning tower. "Battle stations manned in conn," reported the telephone talker.

"Another Jap sub. Maybe just like the other one," said the exec. Tense, muted comments circulated throughout the boat. We were no longer shiny-eyed battle virgins. Ahead was an enemy ship, by now as impersonal as the morning star. But always before, our prey and victims had been surface vessels, a different species. We now deliberately stalked to kill another submarine. We'd had a night and a day to think about that. This was different from anything we had ever done before in all our killing and we felt it, though no one had the words together. The exec joined the captain on the bridge. Black sea and black sky were quiet. Water hissed along Batfish's tank tops.

"Range, six thousand," reported radar.

"All ahead flank," Fyfe called back down to helm.

"Got the feeling we've done this before," I mused.

In the long minutes of silence in the red light of the conning tower I could feel the throb of the diesels and the roll of the boat. On the bridge, all eyes probed the blackness, straining for first sight. The lookouts knew all the steps to maintain the keenest night vision. A low-profile submarine could be seen if the Japanese lookouts were looking as hard as we were. We believed we had the edge; our swift approach assured it. From the shears, the forward lookout called, "Jap sub dead ahead."

Fyfe swung his glasses on the reported bearing and saw what the lookout was seeing: Japanese submarine, unobtrusive shears, very low in the water.

"She doesn't appear to be zigzagging, captain," commented the exec.

"Radar bearing dead ahead, range, one thousand three hundred," said the radar operator through the open bridge hatch. A few moments later, the range to the target was 2,200 yards. I had cranked in the inputs from radar and the bridge. The TDC was tracking and we had a solution light on the angle solver. Batfish was on a course for a ninety degree starboard track. Fyfe had made up his mind to shoot when the gyro angles decreased 10 more degrees to ten degrees left.

"Clear the bridge," called the captain. Pressing the alarm, he hollered, "Dive! Dive!"

As Fyfe cleared the conning tower hatch, Batfish shifted easily to electric drive and slid under the water smoothly. The target had increased her speed from seven to twelve knots. The captain looked at the plot and told me to enter target speed, twelve. I reported that the distance to the track was 1,300 yards and the optimum approach course was 235. In a few minutes, we steadied on course and depth. The captain ordered the outer doors open on one, two and three.

"Set torpedo depth at four feet. Up scope," said the captain. The quartermaster pushed the lever and the periscope raised. For all the light it reflected from its upper eye, our leaking periscope might have been filled with ink. With the target approaching a generated range of 880 yards, it was still invisible to all but our ST radar mounted on the periscope.

"Final bearing and shoot," said the captain. "Set," I said. "Shoot," said the angle solver operator. The quartermaster punched the firing button and again Mk 18 electric torpedoes left the submarine.

Nervous silence settled over the conning tower and control room. The assistant attack officer counted off the running time to the enemy submarine. It was now up to the stopwatch.

From the periscope eyepiece, bright light illumined Fyfe's sweating face. A towering sheet of flame lit up the sea for miles around. At 2202 the submarine literally blew apart and sank immediately. *"We got the sonofabitch!"* sang out a lone voice from the control room. Another muffled hit was heard and felt by all. Eight seconds later, a third muffled explosion. The assistant attack officer conjectured that it was our torpedoes hitting a piece of disintegrating submarine.

"Down scope," Fyfe said quietly. "Course one five zero."

As we leveled off at 150 feet, two more loud explosions reached our ears. Over the next fifteen minutes, sonar reported a variety of noises from the sunken submarine. Feeling the rumbles, we silently envisioned the small internal explosions, escaping air, shifting weights, collapsing bulkheads, scraping, tearing metal then all was silent.

At about 0200 on 13 February, the exec joined Fyfe in the cool, damp air on the bridge. This night was also as dark as it could be. The sea was no longer calm: around us, rainsqualls appeared and disappeared.

"We've got another radar pulse on the APR," said the captain. "This one's at one five seven megacycles. A bit weaker than the other two." He ordered ten degrees left rudder to swing ship and told the exec to have APR pick up the null.

"Yes, sir. Battle stations?" asked the exec.

"Wait for SJ to confirm the contact."

The exec climbed below to pass the word. Batfish began a long, slow swing, searching for the source's approximate bearing. Before the null in the target's radar emission was found, the rumor of another possible submarine contact spread throughout the boat.

"Appears to be about 220, captain," said the APR operator on the 7 MC.

"Come right to course to 220," called the captain to the helm. "All ahead full."

Twenty minutes later, the exec stuck his head into the bridge hatch. "Captain, we've got a solid SJ pip at eleven thousand yards; dead ahead," he hollered.

Fyfe replied, "Call the crew to battle stations."

I began tracking the small pip on the TDC, her base course 120, her speed seven knots. For a few minutes nothing further came from the radar operator. Our position relative to this target was almost identical to our last two; we were surface approaching with the darkest part of the dark sky behind us. We could barely see the heavy cloud cover now rolling over us.

"Contact now bears 015 relative. Range eight thousand yards," reported SJ. I reported that Batfish was approaching an ideal position. The set-up on the TDC was looking good. The target's change in bearing and range indicated it was heading southeast and that *Batfish* was off its port bow.

"Target speed seven knots and steady. Course is 120." called the exec from his plotting board. It was confirmed in the TDC. The fly was coming to the spider; all we had to do was move across the web a little faster. With the target's range now approaching 7,000 yards we had to cross her track to put her behind us at a good range from which to fire the stern tubes down our own wake.

"All ahead flank," Fyfe called back. "Come right to 045." At flank speed, we would cross ahead of her just right and then slow to await her approach. Fyfe pressed the bridge alarm, the lookouts scrambled below and the captain pulled the upper conning tower hatch shut while the quartermaster dogged it. Batfish bored beneath the choppy waves. "Up scope," whispered the captain. The boat leveled off at forty-four feet. Maintaining three knots submerged. It was working like clockwork. The only thing that could prevent us from reaping our set-up would be a radical change in the target's course. Even a change in her speed could be easily compensated for, as long as her bearing remained more or less the same. But a submarine can make one radical course change that no other boat or ship can, it can dive.

"Target just disappeared from radar, sir." an urgent radar operator's voice called out, "Range, 7,150." Why did she dive? We weren't pinging, we were keying our SJ infrequently, and then only briefly on command, our radio was silent, there was nothing aboard they could have heard, if their sound heard our screws, then their equipment was better than our own. That opened a whole range of possibilities for other gear that we had better take seriously.

"Rig for silent running," Fyfe ordered. We crept at radar depth with our eyes and ears open, our mouths shut. "Maybe she'll blow ballast in thirty minutes," someone ventured.

"Could be that's their doctrine." No one replied. "You know, like the last one, thirty minutes".

Fyfe clung to the dripping periscope, awaiting whatever Sonar, APR, and SJ might reveal. Minutes ticked by, then a half-hour. "SJ," Fyfe said. "Key your set briefly".

There was no reason for us to believe our enemy wasn't stalking us even as we stalked him. Five more minutes passed. If she knew we were here, a suspicion that her lengthening submergence could support, then we now shared the same odds with our adversary. In a showdown between submarine and submarine, surprise takes the biggest advantage. But luck gives the biggest breaks. After all, we had sunk two submarines just like this one and in only two days. Could that mean we were lucky? Could it mean we now had strained that luck?

"Where the hell is she?" Fyfe asked no one in particular.

He gave it another five minutes then surfaced *Batfish* to make a high-speed run ahead of the enemy's probable track. Thirty minutes later, we withdrew into the depths for another radar watch. A full hour passed. We listened for our enemy, for her pinging, for her torpedo. "APR contact. 157 megacycles," reported the 7 MC. The report startled us. There she was. The pip appeared on our SJ scope, seventy minutes after it had abruptly disappeared.

"Range 9,800 yards, bearing 166." radar announced. I cranked in the information and kept the speed we had used earlier. I quickly calculated the distance to the track and told the captain.

"Take her up," Fyfe called down the control room hatch. To close for a new approach, we would need surface speed. When we broke the surface he climbed to the bridge for our third high-speed, end-around on the target. They had had their chance, such as it was. Now it was our turn again.

With the target at 7,000 yards, we ran across her track, then dove. We leveled off at radar depth. She approached steadily. Again, our stern tubes were lined up for a near zero torpedo gyro angle. On the TDC the set-up looked good. Her long submergence seemed to have been no more than a routine dive, for her radar was chatterboxing just as before. We were now back off the pass between Calayan and Dalupiri islands. The strong tide streaming through the pass was making depth control and steering difficult. The tide rips could also affect our torpedo run.

"Open the outer doors aft, make ready after tubes," Fyfe ordered. "Stand by to fire".

"After tubes flooded and ready, captain," reported the telephone talker. We waited, checking and double-checking our fire-control set-up. The target was approaching the bulls-eye on our plotting board and TDC. The torpedoes were set to run at six feet, slightly deeper than before so they wouldn't broach.

"Stand-by," Fyfe said.

"Bearing steady at 165. Range is now 1700 yards," I said.

"Commence firing," said the captain. "Set," I said. "Shoot," the angle solver operator said. The first of three torpedoes left the after tubes when the quartermaster pushed the firing button.

"Seven, eight, and nine, fired electrically," came over the 7 MC. "Torpedoes running straight and true," called the sound tracker from the torpedo room.

"Up scope," Fyfe said as he turned to the assistant. "How long now?" "Fifteen seconds. Twelve, eleven, ten . . . " responded the exec.

The ticking of the watch was joined only by the count. The stopwatch went on ticking. As Fyfe started to turn to the PPI [Plan Position Indicator radar] scope, the flash through the scope's eyepiece lit the conn. A yellow fireball consumed the Japanese submarine as she blew apart. The thundering shock struck Batfish resounding through her hull hurting our ears.

SJ [surface-search radar] picked up a wide diffusion of pips on the screen as the target completely blew apart. She had shattered so completely, her pieces sinking so quickly; there was nothing for the succeeding torpedoes to hit. The men around the PPI scope stared at a blank screen.

We surfaced in the hopes of finding survivors amid the oil slick. As we ran through the oil and wreckage, the searchlight was again not effective in the surface haze. Since dawn was close, we waited on the surface for its light. Radar would alert us of danger.

The sun began to slide up behind the dark, hazy horizon, casting dim light on slimy bits of wood and paper. Running back and forth through the oil slick, our search for something tangible was finally rewarded. We recovered a wooden box containing Japanese navigation equipment, papers, and a book of tables. If this blew off the bridge, her navigator may have been waiting for a navigational fix by dawn's first light. From the positions listed in his workbook, it looked as though the enemy had come all the way from the Indian Ocean to Formosa before heading down toward Luzon to join his ancestors.

We reported our third successful strike against the Japanese submarine force. At 0630, we dove for the day's submerged patrol. Oil was still bubbling to the surface.

Captain Fyfe's voice came over the 1MC general announcing system: "Within three days, we sank three enemy submarines. There were no survivors. Those men aboard the Japanese subs who died as a result of our actions were combatant enemies. They knowingly risked their lives in war, just as we do. We attacked and sank them in the course of our duty. Within our good fortune, there is of course some sadness that these submariners have died, and by our hand. The only way that could have been otherwise in this war, would it have been for us to die by theirs. Thank you for your excellence, and congratulations on your success.

Chapter 38
MARCH 1945
BING IS MISSING
BY BILL GLEASON

> Bill Gleason tells the story of his friend Leroy Bingham, who nearly lost his life when he was left on the bridge of *Gurnard* (SS-254) when it submerged.

Leroy J. Bingham was a typical sub sailor. He had a nose that looked as though some stevedore had smacked him in the puss with an eight-pound sledge, but he actually acquired it in the boxing ring before his enlistment.

We sailed out of Fremantle on our way in USS *Gurnard*'s (SS-254) ninth patrol run, underway with our second skipper, Cdr. R.N. Gage.

The watch was informed that the boat was coming about, to head back to Fremantle. I saw the captain come down from the conning tower in an almost grotesque posture he was being helped to his cabin by a Junior Officer, Mr. Rittenhouse. As he went by me, he looked terribly ill.

We made flank speed back to Fremantle. The crew felt bad for the old man, but happy to get back to our home away from home. Many had girl-friends, some had wives, some friends, and some had a feeling of a moment of reprieve, such as myself.

We were given liberty for twenty-four hours with orders to report back aboard at 0800 the next day. We drank Emu Bitter beer at our favorite pub.

Our new captain was our previous executive office, G.S. Simmons. He was a good officer, a super navigator and now our skipper. Reporting back aboard, all hands were informed we would undergo training exercises to acclimate the new commanding officer. He put the *Gurnard* in commission and had already completed eight patrols on board her, but somehow he saw the need for more drills. After five days of dive, dive, dive—fire, fire, fire and all the routine maneuvers, we pulled back into Fremantle and again got shore leave. Little did I know at the time, this would be the last time I would set foot on Aussie soil.

We stood out of Fremantle, bound for the South China Sea on our ninth war patrol. It was becoming routine; up through the Indian Ocean, a stop at Exmouth Gulf, through Lombok Strait, Makassar, past Borneo. Our patrol was to be in the Sulu Sea.

To be a lookout on a sub was the most tedious and most responsible job on a sub. We were steaming towards our patrol area. The night was starless, the wind was about sixteen knots, and all was well. There were no targets, no Jap planes, and no harassment from anyone. While cruising in the Sulu Sea, off Zamboanga Island, we ran all night looking for some kind of target. During the preceding day we had seen several small barges, but practically nothing to expend a fish on. It was 0745 and the watch was about to change. I could feel a relaxed atmosphere aboard the *Gurnard*. The war was coming to an end. There were jovial feelings and much cama-raderie, and "Cookie" was always doing something that could rival a chef from France; steaks, bread, and goodies came out of his galley.

While running on the surface in this atmosphere of leisure, the klaxon sounded and the OD's voice came over the 1MC, "Dive, dive!" I was on the high-pressure air manifold. Down came the bridge watch standers. The lookouts came down through the lower conning tower hatch. There were four of them on Gurnard; port, starboard, high, and one standby that was always ready to rig out the bow planes on the second blast of the diving alarm. The port lookout took the stem planes, the starboard the trim man-ifold, the standby took the bow planes and the high lookout became the standby.

This was all routine. "Green board, pressure in the boat," shouted the chief of the watch. The diving officer gave the depth to his bow planes-man and all was well. As it turned out, this was just a normal trim dive. We all breathed a sigh of relief, for it had been a long war and it was nice to realize that we were safe for another dive.

Watches on the manifold and planes would change every twenty min-utes. The first rotation was due, but there was no one to relieve the trim manifold operator. It was supposed to be Bingham, the high lookout. I was on the stern planes and looked around to see what was happening.

The word was passed over the 1MC, "Bingham to Control!" No Leroy! It was passed again. Then the search began. Thinking he might be in his bunk or asleep somewhere else, no one was particularly concerned. All hands looked then it dawned on the diving officer who had been officer of the deck that he had not counted correctly the men going below when

Gurnard started to go under. "God," he yelled into the conning tower, "I left him topside."

"Standby to surface," came the shout from the conning tower when the diving officer explained his goof. Upon surfacing, we reversed course on the batteries. The captain was on the bridge and he wanted to go ahead full, but as silently as possible to hear poor Bing out there in the water. The battle station lookouts were topside, searching and searching, with no sign of Bing.

The executive officer checked the chart, plotting our dive. We went to all ahead flank.

At this time we were off Zamboanga Island in the Sulu Sea. The wind was nearly sixteen knots. Still no Bingham. We kept maneuvering, back and forth, back and forth. The skipper ordered, "All personnel not at a critical station go topside with binoculars."

The deck was awash with the crew looking and looking and searching and searching. Bing was special; he was an expert lookout. He had been the high lookout who spotted the Jap convoy early on the morning of June 6, 1944, in the Celebes where we sank four ships, and eventually caused a whole Jap regiment to retreat from landing on Saipan for a counter offensive. In this one attack we killed an estimated 3,000 Jap troops.

Eyeballs were popping out of heads; search, search, look, look, look. Then came a yell. I was the port lookout and turned to see S.W. Pencak, second class torpedoman pointing off the port beam. "There! There! Way out there!" Pencak hollered.

I could barely make out a splashing in the water, just abaft the beam. Thank God, it was Bing, sending salt sprays high into the air. No one cared if the Japs showed up with ten tin cans we were going to get Bing no matter what. We maneuvered towards him and got him alongside and up the superstructure onto the forward deck. He was stark naked and red all over. He had been in the water several hours. When he got on deck he passed out. We took him below and doc gave him a stimulant. He came to and related his amazing experience, "I was on the high lookout. The watch was really getting boring. The sun was a beautiful fireball. I was thinking of home and my girlfriend. I felt good. I knew the war was over. I felt a sudden surge grasping me. My God, we were going down. I looked around. All I could see was water.

I tried to get to the bridge hatch, but the water was already covering the bridge. I dove off the conning tower and started to swim. I was alone in the water."

Bing apologized, "I was the top lookout and as all lookouts do, rested my elbows and held the glasses. The wind was blowing. I swear, I didn't hear the command to clear the bridge, or the cry, 'lookouts below!' I saw the boat surface about a mile away, but looking more closely I saw the stern of the *Gurnard*, going away. It steamed away, out of sight. I started to strip, shoes first then everything except the binoculars. I splashed water high into the air, to no avail. I said some prayers among them one really emphatic, `God, if I ever get out of this predicament alive, I'll never take another drop of booze!' Finally, I threw the binoculars away and started to swim as hard as 1 could. I knew I was a gonner, so I stopped swimming. I took my last gasp, then saw the old *Gurnard* coming at me. I jumped with the last ounce of strength I had, again splashing water overhead. I think I passed out once and then I felt these hands slide me up somewhere. I was in a daze. I thought that I was in heaven. I was dead and Davey Jones had me and I was on my may to meet my maker.

Bing was pulled aboard and you never saw a happier crew! We could have shot *Tojo* and never celebrated so much, but Captain Simmons said, "That's enough, get him below and we'll splice the main brace." In celebration all hands were awarded a drink of brandy. It was hospital brandy, for medicinal purposes, kept by the doc. It took the captain's order to break it out. We all lined up in the after battery and one by one took our individual shares.

When Bing was offered an extra-large dose he looked up from his sack and said, "No thanks, you can have mine." I'm not sure old Bing was that religious, but he never again took a drink.

Chapter 39
MARCH 1945
ABSENCE WITHOUT LEAVE, MARCH, 1945
BY JOE O'ROURKE

Commander Joe O'Malley took an interest in a submarine sailor who was AWOL for three years during the war. The boy's story was so remarkable; O'Malley intervened on the boy's behalf.

Commander James J. O'Malley, reported to Submarine Squadron 2 head-quartered at the U.S. Naval Submarine Base in New London, Connecticut. He had completed eight submarine war patrols in the Pacific; four as executive officer and four as commanding officer. Before reporting, O'Malley had been welcomed at home as a hero by his family and friends during his month on leave.

In the squadron operations office, it became customary for Commander O'Malley to start his day with his cup of black coffee; then scan the daily submarine status board. Following that, he read operational and administrative communications that had been received during the night hours. One morning, a teletype message intrigued him. In concise and cryptic naval message language, it read:

From: CO SuBase NewLon

To: ComSubRon 2

Subj: Newmark, Noel, USN surrendered SuBase NewLon main gate 1216630Z X AOL from USS 02. X Absent without authority since 020400Z 1942 X Awaiting disciplinary action Brig, SuBase New Lon

In plain language this message meant that Seaman Second Class Noah Newmark turned himself in after being absent without leave for more than three years. The commander envisioned a General Court Martial. The long period of absence was prima facie evidence of desertion; wartime desertion. With his legal background and training O'Malley wondered why Newmark would surrender with the war still going on. With his legalistic curiosity aroused, he asked the squadron yeoman to locate Newmark's files and records so that he could review them.

Days later, he was still unable to find reasons. At Captain's Mast, the initial hearing, the finding of desertion in time of war resulted in the sentence of General Court Martial, or "GCM" for Noah Newmark. The Articles of War that governed the military could call for the death sentence for wartime desertion. Knowing this, O'Malley was even more than curious about the case. He decided that the only way for him to learn of Newmark's reason or reasoning for the surrender was to voluntarily involve himself to act as Newmark's defense counsel. He expressed this interest and his concerns to the senior members of the legal staff of Commander, Submarine Force Atlantic Fleet (ComSubLant) and was duly appointed defense counsel for the accused.

Since the GCM was to be conducted at the Submarine Base in New London, it was not necessary for Commander O'Malley to travel. It was arranged with SubRon 2 for him to maintain his responsibilities as the squadron operations officer concurrently with defending the accused wartime deserter.

O'Malley obtained a copy of the charges from SubLant staff and discussed them with Captain Ed Hannon, the senior legal advisor. "This will be an open and shut case," said Hannon. "We are going to try, and then hang this guilty bastard. I know you want to get yourself ready for your peacetime return to the legal profession, but I can't understand why you want to associate yourself with this case. It's a losing proposition."

Commander O'Malley made his way to the SuBase brig for his first interview with prisoner Noah Newmark. He identified himself to the guards and was escorted to a small, but secure, private room. Noah Newmark, clad in denims on which a large, white letter "P" was stenciled, entered and sat down at a plain table with O'Malley.

Newmark appeared to the commander to be an unprepossessing young man. Although somewhat in awe of his defense counsel's rank, Noah never avoided O'Malley's eyes. His answer to all the questions was or followed by a respectful, "sir". After one full hour, the meeting was concluded. Brig guards took Newmark back to his cell. The commander, troubled, made his way back to SubRon 2 operations. All through the questioning, Noah stuck to a story that O'Malley found hard to believe. Not only did he disbelieve it, he knew that the General Court Martial board members would also disbelieve it. Noah Newmark told O'Malley that he had been ordered to the submarine 0-2 after completing submarine school. He had been aboard about a month, assigned as mess cook, before he went to New York for the weekend in February 1942. Noah said that he had lived with his aunt from the time he was an infant; his parents died shortly after he was born. His aunt was his only known relative. Noah told O'Malley, that when he arrived at her apartment, he found her alone, critically ill, and, as he found out from the doctor he had called in, near death. With little money, a hospital was out of the question, so Noah stayed there to take care of her. She was truly helpless and during her worst periods, she was so weak that he had to feed her and perform all the nursing functions necessary for a patient near death. He moved to another nearby, and more convenient, apartment. Weeks passed, and his aunt began a gradual convalescence. Noah took a job in a nearby store, bagging groceries. He prepared her breakfasts and dinners, racing home each working day to prepare and feed her during his lunch break. Because she would never fully regain strength, he bought a wheelchair so that they could take walks and shop together.

It took three years for arrangements to be made to assist his aunt, through social government agencies and charities that would provide financial and other support for disabled and elderly persons. His aunt had repeatedly brought up the subject of the time that Noah still had to serve in the U.S. Navy. With the additional help she was getting, she told him that he had to go back to the Navy. He donned his uniform and took the train to New London and the bus to the base to surrender.

Later, reflecting on Newmark's story, Commander O'Malley could visualize Noah's face and expression as he related the details without guile; with the unshakable belief that there had been no choice; that there was nothing else for him to do but take care of his aunt because she was all he had; that the Navy's time would have to be served when she was able to get along without his personal help. "Noah", O'Malley thought to himself, "It's not that clear-cut. You had no idea what you were letting yourself in for. The offense you are charged with carries the ultimate penalty, death. All of the reasons you had for staying at home might be enough to avoid a death sentence, but even if you are very, very lucky, and a model prisoner, you will probably face ten years in Portsmouth Naval Prison at hard labor."

Interview after interview with the accused brought O'Malley to the realization that he had no hope of changing the charge of desertion to absent without leave. The court would be primarily influenced by, and there was no denial for, the very long period of time that had elapsed away from the naval service.

As the date for the general court martial drew near, the commander sensed foreboding gloom and a lack of confidence in his ability to be effective as Noah's defense counsel. He didn't want to be seen as simply going through the motions for an obviously lost cause. He didn't go so far as to regret that he asked for the assignment as defense counsel; he knew that someone would have had to fill it. His questions about himself were, "Did I do enough? Did I do the right things? Have I been away from the courts too long? Am I missing something?" The day came for the general court martial to begin. All the people involved or interested filed into a special room. Five senior naval officers sat at a long table with a green baize cover. There were tables for defense counsel, prosecution counsel and the appointed recorder. There were two rows of chairs placed in the room for any spectators or interested parties. Formally, the charge of desertion and its particulars were read; then the prosecution began opening remarks. While the remarks were brief, they seemed to present an ironclad case for wartime desertion against Noah Newmark. O'Malley could sense the agreement of guilt in the midst of the court martial members in the face of undeniable evidence. There was nothing he could say in rebuttal to the charge; therefore, he elected to forego the procedure that called for opening remarks by defense counsel.

Prosecution witnesses verified details of Newmark's absence from 0-2 and his surrender, three years later at the submarine base.

O'Malley called Noah Newmark to testify for himself and then carefully led him through questions to relate the story of devotion as it had been told him. He sensed that the court martial board had sympathy for Noah, which would only be applied as mitigation for sentencing. Clearly, the case for desertion was being firmly established. There was only Noah

Newmark's uncorroborated word that he intended to return to the Navy. At the end of the week the evidence was even more reinforced. It was likely that Monday would be the last chance for the defense to present anything in favor of Newmark's case.

Friday night and Saturday morning the commander agonized over his seemingly lackluster performance as defense counsel. With his confidence in himself shaken, he wondered, over and over again, what had been overlooked. With a start, the realization came to him that if there was an answer it was not in New London. He set his alarm to rise before dawn on Sunday and drove to New York to visit with Noah's aunt.

Court martial proceedings resumed early Monday morning. The members of the board, the accused, prosecution and defense counsel, and other functionaries and spectators took their seats. Heads turned to the back of the room when a wheelchair, occupied by an elderly woman was brought in.

Commander O'Malley requested and received the special permission of the president of the court to present a witness for the defense. The court was in silence as the wheelchair was placed near the witness stand. In response to the initial questions, the woman identified herself as Elizabeth Newmark, giving her New York address. O'Malley went right to the heart of the matter. "Why did your nephew, Noah, have such a strong sense of obligation to take care of you during the early part of 1942? So strong, in fact, that he remained absent over leave for a period of approximately three years?"

Elizabeth Newmark wept into a handkerchief, then raised her head to state, "Noah himself didn't realize why we were so close. I never told him that I am his mother. I never married, but was determined to raise my son the best way I could."

"Mother!" Noah shouted from the defense counsel's table. The court room buzzed with this revelation. The court could not find that Noah was a bona fide deserter.

The trial ended soon after with a finding of guilty of the lesser offense of Absent Without Leave. Noah, fined the sum of one dollar, had to serve the remainder of his initial enlistment. He re-enlisted repeatedly in the submarine force until his retirement as a Chief Engineman.

Chapter 40
MARCH 1945
FROM KAMIKAZE ATTACK TO TYPHOON
BY K.F. WELTY

K. Welty was a crewmember on *Devilfish* (SS-292) when the boat was struck by a kamikaze aircraft. The experience was extraordinary and was capped by the boat's tussle with a terrible typhoon.

The USS *Devilfish* (SS-292) was built by Cramp Shipbuilding Corp., in Philadelphia, PA, during 1942 and 1943. I was assigned to the *Devilfish* in late June of 1944. We, the pre-commissioning crew, lived on a barge moored at the shipyard. We were present and witnessed the final phase of her construction, the launching, the final outfitting, and the trial trip. At this stage of the war, American submarines had a search periscope, a narrower attack periscope, a mast-retractable surface search radar, a stationary-mast air search radar and a primitive type electronic countermeasure device called APR. This optical and electronic sensing equipment was mounted externally in the periscope shears and on masts that lowered through the conning tower into the boat. *Devilfish* had an elongated conning tower to house three masts; two for the periscopes and one, aft of the periscope masts for the SJ radar. In addition to the masts, various antenna trunks for radar, radio and APR accommodated seals for the heavily insulated wiring that extended from the conning tower interior to the exterior equipment in the shears.

After having made the trip through the Panama Canal to the Pacific we continued our training on our way to Pearl Harbor. There, minor repairs were made. Then on December 31, 1944, we left Pearl Harbor on our first war patrol. We stopped at Saipan, and topped off the fuel tanks, loaded provisions, and left the island on Jan. 15. Our first patrol area was in the waters in and around Bungo Suido, off the coast of Japan. It proved to be fruitless since most of the Japanese ships had been sunk by then.

On March 15 we arrived on station and commenced our second war patrol, with Lcdr. S. S. Mann Jr. as commanding officer, and Lcdr. N.G. Harrison Jr. as executive officer. We were in company with USS *Spadefish* (SS-411), to Saipan. Both boats were reassigned to the waters between Tokyo Bay and the Northern Nanpo Shoto Islands, and to provide life-guard service. On March 19 at 0800 the bridge watch consisted of myself as quartermaster of the watch; the OD, Lt. Victor Krygowski; the JOD Ltjg. Charles C. Rust; and three lookouts in the periscope shears.

At 0842, Rust said to Krygowski, "Hey Vic, there's a plane back there." He pointed astern. "Do you think we ought to dive?"

Krygowski replied, "By all means!"

He then shouted, "Clear the bridge! Dive! Dive!" and sounded two blasts on the diving alarm. I counted all three lookouts as they went down the hatch. Krygowski hung on the hatch lanyard waiting for me to spin the dogging wheel. When I reached up to crank the wheel to engage the dogs and secure the hatch, seawater was already slopping in. We were going down fast.

While we were passing fifty feet, we heard a small explosion, which sounded like a light bomb, and not close. In about ten seconds water commenced pouring through the bottom of the SJ mast, at the rear of the conning tower and through the APR lead-in trunk. We were able to close off the latter leak by cinching up on the seal nut, but could do nothing about the SJ leak.

We leveled off at eighty feet while the shallow conning tower bilge filled rapidly and spilled over down the lower conning tower hatch into the control room. The diving officer below me swore as a regular waterfall splashed down the ladder rungs and onto his shoulders. In order to prevent a fire, circuits were pulled to the conning tower electronic equipment, which was being showered by spray from the SJ mast. We piled all loose canvas, rain clothes, etc. over the electrical equipment in the conning tower. In a while, we managed to trough the water from the SJ mast into the periscope well, and thus decrease the cascade into the control room. The well housed the attack periscope, just forward of the SJ mast and extended into the pump room bilge.

It was difficult to imagine how so small an explosion could have done so much damage. Prior to surfacing, we discovered that the SD radar and APR were inoperative. The attack periscope could not be raised.

The search periscope could be raised, but neither trained or seen through. Because of the extensive damage, we decided to repair what we could while submerged and wait until dark to surface.

We surfaced on a course for Saipan. As usual, on surfacing, I opened the hatch and was the first topside. I looked all around the horizon, nothing in sight, then I looked at the deck and the periscope shears. There were hunks of aluminum, some large, some small, all over the cigarette deck, behind the shears. I picked up a small piece of the aluminum and carefully examined it. By then the lookouts, the captain, the executive officer, and the OD, were also topside.

In the patrol report, Captain Mann wrote, "The following damage was found topside: SD and SJ radar masts sheared completely off, an eight-inch hole in the after periscope shears, APR and VHF antennas destroyed, underwater loop destroyed, and upper periscope bearings distorted."

Amazingly enough, the searchlight was intact. Draped across the shears were several large pieces of aluminum which looked like part of a plane wing section. On the cigarette deck we found a piece of tubing which looked like a section of a plane's landing gear. Closer examination revealed Japanese symbols on some of the pieces. A nameplate in Japanese was also found. It never occurred to us that we had been the victim of a suicide attack until we had surfaced. The captain decided to attempt no topside repairs during darkness, as we felt we might make matters worse. As it was, we could dive, in an emergency to ninety feet.

At 0830 on March 21 we sighted the USS *Tinosa* (SS-283) on an opposite course. We exchanged calls and reported to *Tinosa* our condition for further transmittal to ComSubPac. We sawed off the SJ mast and plugged the opening with a wooden plug. Our hope was that this would stop some of the leakage. We closed off the stationary SD mast at the bottom, although it was not leaking badly. No other repairs at sea were practicable.

The weather during our transit from western waters to Saipan became more stormy as we went. The sea was stormy ninety percent of the time with waves and wind over a Force 4-7 as logged by me. The prevailing wind and seas were from the east, making for an extremely wet bridge. The temperature was mild and that gave us some relief, but each bridge watch for the OD and lookouts was a terrible strain on muscles and nerves. Much green water was taken over the bridge as the boat rode up one giant wave, then plowed through the next one. The heavy seas accounted for numerous bruises and lacerations.

One lookout sustained a broken kneecap, when he was swept off the lookout platform by a very high wave. I was standing on the bridge's starboard side as a roller swept over the bridge. We all hung on and I felt the starboard lookout bump against me. I grabbed his arm and held him down on the bridge deck as the water drained off. In doing so I kept him from being washed overboard, where he would have drowned in seconds. He gasped for air and couldn't stand. I helped him down the hatch. Our pharmacist mate laid him out on a table in the crew's mess and examined his legs. The boy's patella had been shattered and doc put a splint on the knee. The lookout rested in the after battery until we got him to Saipan where a surgeon put the knee back together.

On numerous occasions green water was taken down the conning tower hatch into the conning tower, and into the control room. Green water taken down the engine air induction caused grounding of the auxiliary generator and other electrical grounds. We fought the seas and our damp electrical equipment all the way to Saipan.

After making the transit from our operating area to the Marianas, we rendezvoused with the destroyer escort, DE-966. It accompanied us into Tanapang Harbor, Saipan where we maneuvered the boat alongside, USS *Fulton*, our submarine tender. The captain discussed the state of *Devilfish* with the squadron commander after which repairs were made and the boat was put out on one of the war's last patrols. We had the distinction of being the only American submarine to be attacked by a kamikazi, but our biggest test was not from the Japanese, but the rough seas of spring, 1945.

Chapter 41

MAY 1945

THE SINKING OF *HATSUTAKA*

BY WORTH SCANLAND

> The famous submarine captain Commander Worth Scanland tells of how he sank the
> Japanese warship, *Hatsutaka* with the longest torpedo run in the war . . . and all
> while stark naked.

This story begins the day following our sinking a small convoy, when on
the evening Fox radio schedule from Pearl Harbor we heard a message
from ComSubPac announcing the loss of *Lagarto* in the Gulf of Siam
when depth charged by the destroyer *Hatsutaka*. The skipper of *Lagarto*, a
sister boat of ours built at Manitowoc, was a wonderful friend of mine
named Frank Latta. When I received the news of his loss I went immediately to the charts and after some study came to the conclusion that the
Hatsutaka must have been escorting a convoy from Singapore to Saigon.
Most likely she would have to return to Singapore for another convoy and
thus provide my boat, *Hawkbill* with an opportunity to avenge the loss of
Lagarto. So we sent a message requesting permission to deviate from patrol
orders long enough to take on *Hatsutaka*. Our request was approved by
ComSubPac.

Taking up position a mile or so off Pulo Tengol, which is located approximately at the southeastern corner of the Gulf of Siam we anticipated
intercepting Hatsutaka, which ever-way she chose to return to Singapore.
I wrote in the captain's Night Order Book orders to maintain a sharp lookout and to use the emergency call bell at the head of my bunk if any contact of any kind was made. Because it was a rainy night and we were quite
near the Equator, I stripped down to the buff and fell asleep on my bunk.
We were on the surface, charging batteries. The next noise I heard was five
buzzes on the emergency buzzer from the bridge, telling me in no uncertain terms, "Captain to the bridge, on the double!"

I hit the deck running and was halfway up the ladder between the control room and the conning tower when I realized, in the excitement, that

I had neglected to put on some clothes. I arrived in the conning tower to be told that the target was within torpedo range and we had a firing setup on the torpedo data computer (TDC) where Lou Fockele was busy twirling knobs and urging me to hurry. Reaching the bridge, I grabbed the target bearing indicator and positioned the crosshairs on our target, which was still standing southward down the Gulf Coast just as we had guessed she would.

When our stopwatch had counted off about one minute from launch of the torpedoes, we, on the bridge, were rewarded with the sight of a large explosion on the target, quickly followed by a report from Lou that the target had come to a stop. Then she apparently sighted us or her radar picked us up as we found ourselves coming under fire from a number of ship's medium caliber guns. We turned away and sought safety by opening the range between us and our victim, and, about this time, some kind shipmate quietly reminded me that I was still quite naked!

During the remainder of the night, our target remained stationary, and we sat on the surface awaiting dawn to assess the situation. We recognized that we were in very unfriendly waters. The Gulf of Siam averages about 15 fathoms or 90 feet throughout, and our keel was therefore only 26 feet from the bottom when submerged. In addition, there lay between us and the drifting enemy a large U.S. laid minefield which I was reluctant to enter. At daylight I saw that the enemy ship was the *Hatsutaka*. A Jap float plane was circling lazily around the destroyer, and eventually a seagoing tug showed up, with the obvious purpose of stealing our victory from us.

By this time, perhaps 0900, we had submerged, and a range with our radar equipped periscope showed us to be out 5,000 yards from *Hatsutaka*. Our torpedoes had two options in speed, thirty knots and forty-five knots, with corresponding ranges. At slow speed the Mark 14 could go about 5,000 yards and about 3,000 yards at high speed. In any case, were we to fire a fish at the enemy as a last ditch effort to avert her escape. We would have to be very, very lucky. As every man aboard *Hawkbill* was the best in his field, I had full confidence in our torpedo gang to give us a, "hot, straight and normal" run and ordered a forward tube to be readied for firing. We set the torpedo at maximum range, slow speed and because of the minefield, zero running depth. At slow speed, the minutes ticked by. For five eternally long minutes the torpedo left a trail of blue lube oil smoke in her wake. I can give you my word that the sight of that fish coming inexorably at them must have had the crew of the *Hatsutaka* firing every gun they had at it, but to no avail. As I watched, the luckiest torpedo in U.S. submarine history struck the target squarely between the smoke stacks and blew her into two quickly sinking pieces. *Lagarto* was avenged!

"Not only did *Hawkbill* probably fire the longest successful torpedo shot in U.S. submarine history, but most certainly she was the only submarine in anybody's navy to sink an enemy man-o-war while under the leadership of a 'buck-naked' skipper.

Chapter 42
JULY 1945
THE MAN WHO NEVER MADE A MISTAKE
BY JACK BLUMEBERG

> Jack Blumberg described an event in the control room of *Dentuda* (SS-335) that signaled the need to never brag about one's competence as a submariner.

There we were, in the *Dentuda*, a 335 boat out of EB at Groton. It was the first patrol and our only wartime patrol, but we were there, somewhere off the coast of Formosa. The war was winding down in this July of '45, and targets were far and few between. And here we were at eighty feet and the going was slow. So let's go up to fifty feet and see what the world has to offer.

The chatter in the control room was a bit loose and the COB (Chief of the Boat) was at the manifold. So it was then, that the COB spoke up and said, "As long as I have been in submarines I have never made a mistake." That in itself was a tip-off of things to come.

Up into the conning tower came the captain while the exec stayed in the control room to watch the newly qualified diving officer. With a sweep of the horizon and seeing nothing of interest, the order came to surface. As we broke the surface the captain and Upchurch, the quartermaster went to the bridge. I was just below the upper conning tower hatch, on the sound gear, and could see a bit of daylight above, while at the same time could hear the subtle conversation between the captain and the quartermaster.

Suddenly the captain said, "Uppy, something's wrong." After a very brief pause and in a much more excited voice the captain yelled, "Clear the bridge." We jumped down into the conning tower. As I glanced up the hatch, I could see a wall of water closing in on the opening and simultaneously Upchurch was reaching for the lanyard and with a swift gymnastic swing, pulled himself into a completely inverted position. With his feet planted firmly on each side of the upper hatch rim, and with a mighty lunge, he pulled the hatch closed as water gushed into the conning tower. Fortunately the lower hatch was on the latch so the control room only got sprayed.

After draining the conning tower of sea water into the pump room bilge, the captain descended into the control room. This was followed by a heated discussion. Those of us remaining in the conn could easily overhear the exchange of words below. The discovery that the surfacing was made with the ballast tank vents open was the main topic being discussed. Meanwhile the diving officer and two others at the bow and stern planes were trying desperately to regain control of the boat. I visualized the men in the maneuvering room and those at the engines scrambling to keep up with the quick evolution.

The combined effort resulted in a dismal wallowing of the boat as it settled down to the depths. Finally, with a little forward propulsion on the batteries the boat seemed to be stabilized and voices from the control room indicated that all was well.

I was relieved on sonar and as I descended from conn to the control room I glanced at the deep depth gauge. The needle was passing the 600 foot mark as *Dentuda* continued to settle. Since our test depth was 412 feet I was more than a little interested in what was going on. My eyes stayed glued to the deep depth gauge as we rigged ship for deep submergence and took a big up angle. Maneuvering told control on the 7MC that their sea pressure gauge was reading the equivalent of 720 feet. The pressure hull groaned and squeaked in protest. A zirk [grease fitting] in the after battery compartment popped. By this time we had the sound powered phones manned and the seaman with the headset announced that after battery was flooding. It was an unreal scene, because he said it in a matter of fact voice as if telling a two year old sea story. It seemed to me at the time that a little more concern should be shown by the diving officer. But he took it all in stride and the auxiliaryman on the trim manifold shifted to series and continued pumping auxiliary tanks.

The captain, who had gone to the wardroom after having had his say with the COB, slid into control. (The angle was really big by then.) He didn't wait to assess the situation. He grabbed the air manifold handle and blew all main ballast tanks. The boat started to rise and the angle increased. The old *Dentuda* was pulling herself out of the depths, but the captain was not a happy man. As the needle passed the hundred foot mark on our way to the surface, the captain asked the COB at the hydraulic manifold if the ballast tank vents were shut. He was assured and could see for himself the status of the vents on the Christmas Tree. I was impressed by how the captain controlled his voice as he told the diving officer to get a decent trim for the next dive. He then ascended the ladder and went on up onto the bridge. Everyone in control breathed a sigh of relief and the COB was as quiet as a mouse.

All that excitement took place within a twenty minute window, and to this day my ears perk up whenever someone says, "I never made a mistake."

According to Joe Yaklowich MM1, *Dentuda* went down to 690 feet while on sea trials after an overhaul, so *Dentuda* was not foreign to the deep depths. The submarine participated in the nuclear tests off Bikini Atoll after the Second World War and was later assigned to the 12th Naval District as a reserve training submarine.

Chapter 43
JULY 1945
GABILAN'S AVIATOR
BY ROBERT TALBOT

> Naval aviator Bob Talbot became an honorary USS *Gabilan* (SS-252) crew member when his plane was shot down over Tokyo Bay. He was happy to fight the Japanese in the air and under the sea.

July 10, 1945 was a day I shall never forget. On my second flight of the day, I was assigned to a fighter sweep on the naval base of Yokosuka, just outside of Tokyo. The raids on the day were on the order of 1,000 planes from fifteen aircraft carriers. What a force! I was thrilled to be part of it. It is hard to describe the feelings one has when he is part of such an armada.

The takeoff, rendezvous and climb-out were all pretty normal. We crossed the Japanese coast at 25,000 feet, and met a solid curtain of flak [antiaircraft fire]. I certainly had never seen so much. The air was just black. I got a good hit on a gun emplacement and pulled up to start another run. While flying through the flak, I was hit. I advanced my propeller pitch and throttle. Nothing happened. I could climb by bleeding off the speed I had gathered on my dive, but could barely maintain altitude afterward.

As a result of my loss of power, I could not advise my squadron mates via radio of my predicament. I just headed out to sea over Tokyo Bay, maintaining flying speed by losing altitude. My division leader saw my predicament, and as he came alongside, I tried to spell out "SUB" in dots and dashes with my hand on the canopy. He pointed, and I took that direction.

The U.S. Navy had submarines, which were on routine patrols, to act as lifeguards for downed airmen when we flew missions against the Japanese homeland.

It didn't take long for me to run out of altitude, and I ditched my plane in the outer reaches of Tokyo Bay called Sagami Wan. Wow, did I ever hit the water! I couldn't believe how hard the landing was. I was thrown against the shoulder straps so hard that I had black and blue marks on my shoulders, and my left shoulder hurt for weeks. The engine, being hot, sizzled and smoked; the windshield, even with the thick bullet-proof glass, cracked into a million pieces, and water filled the cockpit almost immediately.

I unbuckled everything and got out as fast as I could. As I reached back into the airplane to retrieve my plotting board, the plane sank. I was left floundering in the water, having retrieved nothing.

I watched the plane go down, tail-hook up in the air, and slipping through the water fast. I thought I was sinking below the water too, from the weight of my clothing. I treaded water like mad to keep my head above water until I got my life jacket toggles pulled, releasing carbon dioxide into the bladders to keep me afloat. Even though I could breathe all right, I was still up to my eyes in water. I just couldn't seem to get any higher no matter how much I kicked, and I thought I must be drowning. I finally realized that my goggles were about half full of water, and that my head was well above. I have never liked swimming in salt water because of the salty taste. This water sure was salty!

Actually, I was not that bad off. I had gotten way out in Tokyo Bay. I don't remember just how long it took them to get to me, but the next thing I do remember is that huge submarine right on me, its decks rising and falling in great lunges. The rescue submarine saw me and took me aboard. I remember the big holes between its hull and its outer plates, and its diving planes rigged for surface running. At this time I did not know if it was an enemy sub or one of our lifeguard submarines. There were no visible numbers or markings. The men on the deck soon calmed any fears I might have had. It was one of ours.

I tried to climb up some little steps on its side, but I was too heavy with survival gear and water-soaked clothes. I fell back into the water. Two men of the crew dove into the water and helped me up those rungs. I was sure a happy guy. From the time I ditched until the time I was picked up, my mind was a blank. I guess I was in shock, as the first time I connected with myself was at dinner in the wardroom that evening.

While we were eating dinner, the officers questioned me as to my name, rank, squadron, ship, where I was from, etc. When I said I was from Cumberland, Wisconsin, the torpedo/gunnery officer said he was from Almena. His name was Carl Klug, and his brother had been a classmate of mine at the University of Wisconsin in River Falls. At that instant, everything came into focus and I was mentally OK. The emotion brought tears to my eyes. I guess the shock phase was over. The submarine which picked me up was SS-252, the *Gabilan*, commanded by Cdr. William Parham. The sub was standing lifeguard duty that day.

I gave my .38 caliber pistol and ammunition to the captain. I don't know what happened to my parachute. Since at that time parachutes were made of silk, some crew members had some nice material.

About the first thing I remember at that dinner table was someone suggesting to another officer that I should be checked out in the use of the head. I thought it was some kind of joke and laughed. It was not a joke. I had to qualify on the head, before I could use it. I memorized the various valves and the sequence of opening and shutting them. Airplanes are complicated, but we don't live in them. Submarines are also complicated and life's necessities have to accommodate that complexity.

The thing most feared by submariners is an attack by airplanes. Because the captain felt I could identify friendly vs. enemy planes as well as anyone else, he let me be topside as a lookout during daytime surface running. I could always go up during darkness. I never felt confined while I was on this boat. The officers and crew were extremely cordial, and I soon felt right at home on the *Gabilan*.

There was another big strike having over 1,000 carrier-based planes that hammered the Tokyo area on July 18th. The *Gabilan* was again assigned lifeguard duty. This time a division in VF-47 (my squadron) was assigned to be SubCap. Squadrons were assigned coded call signs. Ours was "Pelican." When I had flown on the 10th, I was the fourth plane in the fourth division, so my call sign was Pelican 4-4. I radioed our planes on SubCap duty overhead that Pelican 4-4 was just fine and enjoying his new home.

While on lifeguard duty, the *Gabilan* rescued seventeen airmen. Most of these were TBM [Torpedo Bombers] crews, but one was an Army Air Corps P-51 pilot, and I was a Navy F6F pilot. To keep us busy, and to help a little, we were all assigned duties. Mine was to help in the radio room by operating the decoding machine.

When we were running on the surface, I was usually topside. It was really thrilling to watch wave after wave of those planes pass overhead on the way to their targets. About twenty minutes after they passed, they would return, heading home to their carriers. As one wave was returning, another was on its way to Japan. Most of the time, I was watching to the west to see if any of our returning planes were in trouble. I saw one plane falter and fall into the water. We picked up that crew and another one later.

Late in the day on the 18th of July, our sonar picked up what was thought to be an enemy submarine. We were in a "shoot first" area. We dove and tracked it into the night, therefore did not get any of the messages from headquarters at 1800. We surfaced after dark and got the repeat messages. One was addressed to the *Gabilan*. I decoded it, and rushed to the captain with it. The message was for us to vacate that area immediately, as a destroyer/cruiser sweep was going in to get what was thought to be an enemy submarine. It was probably the one we had been tracking.

The captain ordered flank speed and we headed northeast to get away. We didn't make it. In a few hours our radar picked up the U.S. surface force bearing down on us. Our quartermaster flashed recognition signals but the surface group kept coming. The captain ordered flares to be shot into the air. Naval units had a schedule of flares where every hour of everyday a different combination of colors would identify a vessel as friendly. We shot the flares and still the ships came at us. He tried voice radio, and he again used our signaling lamp. The last brought a barrage of shells down on us.

Sometime after giving the captain the message, I went down to the wardroom and had a cup of coffee. The first shells hit us while I was there. The eyes of the mess steward looked as big as saucers as he peered out of the little opening between the pantry and wardroom. I said I thought the shots were from a .50 caliber gun, as they sounded like ours did when our shells hit the water during the times we shot at a towed spar.

He replied, "They ain't .50 calibers, they're five-inchers."

He was right. The ships fired six salvos before we dove, and fired many more as we were diving.

The *Gabilan* had been rated to 300 feet maximum emergency depth. Carl Klug told me that we went to 500 feet. We immediately, "rigged for silent running" and started evasive maneuvers.

We were under attack that night and into the next day. The air in the submarine became pretty foul and lacked oxygen. I am sure we were all breathing harder than normal, and of course, there were extra people on the boat now, too. I spent some of this time playing cards in the wardroom. The sonar, which was located just forward, was picking up a strange sound. It turned out to be me, shuffling the cards. I quit. Even with our sandals to deaden noise, we were asked to try not to walk about any more than necessary.

We evaded this destroyer/light cruiser fleet, and finally surfaced. It was a close call, and Clay Blair Jr. wrote about this in his book, *Silent Victory*.

A night or two later, the weather turned bad. A typhoon was approaching, and we needed to run on the surface to charge batteries. I don't know if it was the high seas, but I felt kind of woozy. We sure did pitch and roll. It seems we would ride up on a wave top, dangle there a while, and roll one way or the other while plunging down into a wave trough. I was sure glad when the batteries had a sufficient charge to allow us to dive and travel in somewhat smoother water.

The submarine, *Runner* was about to return to the sub base on Guam for resupply. Although it would result in a very crowded boat, we survivors were told to get ready for a transfer to it, for transportation to Guam. This transfer was to take place at night while both boats were surfaced to charge batteries. When I went topside to transfer, I found it was so dark I could barely make out the other submarine about hundred yards off our beam.

I was to go first. I climbed down the rungs on which I had entered the boat several weeks before, and got into my life raft again. The torpedo bomber pilots and crews followed, getting into their three-man rafts. We were all tied together with lines, and paddled across the sea between the two submarines.

As I approached the *Runner*, a deck hand threw me a line to enable me to arrive at the proper spot on the boat. I pulled myself to that point and climbed up the rungs. Just as I got onto the deck, a huge wave lifted us way up and I lost my footing on the slippery deck. While I was slipping, I hung onto the rope so tightly that my Navy class ring slipped off my finger, went down between the deck and the hull, and into the sea. I sure hated to see it go, but at least I hung on, and was soon going inside this new home. The others all followed successfully.

At the submarine base on Guam, I was getting off the boat when I met one of my classmates from the photography school in Pensacola. He had been assigned to a sub tender which was now in port at Guam. We exchanged stories as time permitted. However, we were soon told to get on a bus for transportation to a debriefing session at headquarters. This would be followed by our reassignment. I had left Guam on April 29th to join the Fifth Fleet, and returned on July 24th—about three months of combat. Not much, but the war was still going strong, with Navy planes hitting Japan almost every day. I was anxious to get back to my squadron.

Chapter 44

AUGUST 1945

THE CAPTURE OF I-401

BY ALEX LEITCH

Alex Leach was a crew member on *Segundo* (SS-398) when, at the end of the war, it shadowed a Japanese submarine. The capture of the giant I-401 is a unique story in submarine history.

USS *Segundo* (SS-398) departed Midway Island on 10 August 1945 for her fifth and final patrol of WWII. Her patrol area was the Sea of Okhotsk. Segundo was under the command of Lcdr, S. L. Johnson, USN, who had just relieved Cdr. J.D. Fulp, USN. On 15 August 1945 we received word of the surrender of Japan. Captain Johnson immediately granted a warm can of beer for all hands. On 18 August 1945 we were ordered to patrol outside the Kurile Island Chain and await further orders. On 24 August 1945 we received orders to proceed to Tokyo Bay and we left station, heading south.

I was a qualified seaman and stood helm and radar watches. The routine was half hour radar, half hour helm and half hour messenger in the control room. Standing the mid-watch (0000 to 0400) I had just relieved the radar watch at 1145 on 27 August 1945. There were no contacts on the screen. I was munching away on a sandwich and cup of coffee, when an intense blip appeared on the screen about 3,000 yards away. I jumped to the upper conning tower hatch, and hollered up to the OD, "Radar Contact, 3,000 yards, port beam" At the same time one of the lookouts yelled, "Ship, bearing 275, close aboard." I went back to the radar and soon Captain Johnson climbed through the conning tower on his way up to the bridge. As he passed, he told me to keep giving him bearings and ranges.

Since hostilities had ceased on 15 August and the target had not made any move, except to turn away, the captain did not send us to battle stations. It quickly became apparent that the target was picking up speed and trying to outrun us. Gunner's Mate Joe Brown, was on the helm and I was still on the radar. As radar range increased, the captain ordered flank speed and began giving course changes to Gunner Brown at the helm. As our speed increased to maximum, nineteen to twenty knots, it was soon clear that we would never be able to close the target. However, we could maintain our distance and position. We stayed on his tail, about 4,000 yards, and so it went throughout our entire watch.

We were relieved at 0400 and went below. Just about all of the offgoing watch assembled in the after battery, drinking coffee, and talking about the mysterious ship we were chasing. As dawn was breaking, the captain had the quartermaster send out the international signal to stop. He sent the message on our twelve inch searchlight which he mounted on the bridge. The captain now ordered all hands to battle stations, gun action.

As we manned our battle stations, I found myself in a most advantageous position. As gun captain on the forward 40mm [gun], just forward of the bridge, I could hear all the dialogue between the captain and everyone else. Our quarry had stopped dead in the water and we were in an ideal torpedo-firing situation. As it became brighter, it became apparent that our contact was a huge submarine.

It turned out to be the LIN 1-401, a boat over 400 feet long, displacing 5,500 tons and equipped to carry aircraft. In fact, the 1-401 was an extremely unusual craft. She, and two sister subs, were originally built for a single mission to destroy the Panama Canal. But the events of the war made it impossible for that operation to ever be undertaken. The boat was designed to handle two seaplanes, but had been modified, so that when Segundo came upon her, the deck hangar space had been enlarged to handle three seaplane bombers. Compared to her, the 1,500 ton, 311 foot long *Segundo* was a lightweight.

When the sun came up, the captain decided that we would try to board the I-boat. After exchanging blinker light signals, a rubber raft was put over the side, and preceded to the side of the I-boat. On its return, it carried a Japanese English-speaking officer. The captain gave our terms to the Jap officer, who then got back in the rubber raft and was taken back to the I-boat. To the best of my recollection, at least three trips, with officer representatives from each side, were made before an agreement was made.

According to the agreement, the Japanese captain would allow a prize crew of one officer and five enlisted men to board the I-Boat. They would then proceed to Tokyo Bay with us, as our captive.

The boarding party consisted of Lt. J.E. Balson, CMT. E.A. Russell, MoMM1 R.S. Austin, QM3 C.M. Carlucci, EM1 K.W. Diekmann, and TM2 J. V. Walton.

It was my understanding that all the enlisted men above received the Bronze Star for this action. I do not know what Lt. Balson may have been awarded. The Bronze Stars were sent through the mail, much later, I understand, and not awarded as a general ceremony in front of the crew.

We then began our two-day trip towards Tokyo Bay. The boarding party removed the I-401's conning tower hatch, to prevent the Jap from diving. None of our guys ever went below decks beyond the ladder. We still had a lot of mistrust, considering their actions in the past. Every time our guys hollered down for some water, they were presented with a bottle of Saki. It's a good thing they weren't conning the ship. The *Segundo*, meanwhile, maintained a position on the I-Boat's quarter, with our forward tubes loaded with warheads. At any suspicious maneuvering by the I-Boat our quartermaster would signal the boarding party to get over the side and away from the submarine.

Our skipper struck me as a man who wouldn't hesitate two seconds to blow the Jap out of the water. At any rate, there were no problems with the 1-401. We escorted the monster south into *Sagami Wan*, the body of water just south of Yokohama and Yokosuka. We arrived at 0500, on the morning of 31 August 1945, and at this time the American flag was raised aboard the 1-401. At 1100 that morning, the Japanese captain delivered two swords, as a symbol of surrender, to Lt. Balson. We were then relieved of our prize by the USS *Gatling* and were told to proceed up to the Tokyo Bay Approach and go to Yokosuka Ko and moor in a nest of submarines alongside USS *Proteus* (AS 19). The *Proteus* had just arrived from Guam with Admiral Charles Lockwood, ComSubPac, aboard.

The *Segundo* participated in the surrender ceremonies aboard USS *Missouri* on 2 Sept. 1945. On 3 Sept. 1945, *Segundo* departed Tokyo Bay, in company with 11 other submarines, en-route to Pearl Harbor, where on 12 Sept. 1945 the *Segundo* terminated her fifth and final war patrol.

Chapter 45

AUGUST 1945
FROM *PERCH* TO PRISONER

BY B.R. VAN BUSKIRK

> After being one of the few to survive the sinking of *Perch* (SS-176), Petty Officer Van Buskirk was interned by the Japanese. At war's end his liberation was an exhilarating event.

Just before dawn on March 3rd, 1942, we scuttled our own boat, the USS *Perch,* (SS-176) in the Java Sea. As it slid gently out from under us, we stepped off and started swimming. For the last 24 hours we had taken relentless depth charging and been without lights, except for emergency lighting. It must have been natural for us to pick up flashlights in our abandon ship drill. When we hit the water it was still dark. One of the boys asked, "I wonder if they are going to pick us up?" Another suggested, "Let's turn our lights on them." That seemed like a good idea, so we started shining our lights toward the Jap destroyers that had finally taken the life of the *Perch*. In response to our flashing, they started shooting.

We now found ourselves in the same old routine, with projectiles whistling overhead and splashing all around us. We tried to turn off the lights, but they wouldn't turn off. The salt water had shorted them and they simply burned, even though the light was exposing us to gunfire. I think we must have been treading water for about five minutes while trying to get those lights out, when our chief machinist mate yelled, "Why don't we drop the damn things?"

That is all it took. They kept burning as they descended until out of sight. Out of sixty-four of us in the water at night, one was thinking and sixty-three were not.

In a short time we were all picked up by one of the destroyers. Two hours later I was on board the heavy cruiser *Ashigari*, the flagship of the Third Japanese Fleet, being interrogated by the chief of staff of the fleet commander. The first thing I learned was the fact that the *Perch* was the sixty-sixth submarine they had sunk during the first three months of the war. It was nonsense, of course, but I shook my head gravely.

Among the many questions they asked me, were three that were vital to our operating forces, so I claimed ignorance. My interrogator wanted to know the number of submarine tenders in the Asiatic Fleet. He wanted to know their locations. He was interested to learn the minefield locations guarding the entrance to Surabaya and where our boats were being refitted.

I answered, "I don't know." And indeed, I didn't know the answers to most of his questions. I was then asked if I understood the meaning of an unpronounceable Japanese word for beheading. I again claimed ignorance, and the officer went out of his way to explain the meaning. Still, I refused to answer, claiming ignorance. He must have thought I was very stupid or very obstinate. I was just playing my cards close to my chest and succeeded in bluffing my way that morning.

In a couple of days we were landed at Makassar in the Celebes Islands and placed in a large compound surrounded by a barbed wire fence. My skipper, Dave Hurt, expressed the desire that I try and get some paper and write a report, pointing out the structural weaknesses of the Perch discovered as a result of the depth charging. It was his hope that I would be able to smuggle it through the line so that the navy could correct those weaknesses.

We had a Dutch officer in camp. He had been stationed in Makassar before the invasion. He was able to get his houseboy to smuggle a tablet and pencils through the fence. I began interviewing the officers and leading petty officers, and in a short time I had a very detailed twenty page report on the subject, which I turned over to the officers to memorize. A month later, the officers and our three radiomen were put on a ship heading for Japan.

We arrived in Yokohama on Easter Sunday, 1942. I folded my report and stuffed it in my shoe. After a brief train ride, we had a five-mile march to Ofuna, an interrogation camp. During the march I did not dare limp, because I did not want to attract the attention of the guards to my foot. As soon as we arrived in the camp, the commandant through an interpreter, ordered us to take off all of our clothing. "You mean shoes, too?" I asked.

"No, leave your shoes on." said a guard. The guards went through the clothing as if they were looking for a needle in a haystack. It turned out that they were looking for pencil and paper so that we could not exchange notes with each other on questions that we might be asked during the long sessions of interrogation. As soon as this inspection was over we were assigned to our cells. I removed the report from my shoe placed it in my hip pocket and with needle and thread, which I had obtained in Makassar, I sewed the pocket closed. As useless as this effort may have been, it seemed logical at the time.

The first thing the next morning the guards came running through the passageway yelling for us to get out on the parade ground. Needless to say, I was the last one out. As I stepped out into the center of the line, I noticed that the guards were frisking everyone. They worked from each end toward the center. I recalled that the last sheet of paper of my report had no writing on it, so, with tongue in cheek, I stepped out of line. The guards were all over me. They called me things that morning that must have been the extreme of Japanese profanity. Even the interpreter was yelling at me, and I kept yelling at him, "What are they looking for?"

He finally said that they were looking for paper. I told him that I had paper. "Where was it?" demanded the interpreter. "I think it's in my cell."

"Well, go get it," ordered the Japanese guard. I went out of there so fast they didn't think to follow me. While running down the passageway, I was trying to get my pocket open. I did too good a job sewing it closed. When I got to my cell, with my pants down, I practically tore the pocket off. I grabbed the report, took off the last page threw the rest under my blanket and as nonchalantly as possible, walked back out to the assembled prisoners. I waved the piece of paper in their faces. They marched me back to my cell. It was about four feet wide eight feet long and on the outer wall was an opening with wooden bars. On the opposite end was a solid door leading to the passageway. The door had a small peephole so the guards could look in and watch me.

Sitting on the floor in a corner, with my back to the wall, the guards could see the lower part of my legs, but not the upper part of my body. In that position, I ate this report. Twenty sheets of pencil paper without any water was tough to swallow.

In Ofuna, we were not permitted to talk with each other at any time. All the guards carried clubs about the size of a softball bat, but at least a foot longer. They used them on the least provocation. In fact, they didn't need any provocation. The standard punishment for being accused of talking was eighteen swats across the small of your back. With six guards present, each guard gave three swats. He put his all into it, just in case he did not have another chance. One or two swats across the small of your back would cause you to pass blood in your urine for two or three days. During the seven months I was in this camp, my weight dropped from 155 to ninety-six pounds.

In December of 1942, I was transferred to a camp in Yokohama. There we worked in Mitsubishi's shipyard, helping to build Jap ships. I was the senior American officer and kept track of the work records. The Japs furnished me an old Underwood typewriter to keep those records.

As soon as I had a chance to case the joint, and see how the guards operated, I rewrote the report on the front and back of one sheet of paper. I used very few spaces, and one or two letters to represent a word. The boys then smuggled in some thin sheet metal and soldering equipment. We made a small capsule, placed the report in it, heated it up to drive out the moisture and then soldered it up tight. I thought of a place to hide the capsule. The inspiration came when I realized that the Jap guards, for some reason, had a terrific fear of venereal disease. With this in mind I asked the boys to smuggle in something that looked like medicine. What came in was an opaque jar of cold cream. We inserted the capsule in the bottom of the jar, smoothed the surface, placed the cap back on and then placed it in plain sight at the head of my bunk.

When a new guard would come by, he would point at it and ask what it was. Well, with my poor Japanese, but excellent sign language I was able to convince him that I had a terrible case of venereal disease and this was medicine for it. I would then hold the jar up for him sample. He would back away from it like it was the source of the disease. Needless to say, I had no more trouble with my little jar of cold cream for the duration of the war.

During the winter and early spring of 1945, the excitement was building up to a feverish pitch. The B-29s were not only making the night fire raids over Tokyo, but also daylight raids of Tokyo and Yokohama. Fighter planes from our carrier task forces were hitting us during daylight hours.

Mitsubishi finished the small aircraft carrier. When it went to sea, the Japs didn't know that our boys had dumped steel shavings into the reduction gears. Two days after that it limped back into port and anchored in the bay off our camp. Two months later it was still there and the carrier bombers turned it over on its side for the duration. After dropping his bombs on the carrier, one of the fighters roared across our camp rolling his wings and waving at us.

Tokyo was burned down in three fire raids, each raid destroying about one third of the city. By May 1945, two thirds of Tokyo had been burned to the ground. The landfall for the B-29s coming in from Saipan was Mount Fujiyama to the south of us. At that point they apparently set their gyros on automatic pilot for their final bombing run to Tokyo. It brought them directly over our camp. We could see them coming for miles, since the Jap searchlights followed them in. The intensity of the antiaircraft fire was unbelievable, yet the only B-29 we saw shot down fell close to our camp.

Just before the third fire raid we were moved. On that raid they finished Tokyo, Yokohama and the camp that we had just vacated. During the first winter in Yokohama, if a prisoner caught a cold he got pneumonia, and if he got pneumonia, he died. Out of 550 we lost forty-five the first winter. The primary cause was low resistance as a result of a starvation diet and the slave labor working conditions. That was my first experience with *"give-up-itus."* When a person who was very sick, decided that he would rather die than fight on he pulled the blankets over his head and was dead in two days. Those were isolated cases.

Our breakfast consisted of a small boiled potato. For the other meals, there was some soup and a small serving of grain. One of our boys went three and a half years, then lost his faith one-day too soon. On the 14th of August 1945, while scavenging for weeds, he ate a berry he knew was very poisonous. He was dead in two hours.

In those closing days of the war, our camp was located in a wild mountainous region of northern Japan. The men now worked in a copper smelter. If they were too sick to work, but could still walk, we sent them up on the hill to scavenge for weeds. The cooks would boil them in water, add a little soy sauce, and call it soup. About once every six weeks we had a change in the menu. The city fathers of a nearby village would permit the slaughter of a couple of cows. When blood is poured into boiling water it coagulates into large chunks. The cooks would break them into small bits. It would taste just like giblets.

On the 18th of August the men did not leave for work at the smelter. On the morning of the 22nd, we were ordered out of the barracks. Through the interpreter the commandant announced, *"The war is over. It was a very bad mistake. So sorry."*

I immediately took charge of the camp. The first thing we did was to make a large "PW" sign on the hill behind our camp out of rocks and then painted it white with a paste of rice flour and water. We had hopes that one of our planes might see it. I then took charge of the guards' radio so we could listen to Radio Tokyo. Soon we received instructions from MacArthur's staff to stay where we were until they could arrange for a train to take us to the coast and ships to take us south to Tokyo.

On the morning of the 25th, we heard a roar of airplanes. We rushed out. It looked like a squadron of carrier based planes flying over from east to west, and a little to the south of us. They were soon out of sight. After awhile, back they came. Just before they went out of sight to the east of us, one of them must have seen our sign. Two of them left formation, headed in our direction, and soon was followed by all the rest. They arrived over our camp at about 15,000 feet. They circled and circled. We thought they would never come down, but when they did, it was like a dive-bombing mission.

I don't think there has ever been in our history, an air show like the one they put on over our camp during the next fifteen minutes. They did everything but knock us off the rooftops. They even dropped us messages. One I will never forget: "Take heart boys. Texas is still a state of the Union." Another said, "We have to go, but we will be back."

When they came back, it was TBF Avengers loaded with mail sacks. They would swoop down over the camp a little hatch in the tail section would open and out would come a mail sack on a little parachute. Everyone was a direct hit into the center of the compound. These sacks were loaded with everything you could think of; food, medicine, razors, magazines, candy, chewing gum and cigarettes. These planes just kept coming for two full days. What excitement!

On the 27th we heard a different roar. It turned out to be two B-29s. We thought they were on a reconnaissance mission. They circled for awhile and then left. One of them started to lose altitude very rapidly. About ten miles out, he turned and headed in our direction, with his four engines wide open and at an altitude of about fifty feet.

In the center of our camp was the compound or parade ground. Around the whole area was a six foot board fence. Just as the plane crossed the lower fence someone yelled, "His bomb bays are open." During the fire raids in Yokohama, that was time to hit the dirt. I yelled to the man next to me, "Boy, what a show this is going to be."

That was like releasing the firing pin, for at that instant, more stuff started coming out of the forward bomb bay than I thought could be carried in a freight car. The first thing out was two fifty gallon oil drums, welded together, then six single drums. These drums turned out to be carrying 100-pound bags of flour, powdered milk, sugar and stuff like that. Then crate after crate of canned goods. By crate, I mean ten to twelve cartons of canned goods strapped to wooded platforms. These crates just kept coming. The first point of contact was the covered way. With a swoosh it disappeared from view, and the Jap guard was gone, and the area between the second and third barracks was filled to the eves with food. They all had parachutes, but no chute has been designed to operate from a plane traveling between 300 and 500 miles an hour at an altitude of fifty feet.

The best place for the drop was the center of the compound, but 350 of us were standing there waving at him. He picked the next best spot, and he did it perfectly. We started digging through all the goodies dropped from the B-29. Under the crates we found the single drums, under the single drums, the double drum, under the double drum the covered way and under the covered way, the Jap guard who now was about two feet underground.

The plane returned, coming over the hill to the east and this time it let go with the rear bomb bay. It was the most beautiful sight: colored parachutes, with the drums and crates swinging back and forth under them. It was a perfect drop, with one exception. What turned out to be a bundle with 250 pair of Marine field boots came loose from its chute—headed toward the earth at the mythical speed of 500 miles an hour, destination the roof of the Galley. On top of the roof was Staff Sergeant Smith. He later told me, "I couldn't go to the right or the left I thought it was going over my head and I started forward." With a tremendous bang, they both disappeared from view. We made a rush for the Galley. It was a fifteen foot drop to the concrete floor. When the dust cleared away, there was Smitty sitting on top of the bundle of boots. He was shaken up, yet unhurt, and he was a happy kid.

We averaged a plane a day for the next ten days, each plane, brought about four tons of food, medicine and clothing. After the food, the item most needed came in the second drop from the first plane. In its race to the ground, it was nosed out by the bundle of boots. It was a crate of DDT powder. Who ever thought of that must have been a prisoner of war during World War I. In Japan we had three types of insects—not counting the Jap guards. First, were the lice. We didn't worry too much about them. It was cold in northern Japan. When we went to bed at night, we slept in our clothes, because we had only one blanket in which to wrap ourselves. Next, were the bed bugs, there was nothing we could do about them, except burn the barracks down, and we had no intention of doing that. Finally, we had fleas, millions of them. Needless to say we put the DDT to good use.

On the morning of September 11th, some of the boys spotted an old shaggy horse just outside the gate. They led it into camp, killed and butchered it. They then turned it over to the cooks, who started grilling steaks. At that moment the phone rang. It was MacArthur's staff. We were to break camp immediately. Our train was waiting for us at the foot of the hill. As we headed out of the gate, the aroma from the Galley brought tears to our eyes. We knew we were passing up our first opportunity in three and a half years to have a nice juicy steak.

Chapter 46

SEPTEMBER 1945

THE S-40 LEAVES THE ATOMIC AGE

BY GEORGE STANNARD

George Stannard, a crew member of S-40, which survived nine war patrols and earned a battle star, tells of the days following Japan's surrender and how the dawn of the atomic age spelled an ignoble end for the noble old boat.

S-40's last patrol ended when we surfaced off the Farallon Islands in a gray, wet, clinging fog. We slowly felt our way toward the Golden Gate, sounding the foghorn all the way. The fog cleared just as we were approaching that magnificent span. I was astounded by the size and beauty of that great, orange structure; that signified to all sailors the end of the rainbow. As we passed under it, I wrote a glowing, emotional response in the quartermaster's log. I was quickly told by the OD to be less exuberant in my entries. I replaced it with a more nautical, sober entry as we passed mournful Alcatraz Island with its bleak guard towers and blatting fog horn. We navigated toward our berth in Tiburon Bay.

The last of the sub force of the Asiatic Fleet lay nested together alongside a long, isolated pier at the end of nowhere. In 1945 Tiburon seemed like a remote outpost of San Francisco. Most of the crews had been transferred to other duty or discharged, so only a skeleton crew was left on board the dying subs to make sure they didn't slip the bonds that held them to their fate, and escape back to sea for an honorable death.

It was a lonely, cold feeling that crept over me as I sat in the conning tower on an August Sunday evening and listened to the latest news broadcast about the atom bombing of Hiroshima. After the broadcast I heard the duty watch arguing below me in the control room. I climbed down just in time to hear the old chief slam his hand down on the chart table and exclaim in a loud voice, "Do you people know what this means?"

His normally squinty eyes were wide open and shining with excitement. His face was beaded with the sweat of intense concentration. "It's not just another bomb, for Christ's sake! It's an atom bomb, by God!" he announced to the empty control room. "The war won't last another three months! This changes everything!"

From my perch in the conning tower I listened to the old chief, who had seen too much action in this old submarine. A few of the crew came into the control room in response to the commotion. "It's going to change everything! You just watch!" continued the chief to his newly-formed audience. Lighting a cigarette he ended his lecture with, "Now, everybody out of here! Move it! Get this crappy barge cleaned up!"

I climbed down the ladder into control and was stopped by the chief. He asked, "Ya going to stay in? You could make first class easy, you know. The navy will need experienced people after the politicians get through cutting the military's throat. Everybody will be getting out; driving a truck, selling cars, painting, building houses. All this glory will go up in smoke. There won't be many of us left in uniform, believe me. Is that what you want to do? You want to go out and scratch with the chickens?"

"Gosh, Chief! I really haven't thought about it that much! I wanted to be a thirty-year man at one time, but . . . " I answered. I was flustered because the old chief was pushing me to think too far ahead. This had all happened too quickly for any of us to really understand. It was all too much. It had come without warning and no one was prepared to think about much about the future. We were supposed to think of the next liberty or meal, or the next port, or the next girl. Truman's atomic bomb left kind of a vacuum for submariners.

The chief leaned closer to me, put his sweat-shiny face close to mine and whispered softly, "Listen, I've been through this all before. I know! And I'm telling you it's going to be a mad-house out there when they cut the troops loose. You'll be lost in the shuffle, kid. Keep the uniform on and you can stay in as long as you want."

I saw his left eye droop and smelled the faint odor of alcohol on his breath. He blinked his eyes, turned around and flopped down on the green planesmen's bench. I went up to the forward battery and crawled into my bunk and thought a long time about what the chief said. Maybe he was right, maybe he was wrong, but one thing was for sure; the times were changing real fast.

September was a month for breaking up old things like tired, rusty submarines. It was a sad time. Each week one of the S-Boats would be cast off from the nest and taken under tow by a navy tug for the short trip across the bay to Richmond. Crew members stood solemnly on the pier and waved to yard workers who stood on the S-Boats' decks, smoking as if all was right with the world. Some rendered a hand salute and stood at attention. Then walked away with head down and slumped shoulders.

When it came time for S-40 to make its last trip, the old chief and I stood on the pier. Tears rolled down his cheeks. He watched a short time, then turned and walked away. I never saw him again. It was a time for breaking up old ships and old friendships.

SOURCES

Submarine School
Cornelius R. Bartholomew
Polaris Magazine, August 1985

Sea Dragon's Prop Wash
A. J. Killin
Polaris Magazine, August 2007

A Vanishing Day-dream
Cornelius R. Bartholomew
Polaris Magazine, April 1994

Operational Readiness on December 7, 1941
Frank E. Perry
Polaris Magazine, December 1983

Rest and Recreation
Frank Kimball
Polaris Magazine, June 1995

The First and Only Patrol of S-27 (SS-132)
George J. Herold
"Undersea Encounters," Submarine Research Center

S-37's Voyage Home
Robert B. Lander
Polaris Magazine, December 1988

Bob Rose and Sargo's Australian Welcome
Doug Rhymes
Polaris Magazine, August 1982

Escape by Submarine
Lucy I. Wilson
Polaris Magazine, June 1987

The Doubtful Tale of the S-36
Alfred Sims
"Undersea Encounters," Submarine Research Center

Rivets in the O-2
Stanley Lambkin
Polaris Magazine, April 2008

Aground on a Reef
Frank Bowman
Polaris Magazine, August 2007

Pompon Evades Torpedoes
Charles Foskett
Polaris Magazine, April 2008

Gun Boss Pay
Edward Crawfoot,
Personal Interview, Submarine Research Center, February 2007

Loss of the USS Grenadier (SS-210)
Robert W. Palmer
Polaris Magazine, April 1983

Midway, Our Refuge of 1943
Jack Quade
Polaris Magazine, October 2006

Loose Torpedo at Pearl Harbor
James H. Allen
Polaris Magazine, February 1993

Second Patrol of the USS Bluefish (SS-222)
Edwin J. Shepherd Jr.
Polaris Magazine, August 2007

S-48, My First Boat
Churchill "Jim" Campbell
Polaris Magazine, October 2006

The Ryuho's Last Stand
John M. Good
Polaris Magazine, August 1993

Submarine on the Loose
William Dreher
Polaris Magazine, August 2007

USS Ray's Great Conning Tower Flood
Hal Moyer
Polaris Magazine, August 1999

Ambush on Borneo
Ken Harrington
Polaris Magazine, August 1984

Pogy's Stowaway
W. E. Battenfield
Polaris Magazine, February 1986

The Battle of the Philippine Sea
Ernest J. Zellmer
Interview by Richard Misenhimer of the National Museum of
    the Pacific War, Center for Pacific War Studies, March 2007

Penny Picked Me
Bill Gleason
Polaris Magazine, June 1985

Story of the USS Flier Second Patrol and Its Survivors
Alvin E. Jacobson
Submarine Review Journal, July, 2007; October 2007; January 2008

Left on the Bridge
John Paul Jones
Polaris Magazine, April 1993

Dying of the Emperor on Paulau
Norman R. DiRey
Polaris Magazine, April 1990

Picking Up the Left-overs off Paulauig Point
R. C. Gillette
Polaris Magazine, February 2001

A Total Loss
Farrell Stearns
Steep Angles and Deep Dives, Submarine Research Center

The Sape Strait Shooting Incident of November, 1944
H. E. Miller
Polaris Magazine, February 1998

From the Perspective of an Aviator
C. B. Smith
Polaris Magazine, October 2001

A Submarine Home
Myron Alexander
Polaris Magazine, August 1998

My First War Patrol
Joseph Corneau
Polaris Magazine, April 1995

Bucket Brigade
Hank "Nate" Henderson
Steep Angles and Deep Dives, Submarine Research Center

Three Submarines in Three Days
Hughston F. Lowder
Polaris Magazine, February 1985

Bing is Missing
Bill Gleason
Polaris Magazine, August 1987

Absence Without Leave, March 1945
Joe O'Rourke
Polaris Magazine, August 1992

From Kamikazi Attack to Typhoon
K. F. Welty
Polaris Magazine, October 2000

The Sinking of Hatsutaka
Worth Scanland
Polaris Magazine, June 2007

The Man Who Never Makes Mistakes
Jack Blumeberg
Polaris Magazine, February 2008

Gabilan's Aviator
Robert Talbot
Polaris Magazine, February 2008

The Capture of I-401
Alex Leitch
Polaris Magazine, December 1985

From Perch to Prisoner
B. R. Van Buskirk
Polaris Magazine, October 1983

The S-40 Leaves the Atomic Age
George Stannard
Polaris Magazine, April 1997

INDEX